Ella Baker

THE LIBRARY OF
AFRICAN AMERICAN BIOGRAPHY

General Editor, John David Smith
Charles H. Stone Distinguished Professor of History
University of North Carolina–Charlotte

The Library of African American Biography aims to provide concise, readable, and up-to-date lives of leading black figures in American history, in widely varying fields of accomplishment. The books are written by accomplished scholars and writers, and reflect the most recent historical research and critical interpretation. Illustrated with photographs, they are designed for general informed readers as well as for students.

Paul Robeson: A Life of Activism and Art, Lindsey R. Swindall (2013)

Ella Baker: Community Organizer of the Civil Rights Movement, J. Todd Moye (2013

Booker T. Washington: Black Leadership in the Age of Jim Crow, Raymond W. Smock (2010)

Walter White: The Dilemma of Black Identity in America, Thomas Dyja (2010)

Richard Wright: From Black Boy to World Citizen, Jennifer Jensen Wallach (2010)

Louis Armstrong: The Soundtrack of the American Experience, David Stricklin (2010)

Ella Baker

Community Organizer of the Civil Rights Movement

J. Todd Moye

ROWMAN & LITTLEFIELD
Lanham • Boulder • New York • London

Published by Rowman & Littlefield
A wholly owned subsidiary of The Rowman & Littlefield Publishing Group, Inc.
4501 Forbes Boulevard, Suite 200, Lanham, Maryland 20706
www.rowman.com

Unit A, Whitacre Mews, 26-34 Stannary Street, London SE11 4AB

British Library Cataloguing in Publication Information Available

Library of Congress Cataloging-in-Publication Data

The hardback edition of this book was previously catalogued by the Library of Congress
as follows:

Moye, J. Todd.
   Ella Baker : community organizer of the civil rights movement / J. Todd Moye.
      pages cm. — (The Library of African American Biography)
   Includes bibliographical references and index.
   1. Baker, Ella, 1903-1986. 2. Civil rights workers—United States—Biography.
 3. African American women civil rights workers—Biography. I. Title.
   E185.97.B214M69 2013
   323.092—dc23
   [B]
                                                                    2013018707
ISBN 978-1-4422-1565-8 (cloth : alk. paper)
ISBN 978-1-4422-1566-5 (pbk. : alk. paper)
ISBN 978-1-4422-1567-2 (electonic)

Printed in the United States of America

For Murphy

As far as I'm concerned, I was never working for an organization, I have always tried to work for a cause. And the cause is bigger than any organization, bigger than any group of people. It is the cause of humanity.

~

Even if segregation is gone, we will still need to be free; we will still have to see that everyone has a job. Even if we can all vote, but if people are still hungry, we will not be free.

~

Singing alone is not enough; we need schools and learning.

~

Remember, we are not fighting for the freedom of the Negro alone, but for the freedom of the human spirit, a larger freedom that encompasses all mankind.

—Ella Baker, speaking to a mass civil rights meeting in
Hattiesburg, Mississippi, January 21, 1964

~

Contents

List of Abbreviations ix

Introduction: Strong People Don't Need
Strong Leaders 1

Chapter 1 A Deep Sense of Community 9

Chapter 2 Hotbed of Radical Thinking 29

Chapter 3 Give Light and the People Will Find a Way 47

Chapter 4 The Hard Job of Getting Down and Helping People 77

Chapter 5 Bigger Than a Hamburger 109

Chapter 6 We Who Believe in Freedom Cannot Rest 135

Chapter 7 The Tribe Increases 165

Acknowledgments 169

A Note on Sources 171

Index 177

About the Author 185

~

List of Abbreviations

ACMHR: Alabama Christian Movement for Human Rights
CED: Consumer Education Division
CEP: Citizenship Education Program
COFO: Council of Federated Organizations
CORE: Congress of Racial Equality
FELD: Fund for Educational and Legal Defense
MIA: Montgomery Improvement Association
MFDP   Mississippi Freedom Democratic Party
NAACP: National Association for the Advancement of Colored People
SCEF: Southern Conference Educational Fund
SCLC: Southern Christian Leadership Conference
SDS: Students for a Democratic Society
SNCC: Student Nonviolent Coordinating Committee
SPHR: Special Project in Human Relations
UCM: United Christian Movement
VEP: Voter Education Project
WEP: Workers Education Project
WPA: Works Progress Administration
YNCL: Young Negroes Cooperative League
YWCA: Young Women's Christian Association

INTRODUCTION

~

Strong People Don't Need Strong Leaders

In the middle decades of the twentieth century a mass movement of African Americans and a few white allies successfully challenged and transformed a system that oppressed them. In those years the overwhelming majority of American blacks lived in the southern states, where white supremacy was codified in Jim Crow law, ingrained in social custom, and policed with horrific levels of violence, on the part of both white citizens and representatives of state and local governments. Without economic might or significant voting power, and therefore without reliable allies in any of the three branches of the national government, black citizens worked without government protection or a realistic expectation of access to equal justice under the law. Yet they somehow leveraged the one power they did have—people power—to transform their nation. Others have since followed their example to change the world.

The civil rights movement was the best, brightest, and most powerful display of democratic social change ever seen in the history of the United States of America. In retrospect, it seems almost impossible that a minority of Americans who were so thoroughly marginalized and exploited by the majority could, first of all, have had enough faith in American institutions that they literally risked their lives to reform those institutions not just for themselves, but for all Americans. That they could have succeeded was even more unlikely. But succeed they did, using no more or less than the collective power of ordinary people working in solidarity.

Arguing about who was most responsible for these successes is silly; the multiple black freedom struggles we know as the collective "civil rights

1

movement" was a stew with hundreds of ingredients and thousands of cooks. Yet with the exception of a small handful of people that includes the movement's most charismatic and effective spokesperson, Martin Luther King Jr., no one person—no president or politician, religious leader or cultural figure—could claim more credit for the development of the mass movement or the changes it brought about than Ella Josephine Baker could have claimed had she had been so inclined. She was not so inclined; she came to believe that the worst thing that could happen to someone working for social change was to attract the attention of the mass media and begin playing for the cameras, so she refused to do it. But this reticence only begins to explain why Baker did not become the sort of national figure that other civil rights leaders became in her lifetime.

Baker did not seek publicity for herself and the major news outlets seldom sought her out for comment, but that made little difference to her. Reflecting back at the end of her long career, she said, "[Y]ou didn't see me on television, you didn't see news stories about me. The kind of role that I tried to play was to pick up pieces or put pieces together out of which I hoped organization might come. My theory is, strong people don't need strong leaders." Stokely Carmichael (Kwame Ture), an activist and community organizer in the Student Nonviolent Coordinating Committee (SNCC) who went on to become chairman of the organization, believed, "The most powerful person in the struggle of the sixties was Miss Ella Baker, not Martin Luther King." He was exaggerating for effect when he said this—not for the first time, nor the last—but the fact remains: Baker wielded tremendous influence over a generation of social activists, even if she was invisible and unknown to the vast majority of Americans then and remains so now.

Baker held leadership positions in the three major civil rights organizations of her day—the National Association for the Advancement of Colored People (NAACP), the Southern Christian Leadership Conference (SCLC), and SNCC—among many other activist groups in a long career as a professional community organizer. No one besides Baker influenced all three. (To be fair, the Congress of Racial Equality, or CORE, has a claim to being the fourth major civil rights organization of the era; Baker influenced it indirectly if at all.) She developed a sophisticated philosophy of civil rights activism that she described memorably as "group-centered leadership," which remade the black freedom movement in the 1960s and continues to inform activists for social justice and equality in the twenty-first century. Avoiding the charismatic leadership and headline-grabbing mobilizing campaigns that drew so much attention to the civil rights struggle—in Birmingham, Selma, and at the March on Washington, among other places—Baker preached and practiced a much more intensely egalitarian gospel of community organizing.

This organizing tradition, historian Charles Payne has written, requires "a different sense of what freedom means and therefore a greater emphasis on the long-term development of leadership in ordinary men and women." Baker was committed to this kind of long-term development because she had "faith that ordinary people who learn to believe in themselves are capable of extraordinary acts, or better, of acts that seem extraordinary to us precisely because we have such an impoverished sense of the capabilities of ordinary people," Payne tells us. "You must let the oppressed themselves define their own freedom," Baker said, and she believed that all people have the right "to participate in the decisions that affect . . . their lives." The simplicity of these sentiments is deceptive, their implications profound.

Baker's concept of leadership differed greatly from most Americans' of her time and ours. To understand it, we have to forget what we think we know about the qualities of an effective leader. Leaders, Baker believed, should first and foremost be teachers or facilitators. Strong speaking skills were helpful, but not so much as good listening skills. "I have always thought what is needed is the development of people who are interested not in being leaders as much as in developing leadership in others," she said. To that end, Baker encouraged black Americans not just to march to protest injustice, but to organize among themselves to build autonomous, self-sustaining institutions they could use to better their own lives and their communities over many years. There were no shortcuts in this system. "I just don't see anything to be substituted for having people understand their position and understand their potential power and how to use it," Baker said. "This can only be done, as I see it, through the long route, almost, of actually organizing people in small groups and parlaying those into larger groups." Though she abhorred every aspect of totalitarianism with every fiber of her being, she frankly admired the Communist Party's practice of organizing through cells, or small groups of committed activists.

At every stop along her professional journey, Baker had to contend with personal and institutional expressions of sexism that underestimated or denied her abilities even as she and her colleagues battled racism. "I have never been one to feel great needs in the direction of setting myself apart as a woman. I've always thought first and foremost of people as individuals," she insisted. Yet her very presence in the freedom movement, her insistence on radically democratic thought and action in all aspects of life, and her determination to have her say without first considering how men might respond made her an especially effective feminist ahead of her time.

Baker herself was not the kind of person most Americans have been taught to think of as a leader, but she inspired, taught, and led a generation of civil rights organizers every bit as effectively as any of the other civil rights leaders Americans do know and celebrate. Bob Zellner, a white staff member of SNCC, said that the physically slight Baker "was usually quiet so that you [only] became aware of her immense influence and wisdom gradually. She always wore a little pillbox hat, like Jackie Kennedy, and a suit. She had sensible, classical clothes, and very few outfits. That was kind of the organizers' way." Julian Bond of SNCC found her "pleasingly prim and benignly schoolmarmish, formal but not rigid, proper but not proud or arrogant. . . . She was approachable." The proper looks and unassuming manner could be deceiving. By the time the students of SNCC knew her, Baker was a militant, a radical. When she chose to, she could unsheathe a sharp tongue or dominate a room with her deep, resonant voice.

When she first encountered Baker, Mary King of SNCC was struck by her "dignified carriage. She impressed me immediately as a person of wisdom and intellectual honesty. . . . she appeared to me to be a sage." Baker always dressed properly and spoke grammatically correct English with perfect diction, although she prided herself on being able to speak and connect with, without speaking down to, working-class people who did not. She was content to listen in most situations, but when the situation demanded that she talk, she spoke with immense authority. She had been a champion debater in college and said, "You could hear me a mile away, if necessary." The valedictorian of her high school and college classes, she could win an argument or deliver a hell of a speech.

Baker's style was not doctrinaire or dogmatic; it could in fact be poetic—idealistic without being romantic. She encouraged her protégées to imagine the kind of world they wanted to live in and then to work to bring it about as though their lives depended on it. If they wanted to change the world, she preached, they had to change themselves. If they wanted to organize support for a particular issue, they simply needed to open their front doors, make a connection with someone else, and start organizing the small corner of the world they inhabited. If the cause was righteous and the people were sufficiently devoted to it, the ripple effect would take it from there. When a 1963 SNCC meeting got caught up in a discussion over what roles members of different races might play in the movement, Baker stopped everyone present (including the writer James Baldwin) in their tracks with the observation, "We need to penetrate the mystery of life and perfect the mastery of life, and the latter requires understanding that human beings are human beings." At other times her approach was prosaic. Over and over again, through a career that spanned five decades, she demanded that groups of which she was a part stop whatever they were doing and answer the questions, "What is our purpose here? What are we trying to accomplish?"

Baker's set of beliefs, which the historian Barbara Ransby describes as "a philosophy based on militant antiracism, grassroots popular democracy, a subversion of traditional class and gender hierarchies, and a long-term vision for fundamental social and economic change," was not the result of academic study or armchair philosophizing. It was born of hard-won, lived experience, countless conversations with people from all walks of life, and a commitment to rigorous analysis. It was radical for Baker's time, and it remains radically powerful today. (Why Baker's belief that all people had a right to lead digni-fied lives and deserved to have a voice in the decisions that affected their lives marked her as "radical" is a question worth pondering.) Her ideas in-spired two generations of direct-action activists—the young women and men of SNCC in particular revered her—and she continues to inspire those who learn from her example.

Baker was an empiricist: bad ideas, she believed, could be overcome by bet-ter ideas if they had been formed by the gathering and analysis of evidence, and social activists could be successful if they outthought and outworked the supporters of the status quo. "The problem in the South is not radical thought," she told colleagues in the 1960s. "The problem is not even con-servative thought. The problem in the South is not enough thought." She might have expanded her geographic scope in that pithy statement. Baker considered racism a national, not a southern, problem, and she believed that the South was able to maintain Jim Crow only because the rest of the country allowed it to. In any case, she resolved to outthink and outwork it.

She developed an intense intellectual curiosity, a genuine desire to figure out what made individual people tick and how individuals could best work en masse to improve their collective lot in life. The SNCC organizer Bob Moses recalled being with Baker in Harlem when she stopped total strang-ers on street corners with the greeting, "Hello, brother. And where do you hail from?" For Baker, any social interaction was an opportunity to connect with and learn from another human being. These interactions, she believed, formed the connective tissue of social movements. Her lifelong commitment to learning from others, and to applying those lessons, formed the foundation of her approach to community organizing.

Ironically, however, Baker was also notoriously guarded when it came to her private life. Many of her closest movement comrades never knew that she was married for more than twenty years, and those who did know of her marriage to T. J. Roberts knew better than to ask Baker too many questions

about it. When a pair of interviewers from the University of North Carolina's Southern Oral History Program, Sue Thrasher and Casey Hayden,
both of whom had worked closely with Baker in the SNCC and knew her
well, interviewed Baker in 1977 and asked one too many questions about
her marriage, she shut down the line of inquiry: "Don't ask too many personal questions now." The interview transcript indicates that Baker laughed
off the question, but Thrasher and Hayden wisely chose not to pursue it.

Details of Baker's private life are few and far between even in the collection of her personal papers at the Schomburg Center for Research in Black
Culture in New York. Based on the limited materials she left behind, it is
difficult to find answers to even basic questions about her life and livelihood.
For long stretches of time she worked full time for social change outside of
established institutions and without a steady paycheck. How she was able
to cobble together enough money to live on during these periods is still
something of a mystery. (I suspect that wealthy New Yorkers with whom she
worked closely in the 1950s to raise funds for the southern movement also
quietly supported Baker thereafter, but I have found no evidence to support
the theory.) I am quite sure that this was no accident or oversight on her
part; throughout her adult life, it was entirely in keeping with Baker's modus
operandi to push everything but "the issues" that concerned her or "the program" she devised to deal with them into the background.

This is, therefore, first and foremost an intellectual biography, and it
would be even if Baker's personal archive contained a wealth of private
information. Joyce Ladner of SNCC recalled, "When I asked her about her
husband she would say, 'Oh no, it's not important.'" The marriage "was just
one of the few things she wouldn't talk about," said Bernice Johnson Reagon,
another of the young women in SNCC who looked up to Baker. Everyone in
SNCC called her "Miss Baker," a sign of the respect she had earned, but one
that also misunderstood her marital status. It never would have occurred to
them to address her as "Ella." In any case, in refusing to talk about her personal life, by defining herself as something other than a traditional wife and
mother in postwar America, her charges believed, she refocused attention on
her ideas. I share that belief, so in this book I share that focus.

A former reporter, Baker the civil rights activist also wrote surprisingly
little beyond her official reports for the NAACP and SCLC. Baker was
exceptionally well educated and well read, but she was at base the product
of tradition in which her elders transmitted the most important information
to her orally. She continued that tradition, sharing most of her insights via
the spoken word, in face-to-face meetings, rather than through newspaper
op-eds or academic journal articles. Fortunately, after retiring from public

life she shared these ideas in expansive interviews with journalists and oral historians. I rely especially heavily on these interviews in reconstructing her intellectual biography.

If Baker's ideas and lived example force us to rethink our ideas about leadership, they also force us to rethink what we think we know about the civil rights movement. She understood the movement and the multigenerational black freedom struggle of which it was a part as having two broad stages. First, she said, came "the aspect that deals with the struggle to get into the society as it obtained[,] or the struggle for being a part of the American scene." This was an effort to integrate into American society without changing the society. Next, said Baker, came "the struggle for a different kind of society which will reject, if necessary, the present system. The latter is the more radical struggle." Hers was the latter kind of struggle, which rejected mainstream values and replaced them with ultrademocratic, egalitarian, and radically Christian values. She memorably described this value system when she explained to a wider audience the students' sit-in movement that began in 1960: it was not simply about desegregating lunch counters so that blacks could eat next to whites in public; it was about fundamentally transforming a sociopolitical system that would allow racial segregation to take root in the first place. It was, in her words, "bigger than a hamburger."

The granddaughter of slaves who pulled themselves up by their bootstraps to become successful landowners and rock-solid pillars of their community, the daughter of hard workers who "lifted as they climbed" to improve the lives of their neighbors, the intellectual godmother to a new generation of social activists, and an exceptional thinker and historical actor in her own right, Baker considered herself a participant in a saga with a long history and an unlimited future. "I think what you have is a question of continuity of struggle," she said. The struggle continues, of course, and Baker's ideas continue to animate it. At a time when a former community organizer sits in the White House and millions of Americans identify with groups such as the Tea Party or the Occupy movements that (however disparate their goals) seek to organize grassroots challenges to America's political and economic elites, Baker's ideas regarding movement organizing and the extraordinary power of ordinary people are as timely as ever.

CHAPTER ONE

~

A Deep Sense of Community

In 1903, the year Ella Josephine Baker was born, the great African American intellectual W. E. B. Du Bois published an influential collection of essays titled *The Souls of Black Folk*, which is best remembered today for a prescient prediction. "The problem of the twentieth century," Du Bois wrote, "is the problem of the color-line." Ella Baker spent her life trying to erase the "color-line," along with other lines that separated people and prevented the United States from fulfilling its democratic promise. She was born in Norfolk, Virginia, on December 13, 1903, but her true home was in rural Littleton, North Carolina, where her maternal grandparents bought land that they had worked as slaves and developed into a productive farm.

As an adult, Baker had the habit of beginning discussions on what African Americans needed to do to gain full equality in the twentieth-century United States by analyzing the legacies of slavery, insisting that "the freedom movement has been and is as old as the existence of black people on this continent." Baker thought of her own activism as one part of a long-term historical whole, a point along a continuum. By linking her own civil rights work to nineteenth-century efforts to resist and abolish slavery, Baker both grounded and elevated the work she and her colleagues did to register voters and desegregate lunch counters. Her own understanding of her life story began in "slavery days," so it would be appropriate for this biography to begin there as well.

All four of Baker's grandparents were enslaved in Warren County, North Carolina, in the north-central part of the state, on the eastern edge of the

Piedmont hard against the Virginia border. She did not know her father's parents intimately, but knew that they had been slaves. Her paternal grand-father "must have had a great deal of Indian in him," Baker recalled. "I have no specific indications as to what blood line as far as Indian input came from. Both of [my father's] parents were light. [In other words, they had at least a few Caucasian forebears.] At least his mother was very light. And his father I did not know; he died before I was knowledgeable. But I knew Grandma Margaret, his mother." Her maternal grandparents were much more formi-dable presences in her childhood.

The rolling, forested hills of Warren County supported an overwhelm-ingly agricultural economy—cotton, tobacco, corn, and lumber were the main crops—that relied on slave labor, but very few farms were so large as to be home to twenty or more slaves. Slave communities in that part of North Carolina tended to be small and, compared to some other parts of the antebel-lum South, stable; the slave trade was less active than it was in the coastal part of the state and in other parts of the South. Slave families in the region also interacted with families on neighboring farms to a greater degree than slaves elsewhere. Of course, individual slave owners could be and were unspeakably cruel, and the state placed tight restrictions on their bodies and minds. For instance, by 1830 it was illegal to teach a slave to read and write in North Carolina, and after Nat Turner led a bloody slave insurrection just across the state line in Virginia the following year, white North Carolinians cracked down even harder on slaves' freedom of movement and freedom of thought.

In North Carolina, as elsewhere, slaves typically worked for their owners from sunrise to sunset six days a week, from a young age until their bodies gave out. They had little time available to them in a given day to augment the minimal housing, clothing, and food their owners provided, so they had to learn to be resourceful and reliant upon one another. This was the portrait of slavery that Ella Baker's grandparents painted for her: a profoundly unjust social system that they had worked to resist and change, even as they worked to improve their lives and the lives of others within it. Slavery had not broken her ancestors, Baker believed; it had made them resilient and forced them to forge strong bonds with one another. She looked to their experience for inspiration in her own work, and she made a point of sharing the lessons of slavery that she had learned from them as a child.

As an adult, when asked to address an audience—of students, adult learn-ers, or would-be citizen activists—Baker returned again and again to the stories of slavery her grandparents had bequeathed to her. (She did this long before Alex Haley published the historical novel *Roots*, which encouraged black Americans to search out their own families' oral traditions about life under slavery. In this way, among many others, Baker was ahead of her time.) Baker "had the privilege," as she called it, "of having known my maternal grandmother who was an ex-slave," Josephine Elizabeth "Bet" Ross. She heard the great majority of the stories from her grandmother Bet, internalized them, and retold them for different purposes.

Bet Ross's biological father was her white master, and her mother was an "octoroon," a slave with many more white than black ancestors herself. (If the octoroon term is accurate and the plantation owner's family tree was fully Caucasian, fifteen of Bet Ross's sixteen great-great-grandparents were white— but because she was born to a slave mother, she was born a slave herself.) According to the family's oral tradition, the "mistress" of the plantation, the owner's wife, was so jealous of Bet's mother that she killed her by poisoning her Christmas Day meal, soon after Bet was born, so Bet had to be raised by a grandmother. Bet Ross was, in Ella Baker's telling, "a very light [-skinned] woman, and as such in the pattern of the day, the light slaves were taken as house girls and carriage boys or carriage men." According to the stories Ross told Baker, the plantation owner's young wife wanted her to marry another light-skinned house servant named Carter. "But my grandmother was in love with a man who was very, very dark, who was known as Mitchell."

When the order came for Bet to marry, she refused, and as a result, the plantation mistress ordered her to be whipped. The master—who was, after all, her father—refused to whip her. Instead, he sent her to work a plow in the low grounds by the river. This was hard work normally reserved for men. "She recalls the stories of getting up early in the morning and having to warm her hands under the horses' belly in order to keep going," Baker said. "But to show her defiance, she insisted that no social occasions . . . would take place without her. So she would plow all day, and if necessary, dance all night to show that her spirit was not broken. This was a form of resistance." In case the moral of this story was lost on her modern audiences, Baker emphasized "the fact that wherever there has been struggle, black women have been identified with that struggle."

Bet Ross, like countless others born into slavery, was conceived via rape. Violence, inequality, and injustice were woven into the very fabric of their social system, and they required slave women to make otherwise unthinkable decisions. "One of the other forms of resistance which was perhaps much more tragic and has not been told," Baker said, reciting one of her grandmother's lessons, "is the large number of black women who gave birth to children and killed them, rather than have them grow up as slaves."

Ross also told the story of "one of her forebears who was called 'Stracted Mary.'" Baker repeated the story and its lesson: "Now what does ''Stracted' imply? It meant that she was distracted. They called her crazy, because after Mary had done what she considered her share of the chopping in the corn or cotton field, she'd just refuse to chop anymore. When the overseer would press her, she would act as if she were crazy and run after him with the hoe. This was her resistance to slavery."

Why did Ella Baker pass these stories along? Because, she emphasized, they illustrated "a certain kind of deep *commitment* or *resentment*. Commitment to freedom and deep resentment against slavery. It is not the kind of thing we would advocate at this point, but it shows that the drive for full dignity as human beings goes very deep in the struggle." To be black in America, Baker told her twentieth-century audiences in so many words, was to fight for your dignity and your rights as a human being. The struggle was part of the existence, and the struggle was noble. Baker's slave stories taught them that they had deep wells of strength and perseverance they could draw from and be proud of as they fought their own battles. These were certainly the conclusions she drew from the narratives.

Baker's grandmother Bet "jumped the broom," marrying Mitchell R. Ross, the slave she preferred to Carter, while still a slave. Tall, lean, and dark-skinned, Ross was known as a hard worker and a proud man—proud of his talents and his work ethic, and proud of his skin color. After emancipation in 1865, the couple and many of their family members stayed in the area, making homes either on the plantation where they had been enslaved or very nearby. In the quarter century after freedom came, Mitchell Ross and several of his brothers and cousins were able to do the unthinkable. Growing wheat, corn, and cotton, and raising livestock, they were able to save enough money to buy a substantial plot of land from the estate of William D. Elams, a white man who was in all likelihood Bet's father. (If Elams was not her father, he was her father's close neighbor. The community just northwest of Littleton at the site of his plantation bears his name.) The Rosses made the last installment payment of $250 (the equivalent of more than $6,000 in 2013) on January 24, 1888, a date that became an unofficial family holiday. They immediately donated a parcel of the land for the construction of Roanoke Chapel Baptist Church, which also housed a school for African Americans.

In an overwhelmingly agricultural economy, owning land was the only thing that counted nearly as much as owning one's own labor. Only a tiny fraction of freed slaves ever managed to reach the impossible dream—after all, they entered the world as freedmen with absolutely nothing. In their own particular social context the Rosses were elites, but they chose to share their good fortune. Mitchell Ross subdivided his own fifty-acre plot of rich river-bottom land into smaller farms that he rented out or sold to his sisters, brothers, and cousins and their families.

The Rosses did remarkably well, considering the social and economic forces that were arrayed against them. By the turn of the twentieth century Mitchell Ross had planted fruit orchards and a large garden, and he grew enough corn and wheat to support his family with a bit left over to sell on the market. By his granddaughter's reckoning he had enough cows to produce a dozen gallons of milk a day, along with enough chickens and hogs to keep the family well fed. The Rosses became economically self-sufficient, which allowed them to weather the notorious booms and busts of the post-Reconstruction period and to protect themselves from the worst expressions of white supremacy.

"One of the things my grandfather had was a large production of food . . . there was plenty of food," Baker said. "He believed in that kind of living, so . . . how did I know he wasn't rich? As far as I was concerned, there was plenty to eat. In fact, there was no question; riches never entered into it. It was the business of good living." Just as importantly, she added, "[N]obody ever got turned away. As I understand it, he was certainly [generous] in terms of food. So this was the pattern, and if somebody called and needed help [he helped them]." The lesson Baker learned from her grandparents' example was profound: "Your relationship to human beings was more important than your relationship to the amount of money that you made. There was a deep sense of community that prevailed in this little neck of the woods." But the amount of money the Rosses earned did make a difference: on their self-sustaining farm they were comparatively safe from the worst humiliations that white southerners who were still getting used to living in a nonslave society could dish out.

At some point during slavery or shortly after emancipation, Mitchell Ross taught himself to read and write, demonstrating another passion nearly as great as his drive to own land and support his family. African Americans all over the South considered education a holy grail, and they sacrificed to achieve it. Millions of them, the Rosses included, would have agreed with a newly emancipated slave in Mississippi, who said, "If I never does do nothing more while I live, I shall give my children a chance to go to school, for I considers education the next best thing to liberty." Ross also pastored Roanoke Chapel and filled in when necessary at a few other nearby black Baptist churches.

Bet and Mitchell Ross had a large family—at least twelve children, one of whom was a daughter named Anna Georgianna. (They gave their six sons the names of the apostles: Luke, Mark, John, Peter, Paul, and Matthew.)

Anna Ross grew up with the new South following Reconstruction, and it would have been possible for her to believe that her world was opening with new opportunities and a new, post-emancipation social order. She attended one of the thousands of schools that New England missionaries founded throughout the south for the children of freedmen in the nearby town of Warrenton, and she dove into the work of her church. She met Blake Baker, another son of slaves, at the school and fell in love with him. His family was much less well off than the Rosses, but Baker was ambitious. After graduation he moved to nearby Norfolk, Virginia, where jobs on the waterfront were plentiful, but Anna Ross stayed in Warren County and taught school. They courted during his visits home.

The school where Anna Ross taught was a "community school," as opposed to a public school—it was open to the (black) public, but it received few if any government resources. "In all probability the parents, who were themselves recently out of slavery, were a party to the establishment of the school," Ella Baker said. "My mother's father, being a minister, had several churches, and he gave the land for the school. And of course, the community, I'm sure, lent its labor to doing whatever was necessary to see that there was a schoolhouse." The hunger for education in the freedmen community was so great that the community was willing to cooperate and make great sacrifices to educate its children.

Anna and Blake Baker married in 1896, the year that the U.S. Supreme Court decided in the case of *Plessy v. Ferguson* that a new set of southern local and state laws denying black Americans equal access to public accommodations was constitutional. If their generation of black southerners really had believed during Reconstruction that they were helping the country build a new form of race-neutral democracy, the court's decision made it difficult if not impossible to maintain that belief any longer. After 1896 Jim Crow segregation became the law of the land all over the South, and racial segregation continued to be practiced by custom throughout the rest of the United States. Jim Crow entrenched itself in American social relations, culture, and thought, and it would take a half century even to begin rooting it out.

The couple chose to make their home in Norfolk, where Blake Baker had found a job as a waiter on a steamship that made regular round trips between Norfolk and Washington, D.C. The decision to move away from Littleton and her family network was a difficult one for Anna Ross Baker. Not only would she lose the support network her extended family provided, but she would also have to spend most of her time alone keeping house while Blake Baker was gone for days at a time. Norfolk was not exactly New York City at the turn of the twentieth century, but the rhythms, sights, and sounds of urban life were different enough from those of life in Littleton to be disorienting. Anna Ross Baker came to believe that the city was, in a word, vulgar. Having grown up sheltered from the worst aspects of white supremacy, she was now in a position where she could not possibly ignore them.

The Bakers lived first in a nearly all-black neighborhood near the waterfront among other households headed by skilled tradesmen, and then in a more centrally located neighborhood that was home to more middle-class blacks, many of them highly educated. Many of the shopkeepers in these neighborhoods were African American, but not all were. There was no choice but for a housewife to deal with whites, none of whom considered blacks their social equals, on a daily basis. A proud African American such as Anna Ross Baker had to work hard and constantly in such a situation simply to maintain her dignity.

She gave up her career as a teacher when she moved to Norfolk. Blake Baker made a good wage, and it was important to both of them that they keep up Victorian-era middle-class appearances, which dictated that wives not work outside the home. Reflecting on the arrangement, Ella Baker surmised, "It could well be . . . that my father at that stage, in order to consider himself the keeper of the home," didn't want his wife to work. "You see, people take on the patterns of those whom they escape from, as you well know. And so this was no doubt part of that. She did not work at any point while we were in Norfolk."

According to this way of thinking, no matter what talents she had to offer to the world, the sole job of a proper married woman was to create a loving, comfortable atmosphere for her husband and children, safe from the dog-eat-dog public sphere. The only work outside the home that the larger society expected of a proper married woman was volunteer labor on behalf of her church, or perhaps on behalf of a social welfare society. (The one divergence Anna Ross Baker allowed herself from this ideal was the taking in of boarders. She rented out rooms to the young men of families she knew from Warren County who came to Norfolk looking for work, and she made a little extra income.) But allowing herself to be confined to the private sphere did not mean that Anna Ross Baker was weak, or that she accepted any kind of second-class status. A strong-willed woman with strong opinions and a strong voice, she was the dominant personality in the marriage and by far the primary influence on her daughter.

The Bakers' home life was not entirely happy, for reasons that were all too understandable to a great many American families at the turn of the twentieth century. Anna Ross Baker had eight pregnancies, but four of them ended in miscarriage or stillbirth, and one child died in infancy. Only three

Baker children lived to maturity: Blake Curtis, who was born in 1901; Ella Josephine, born in 1903; and Margaret Odessa ("Maggie"), born in 1908. The U.S. Centers for Disease Control and Prevention estimate that one in ten children born in the United States in 1900 died before their first birthday, and in some cities the ratio was closer to one in three. African American families, even middle-class ones, were statistically more likely to lose children. "There was one between me and my baby sister who died in infancy, I recall," Baker said, referring to a brother named Prince, who was born around 1906. "This was the first death I knew of in the family. I remembered it in particular because my father was the only one who went to wherever the interment was taking place." Her mother was too distraught to witness the burial. "I was very eager to be in the carriage" with her father, Baker said, "but they didn't permit me to go." While still in Norfolk the Bakers took in ten-year-old Martha Grinage, the daughter of Anna's first cousin, and raised her as their own. Anna took the children home to Littleton for long summer visits on the family farm. It was on these visits that Baker began to soak up her grandparents' stories about freedom and emancipation and their "deep sense of community."

The twenty or so years following the Supreme Court's *Plessy* decision were the worst for African Americans in the South after slavery ended. They lost nearly everything they had gained during the Reconstruction era. Southern states systematically disfranchised black voters and prohibited black citizens from participating in public life in other ways, especially by enforcing Jim Crow segregation in increasingly wide swaths of public space. The adjustment was hardest in growing southern cities, whose populations swelled with both blacks and whites from the countryside looking for economic opportunity. The number of black voters in Norfolk alone dropped from 1,826 in 1901 to forty-four in 1910, and "Whites Only" signs went up all over town.

Whites created the new, segregated system because it offered them obvious economic, political, and psychological benefits, and they defended it with violence whenever necessary in dozens of southern cities. In 1910 they rioted over the Fourth of July weekend in Norfolk simply because the African American prizefighter Jack Johnson had defeated white boxer Jim Jeffries in the so-called Battle of the Century. The fight took place thousands of miles away, in Reno, Nevada, but local whites did not want their black neighbors to gain strength or confidence from the victory, so they beat up African Americans and ransacked their neighborhoods. When the dust cleared, forty people had been injured in Norfolk, and two hundred were in jail. Ella Baker had to learn to live within these new realities as a small child. One of her enduring memories of life in Norfolk was wrapped up in racial conflict: as a child she was walking through the downtown shopping district at Christmastime when a young white boy called her "nigger." She immediately began throwing fists, and her father had to pull her off the boy before other whites intervened.

By 1910 Anna Ross Baker had had enough of the city. She took the children back home to Littleton, which she considered more "cultured" than Norfolk, despite its tiny size. She and the children lived for a time with one of her aunts, and then they moved into a rented two-story house in town. It had all the trappings of a nice middle-class Victorian home, Ella Baker remembered: a piano, "a dining room, and dining room furniture, and silver." Blake Baker visited as often as his work allowed.

As compared to Norfolk's, Littleton's middle-class black community was a little more quarantined from the indignities that whites could dispense. "We did not come into contact with whites [in Littleton] too much," Baker said. "I was shielded from having contact with them at an early age. This was a complete black community to a large extent. Even the store on the corner, it was Mr. Foreman's store, he was black. . . . So, this is the kind of insulation that was provided by the black people themselves . . . you didn't have to run afoul of a lot of insults." Of course, Baker's family was more insulated than most; the great majority of African Americans in Warren County were economically vulnerable and therefore dependent on whites. But for families such as hers that could afford it, the circumstances were comfortable.

Baker's childhood in an extended rural family network and a way of life that bordered on the communal had a deep effect on her. Her grandparents' influence was intense. Bet Ross was "my escape valve, because she was very gay," Baker said. "She identified with young people. She played catch ball with us. I'm sure she must have been in her seventies . . . she was very healthy." Mitchell Ross's impact was nearly as great. Ella Baker was her grandfather's favored child, perhaps because she seemed to have inherited his beautifully dark skin, booming voice, and proud personality. He called her "Grand Lady" and invited her along for long buggy rides in which they engaged in deep conversations as he went about his business. He insisted, over his wife's and daughter's protests, on allowing Grand Lady to sit beside him in the chair at the front of his Roanoke Baptist Church that was otherwise reserved for visiting preachers or deacons. Anna Ross Baker had to sit stewing in her pew and watch the soles of her daughter's shoes glide into and out of sight as Ella sat in the pulpit and gaily swung her legs through the course of her grandfather's sermons.

The sermons were memorable. Mitchell Ross did not suffer fools gladly, and he expected members of the congregation to remember who was in charge of his church. He believed that black Baptists generally behaved too emotionally during services, and it was his practice to stop preaching and stare down worshippers who got lost in the spirit. "My grandfather didn't care too much for noise in the church," Baker recalled. "The story goes that if they began to do a lot of shouting and throwing their arms, he'd call them by name and tell them to sit down and keep quiet. And if they didn't, then he had his sons . . . go and take them up and sit them outside the church, let them cool off. . . . In fact, as I understand it, the deacons had to accompany him [to baptisms], because he wasn't going to try to hold them. If they wanted to shout, he'd let them fall back in the water."

Baker believed that her grandfather had such strong feelings about worship because he worked hard to craft his sermons into learned moral lessons, and he wanted his congregations to react to the lessons intellectually rather than emotionally. It is just as likely that he was concerned with outward expressions of middle-class respectability: he wanted this new generation of African Americans to behave differently than they had as slaves, in church and elsewhere. Ross also refused to eat certain foods, including cornbread, that he associated with slavery. Bet Ross seems to have considered such ideas silly—besides, she liked cornbread—but in her husband's presence she did not serve those foods.

White southerners of Mitchell Ross's generation had trouble getting past slavery ways, too. They never accepted the Reconstruction-era amendments to the U.S. Constitution that redefined black Americans as citizens. The freedmen—the black southerners who stayed to make lives for themselves in the places they loved, the only homes they had ever known—had to fight constant rear-guard actions against whites who wanted to return to the political economy of slavery. And they did fight. Mitchell Ross was, Baker said, "a man who had the nerve to fight back." She recalled family stories from the 1880s and 1890s: "It was said that when [black men] went up to register to vote . . . if they interfered, he and his sons would go up and stand by the folks if necessary." Baker's family did not have a tradition of philosophical nonviolence; the men of the family reserved the right to defend their loved ones and property by any means necessary. "The thing that was passed on was not subservience. It was fighting back," Baker said.

Mitchell Ross worked hard to get ahead, and he was recognized as a "big man" in his community, but he demonstrated an unswerving devotion to his family and neighbors. He and Bet Ross thought of their large, prosperous farm, historian Barbara Ransby writes, "not only as a resource for the economic well-being of their immediate family but also as a source of stability for the entire community." His family shared the farm's bounty with neighbors as a matter of routine. When economic conditions got especially rough, Ross mortgaged his farm and lent the money to neighbors in need. It was their Christian duty, the family believed, and it was a way of "Lifting as We Climb," as the motto of the National Association of Colored Women put it at the time. It was "more or less a kind of a Socialistic bit of thinking," Baker said, even though no one in Warren County "called [it] such" back then.

"This was to a large extent . . . an independent community; they were independent farmers," she said. "But they also went in for the practice of co-operative [farming] . . . Helping each other. When I came along, for instance, I don't think there was but one threshing machine for threshing the wheat. And so today they might be on Grandpa's place, and all the people who had wheat who needed the thresher would be there [helping], or at least some from those families. And then they would move around [to thresh at another farm]. There was a great deal of what might have been a cooperative type of relationship at that stage."

Baker chose to be baptized at the age of nine, at the same time as her eleven-year-old brother Curtis. "We hadn't quite planned it that particular year," Baker said, but when they went to a revival and learned that two cousins had confessed their sins, opening the door for their own baptism, "We had to do something about it. . . . I guess we were about to be left out." Baker described the process in terms remarkably free of emotion: "We went to church, and I don't know whether we both got 'religion' the same night or not. We weren't very dramatic about it, but we were ready for baptism, and all four of us were baptized at the same time in the old mill pond. That's where you were baptized."

Perhaps Baker approached baptism with an all-business attitude in defer-ence to her grandfather; but her faith was real, and she approached her con-version with total seriousness. "I took the position that you were supposed to change" after baptism, she said. "And I think the manner in which I mani-fested [the change] was, I was to control my temper. I had a high temper; I was very quick-tempered. And I'd strike back very quickly. I didn't take teasing. I wasn't good at teasing, and I wouldn't take it but so long. I'd say, 'Stop,' and if it didn't stop I'd hit, and it didn't matter how large you were. And so this was my way of demonstrating my change, by trying to control my temper."

Baker's religious faith remained a foundation for the rest of her life, as a person, an activist, and a thinker, which is not to say that she never questioned God, his followers, or religious institutions. Far from it. "It was important for [instilling in me] the sense of the value of the human being," she said. "I look upon it as having had a family who placed a very high value on people." Mitchell and Bet Ross lived according to the ideals of a cooperative commonwealth, and Anna Ross Baker lived a Christian life devoted to service. Ella Baker later drew from these examples and more in her professional life. "I was young when I became active in things and I became active in things largely because my mother was very active in the field of religion," she said. The members of the Ross family acted as they did because they believed Christ had compelled them to do so. That compulsion fueled Baker's later social action as well.

Anna Ross Baker practiced an especially feminized version of Christian service that was very much of its time and place. She exercised her leadership and activism under the auspices of the Baptist church. In fact, she "would have been very much at home leading a feminist movement," her daughter thought, but it may be more useful to think of her as a protofeminist or a womanist. She would not have described herself as a feminist at any point in her life.

"[L]et Christ take the first place in your vocation and life. Inquire of the Lord what he would have us do. Let us stay on the job for Christ," Anna Ross Baker advised a statewide meeting of the Women's Auxiliary Progressive Baptist Convention. This was the work that black Baptist housewives could acceptably do in public in their historical context, and she took it incredibly seriously. Doing the "job for Christ" involved raising money for overseas missionary work and black schools closer to home; tending to the sick, elderly, and orphaned; and attending meetings at which responsibilities for this work were organized. Young Ella Baker attended most of them, and she was often called upon to recite a Bible verse or give a short speech on the importance of one or another of the group's efforts to put their Christian teachings to work. These were her first attempts at public speaking; the affirmation she received made her want to continue to develop the skill.

The women she saw and interacted with at the meetings were "confident, competent, and committed," Barbara Ransby writes. They "operated with considerable autonomy. Women conducted their own meetings, managed their finances, and made policy decisions." Having seen this model of church-based organization and activism at close range, Baker knew that it could be highly effective. She would later have reason to contrast it to another church model, in which a single preacher-leader directed his many congregant-followers. Finding the latter overly hierarchical and male dominated, she would draw lessons from her experience with the former in her civil rights organizing.

Ella Baker described her mother as a "precise-spoken . . . lady" who demanded that others treat her with the dignity she deserved. When a white salesman came to the door and referred to her mother as "Auntie" (a dismissive term whites used to address their African American women elders, a leftover from slavery), Baker recalled, her mother barked, "I didn't know my brother had a son like you" and refused to have anything to do with him. According to Ransby, Anna Ross Baker showed "no deference to white authority and very little deference to male authority." It rubbed off on her daughter.

Anna Ross Baker subscribed to the biblical injunction, "For unto whomsoever much is given, of [her] shall be much required." She was as charitable as she was dignified. Her daughter recalled, "On many a night . . . people would knock on the door in the middle of the night and say, 'Mrs. Baker, So-and-so is sick.' And my mother had one of those very positive voices. They'd knock, and she said, 'Ye-e-es?' She would get up" and do what needed to be done. Anna Ross Baker had a high opinion of herself, but she did not act as though she believed she was better than her neighbors; her charitable work had the effect of breaking down class barriers in the black community, not reinforcing them.

Ella Baker recalled one incident in particular from her childhood that drove home this point for her. On the way to the post office in Littleton she passed the home of Mandy Bunk, a child whose parents were "lacking in mental capacity." (Sadly, the federal and state governments provided few if any facilities for the care of mentally ill and mentally retarded people in the turn-of-the-century South. They were entirely dependent on the charity of others.) From the sidewalk Ella saw Mandy standing in the doorway, bleeding heavily from what was probably her first menses. "I don't know whether it was a hemorrhage or just *what*," Baker said, but "she needed medical attention. So what do you *do*? I mean, she was a *person*. You couldn't just pass by her and say, 'Oh, that's just Mandy Bunk, you see, who raised her pig in one room and herself in the other room.' You don't do that." So Ella ran home to tell her mother, and Anna Ross Baker rushed out to tend to Mandy Bunk.

Young Baker was clearly compassionate, but she was also headstrong and tough. She would have been called a tomboy. She loved to play baseball and was often enlisted to physically defend her older brother, Curtis, a slight and shy boy who preferred to stay at home with his mother if given the choice. Even before she was old enough to attend school herself, Baker recalled, when Curtis's classmates roughed him up "I was sent to school to take care of the situation." In Littleton, as in Norfolk, she was quick to defend herself. Soon after she had the altercation in downtown Norfolk, the son of Warren County's sheriff flung the n-word at her, but she flung rocks back at him and chased him out of her neighborhood. After that, no other white children made that mistake in Littleton. Anna Ross Baker cultivated Ella's physical and mental toughness, but she also forced Ella to conform to her own particular feminine ideal. Baseball or no, Ella Baker would become a proper lady.

A proper lady was educated. Anna Ross Baker taught her children to read and write before they were old enough to go to school, and she used corporal punishment to ensure that they used proper English in her home. (As an adult Ella Baker came to appreciate greatly having learned to speak precisely, but she also worried that it could get in the way of organizing. Using the king's English could bring people together by communicating ideas to them clearly, but it could also emphasize class differences and make people who did not know how to use it feel inferior to those who did. She made it a point to speak clearly and precisely, but without "putting on airs.") A proper lady also displayed Christian devotion and charity. The Bakers knew a farmer whose wife had died and who was too overwhelmed to take care of his many children. Once a week Anna Ross Baker announced that it was time for Ella to attend to her chore, taking care of the Powell children: "Mama would say, 'You must take the clothes to Mr. Powell's house, and give so-and-so a bath.' . . . The kids for the devilment would take off across the field [and] we'd chase them down, bring them back, put 'em in the tub, wash 'em off, change their clothes, carry the dirty ones home, and wash them. Those kind of things were routine."

Ella, Curtis, Maggie and Martha attended a free public, though church supported, two-room school for African Americans at South Street Baptist Church in Littleton. Because she had already learned to read and was considered preternaturally self-confident, Ella was allowed to skip grades. She remembered the school principal, Alonzo ("Lonnie") Weaver, as a stickler for discipline and piety; he led the children in prayer every morning. Ella learned important lessons in gender equality on the school's playground, where she excelled at her favorite sport. At that point in her life, she said, "I would rather play baseball than to eat. . . . we had a mixed team of boys and girls, some much bigger than I, and I played baseball at recess." She began eating her packed lunch on the way to school to leave more time during the lunch period for baseball.

The state of North Carolina only provided education for African Americans through the eighth grade, so families who wanted more for their children had to send them to private schools. Even these were few and far between—as late as 1925 there were only twenty-one accredited high schools for blacks, many of them prep schools run by historically black colleges, in the entire state. But allowing the Baker children to end their educations before high school was apparently never even an option. Curtis attended the high school run by North Carolina A&T College in Greensboro. Ella attended Monroe High School for one year. The teachers at Monroe did not pass muster with Anna Ross Baker, so she moved her daughter to Shaw Academy, a high school in Raleigh connected with historically black Shaw University, for the 1918 to 1919 school year. Maggie, the partier of the family, attended a less prestigious school.

Ella Baker would spend nine years as a student at Shaw, and the school allowed her to blossom, both as an intellectually curious scholar and as a self-confident person determined to engage with the world around her. In Barbara Ransby's judgment, "Next to the church, Shaw was the most important institution in Ella Baker's early life." Founded as the Raleigh Institute in 1865 by a Union Army chaplain affiliated with the Northern Baptist Church, Shaw was initially administered by the American Baptist Home Mission Society. The Home Mission Society's stated beliefs regarding racial equality were far ahead of its time: it affirmed "the thorough humanity of the black man, with divine endowment of all the facilities of the white man." Shaw offered what it called "choice scholarship" to the sons and daughters—almost from its founding, Shaw opened its doors to women, making it forward looking in another way—of freedmen via a classical humanities curriculum. Black Baptist congregations and church societies such as Anna Ross Baker's Women's Auxiliary Progressive Baptist Missionary Association throughout the state raised money for the school and got it up on its feet.

By the time Baker arrived in 1918, Shaw was one of the few historically black colleges in the South offering a classical education. Influenced by Booker T. Washington, the president of Tuskegee Institute, most schools open to black students offered industrial training and "normal" (teacher training) school programs. Shaw trained teachers as well; in fact, Anna Ross Baker had chosen the school for Ella because she expected her daughter to become a teacher. But whereas Tuskegee students studied masonry or agriculture, Shaw students studied chemistry or English literature.

The college president was white, but many of the deans and members of the faculty were black. Many of the high school teachers were white "missionary types" from the North, but others were Shaw University normal school graduates and students engaged in practice teaching. Here Baker had her first real experience of blacks and whites working together with a common purpose. She decided at Shaw in the 1920s that she liked racially integrated institutions—not because the ideal of integration had any special merit on its own, but because she now had empirical evidence that it brought out the best in people of both races, although the sample size in her experiment was admittedly small.

Most of Baker's classmates, all of whom were African American, were fellow boarders from around the state, but many were day students from Raleigh's elite black families. She had no trouble competing with any of them. Baker excelled as a high school student, studying history, English, French, Latin, science, mathematics, the Bible, and home economics. She graduated as valedictorian of her high school in the spring of 1923 and entered the university as a freshman that fall.

Shaw University provided a top-notch undergraduate education comparable to any available to whites in the state. The North Carolina Board of Education awarded it an "A" rating in a 1923 evaluation. The school's connection to the Baptist church dictated a conservative social atmosphere, in which male and female students were kept as separate as possible, even in chapel, and everyone had to abide by a strict code of conduct. Among the prohibited behaviors were dancing, smoking tobacco, playing cards, and engaging in "frivolous conversations or attention to trivial matters." Boarding students like Baker had to attend chapel services every morning, and the women who lived on campus often had to attend additional services every night in their dormitories. "So you can understand why we were good Christians," she joked as an adult. "And why I don't go to church now." While a student Baker's Christian faith remained as strong as ever, but she began to have strong reservations about the church and its hierarchies.

A small handful of Baker's academic work from Shaw survives in the Ella Baker Papers at the archives of the Schomburg Center for Research in Black Culture in Harlem. In one essay, "The Challenge of the Age and the Negro Youth," Baker paired her religious faith with her growing commitment to social justice. She wrote, "In this age of materialism in which we now live, with all its mad ruckus for wealth, its over-spreading waves of jazz, its scientific inventions and appliances, we sometimes question whether there is any room in the world for God or not!" She asked rhetorically, "Is there any room in the world for justice?" and responded, "Have the strong ceased to oppress the weak? Since conditions force us to acknowledge the need of man, through love, truth and justice, we must admit the need of God; for from him cometh all 'good and perfect gifts.'" Baker dedicated herself in the essay to belief in "the fundamental equality of all mankind" and concluded, "The salvation of the world is in its youth." Both would become major themes in her organizing career.

In another essay, titled "Our Heritage and Its Challenge," she championed another major theme. "Social reform has had as its co-partner education," Baker wrote. "We have witnessed the day when education was a personal matter, and therefore the luxury of the rich, through the period when it became a part of the static program, to the present when it is of vital concern to states and nations." She gave all credit due to the African American institution that she considered most responsible for the development of educational systems: "To speak of ideals and visions in Negro education without mentioning the Negro Church would be unpardonable." That was the party line for a student at Shaw, but the essay accurately reflected Baker's evolving ideas about the role of the black church in efforts at social reform.

Baker's favorite professor at Shaw was Benjamin G. Brawley, a poet and prolific scholar of English, American, and African American literature, and of African American history. She found his bourgeois formality a bit off-putting, but they bonded over their common passion for social justice and racial equality. Brawley was enough of a prude that he refused to attend men's basketball games on campus because he thought the players' uniforms were too revealing, and he skipped the racy bits when he presented Shakespeare to his students, but he also sparked Baker's intellectual curiosity and introduced her to new worlds.

Students at Shaw had to develop critical-thinking skills. Baker recalled one class discussion in particular, on a topic that is still very much a subject of debate in the black community: the concept of "good hair." Another favorite professor, Dr. Walter S. Turner, a professor of ethics and sociology who also served as the college dean and as a member of Shaw's Board of Trustees, asked his students to consider how their culture constructed ideas about the worth of certain kinds of hair styles. Black Americans of the time spent millions of dollars a year on hair-straightening and skin-lightening products, placing a premium on appearances and hair styles that more closely approximated whites' fashion sense. According to the popular standards of the day in the black community, hair that was most like whites' was considered "good hair." Turner encouraged his students to recognize the standards as social constructions, and rejections of African traditions at that. "Everybody's got good hair," he said. "All hair is good. It covers your head." Though she had straight hair herself, and though she had been raised to conform to what may appear to have been "white" standards of beauty and comportment, the black pride message resonated with Baker.

She put her critical-thinking and oratorical skills to work for Shaw as a valuable member of the school's debate team. Baker "had a heavy voice, and helped to win a lot of trophies and honors for the school," her friend Effie Yergan recalled. Baker worked two jobs, supervising a chemistry laboratory and waiting tables, to help her parents pay her tuition, but still found time to write for and edit the student newspaper. Journalism and debate were normally reserved for men, but Baker seems not to have given a second thought as to whether she would participate in whatever activity she pleased. At the very least, she refrained from asking for permission. Surely she faced sexist opposition at points along the way, but she apparently ignored it. "My man-woman relationships were on the basis of just being a human being, not a sex object," she said of her college years. "As far as my sense of security, it had been established." Her experience at Shaw taught her that she could "compete on levels such as scholarship . . . And I could stand my own in debate. And things of that nature. I wasn't delicate."

In addition, Baker was heavily involved with the campus chapter of the Young Women's Christian Association (YWCA) and raised money for the Student Friendship Fund, a group that supported Baptist missionary work in Africa and other parts of the world. With so many activities on top of her studies, Baker had little time to socialize. But she was popular, according to a classmate. Effie Yergan said, "She was friendly to everyone, but I don't think she ever had a steady beau." Baker did become friendly with at least one fellow student, her future husband T. J. Roberts, and another classmate remembers Baker as having swooned over a football player. But "you know how men were at that time, and some of them still are today," Yergan said. "They wanted you to be beautiful and dumb. [She] was too intelligent for that. The boys were probably intimidated."

While still a high school student Baker developed a reputation for out-spokenness and leadership. The administration forbade women students from wearing silk stockings to class. A group of college upperclassmen who wanted to wear stockings, but not so badly that they were willing to speak up for themselves, enlisted Baker as a high school senior to speak on their behalf. "I didn't have any silk stockings, but I felt it was their right to wear their stockings if they wanted to," she said. In Baker's telling, when she went to the administration to challenge this aspect of the dress code, she so shocked the dean of women that the woman fainted. The dean subsequently asked Baker to pray with her that the young woman could be made to see the error of her ways and endeavor to change. "I didn't seem particularly penitent, and she was very disturbed about it," Baker said. "But it didn't bother me because I thought I was correct."

On another occasion the white president of the university asked a group of students to sing Negro spirituals for a group of visiting white dignitaries. The students felt humiliated, and Baker refused to sing. Only a young woman with an ironclad sense of right and wrong, coupled with abundant self-confidence, could have challenged the administration in these situations. "I didn't break rules, but I challenged rules," Baker said of her college years. By the end of that experience she was, according to Ransby, "a rebel but not yet a radical, tactically prepared to question but not to defy the rules, and philosophically ready to argue against the limitations of the dominant authority but not to challenge its fundamental validity."

She graduated valedictorian of the class of 1927 with enough credits to claim two baccalaureate degrees and just about all the knowledge Shaw's faculty could impart. "Awake[,] youth of the land and accept this noble challenge of salvaging the strong ship of civilization, by the anchors of right, justice, and love," she urged her classmates in her valedictory address at graduation ceremonies. Her speech reflected the sense of Christian duty she had inherited from her family and from Shaw, and in it she flashed the rhetorical skills she had honed by then. Baker also displayed a crusader's zeal. "Let us resolve that for the welfare of the whole, for the good of all, for the uplift of fallen humanity, for the extension of Christ's kingdom on earth," she thundered, "there shall be no turning back . . . we will strike against evil, strife, and war until the echo shall resound in the recesses of the earth and . . . the waters of the deep." It is tempting to find in any valedictory speech read after the fact only clues of the adult the student was to become, but Baker's clearly signaled the path she was to take in life.

Anna Ross Baker had hoped Ella would become a teacher, and she was certainly qualified to take up the profession immediately upon graduation; indeed, she received several compelling job offers. Baker could have had a comfortable life as a teacher, but she refused even to consider the possibility. Because even the best schools, such as Shaw Academy, were utterly dependent on paternalistic (or worse) whites, black women college graduates, she had noticed, "couldn't teach unless somebody in the white hierarchy okayed your teaching." Baker simply refused to play along with a system that automatically treated blacks, no matter how educated or gifted they may have been, as inferiors. This was "a demeaning sort of thing, and I resented this, and I refused to teach."

Baker had seen that teachers had to compromise their principles to keep their jobs. "One of the reasons I developed an antipathy for teaching was that there were issues that would come up in a school community, and there were sides which would evidence positions," she said. "I noticed that some of those who had taken what I would have called good, positive, or progressive positions prior to their going out to teach, came back and they were no longer that type of person. It didn't maybe necessarily follow that this would be inevitable for everyone, but I think there was a great deal of truth in that. . . . When they'd come back and they didn't have spirit, this certainly turned me off as far as teaching." Besides, Baker candidly admitted, teaching was what everyone assumed she would do, and she had a strong enough ego to resist it just because it was expected of her. Then again, Anna Ross Baker may have been unable to talk her daughter into teaching as a career, but she clearly understood that Ella was a natural-born educator. Education remained at the core of Baker's program for social change.

Baker had decided by then that she wanted to go to graduate school at the University of Chicago, one of Dr. Brawley's alma maters. There she would study sociology on her way to becoming a social worker, or maybe an academic. Or, she thought, perhaps she would go in an entirely different direction, study medicine, and become a medical missionary overseas. Baker was neither the first nor the last American college graduate to enter adulthood with such wildly divergent ideas, or none at all, about what she wanted to do with the rest of her life. It takes some people a little longer to find their respective missions in life.

What separated Baker from the others was that when she finally figured out what her purpose was to be, she had an especially strong foundation to build from in working to achieve it. Baker's family had bequeathed to her a history of which she could be intensely proud, an egalitarian spirit that connected her intimately to the rest of humanity, and a Christian devotion to community service. In church and in school she had taken advantage of opportunities to develop leadership skills, and she had sharpened her ability to think critically. That was a powerful combination. When Baker did finally determine what her mission in life was to be, she was well prepared to act on it.

CHAPTER TWO

~

Hotbed of Radical Thinking

Years of making tuition payments to the children's private schools depleted the family's savings, so Ella Baker could not afford graduate school. Instead, with hundreds of thousands of other black southerners of the time, she migrated to the urban North to look for work. She chose to make her way to New York City because she had a close relative living there and because she had visited once and enjoyed it. There she found the best advanced education no money could buy. Baker took advantage of the educational opportunities she found wherever she looked in New York, whether they were impromptu lessons on communism in Washington Park, lectures on black nationalism on Harlem street corners, salons on social organizing in grand Harlem apartments, readings and lectures at the public library, or the hundreds of other informal classes available to the intellectually curious in fin de siècle Gotham. The child of the South was stunned to find "so many cultural advantages entirely free in New York every day of the year," as Baker put it; she was a long way from Littleton. "Sometimes I was the only woman there; sometimes the only black person," she said of those gatherings, "but I didn't care. I was there to learn."

Baker left North Carolina as soon as she could after graduation and spent the summer of 1927 working as a waitress at a New Jersey resort. She sent her first paycheck back home to Littleton to help the family meet a tax payment on her grandparents' farm. She moved into a roomy apartment on 152nd Street with her "sister," Martha Grinage, at the end of the summer. (They were actually cousins, but Anna and Blake Baker had raised Martha as their own child from the age of ten; she and Ella were close enough that they referred to each other as siblings. Knowing that Martha was in New York made it easier for Baker's family to accept her move.) Their apartment was at the northern edge of Harlem, the economic, social, and cultural capital of black America—"a place of laughing, singing, and dancing; a place where life wakes up at night," in the words of the poet, writer, and civil rights activist James Weldon Johnson. In 1927 the neighborhood was in the midst of arguably the most important artistic outpouring in the history of the United States, the Harlem Renaissance.

Novelists, poets, painters, sculptors, musicians, and artists of every possible stripe flocked to Harlem after World War I. During the period, black capitalists also built some of the first black-owned business empires based in Harlem, and denizens of Harlem nightclubs set fashions for black (and, to an increasing extent in those years, white) America. Blacks in the area began to assert a public personality that the philosopher Alain Locke first called the "New Negro" type. If white America expected blacks to be lazy, ignorant, and helpless, the New Negro would be vigorous, cultured, and assertive. The explosion of artistic, entrepreneurial, and civic talent produced a grand synergy in Harlem, a total greater than the sum of its parts, and it attracted ever more African Americans who considered themselves New Negroes. It was no coincidence that Baker ended up in Harlem. Where else could a young black adult with such a bright mind and a determination to make her mark on the world have moved in 1927?

Nearly all black, Harlem was at the same time a fascinatingly diverse place. Home to more than two hundred thousand people, Harlem's population had surged with the Great Migration of rural black southerners to the urban North in the economic expansion during and after World War I. But it was also home to a significant number of Caribbean newcomers and a smaller but still significant population of West Africans. According to the 1930 U.S. Census, 55 percent of all of the foreign-born "colored" residents of the United States lived in the neighborhood. With its mix of longtime residents, recent transplants from the rural South, and international immigrants, Harlem was a melting pot of cultures and ideas in its own right.

When Baker arrived Harlemites were still talking about Marcus Garvey, the Jamaican immigrant who had led a black pride movement in the years surrounding World War I. Garvey's fiery rhetoric stirred crowds and built support for black nationalist and pan-Africanist ideas, but he was convicted of mail fraud and deported from U.S. soil the year Baker arrived. Harlem had no shortage of small-time capitalists, but it also attracted the nation's young black socialists and others who rejected political, cultural, and social orthodoxies. Even before the stock market crash of 1929, the event that caused millions of Americans to question the nation's economic institutions, Harlem street corners were the sites of intense debates on the subject.

In fact, blacks all over America in the 1920s were engaged in a great debate that still resonates. According to historian Jeffrey O. G. Ogbar, one school of thought associated mainly with W. E. B. Du Bois, who was then the editor of the NAACP's magazine, *The Crisis*, and a great patron of the Harlem Renaissance, held that white Americans "could be convinced that democracy, freedom, and civil rights were good for all, not just for whites." In stark contrast, Marcus Garvey, who "did not believe whites could be reformed . . . was a staunch supporter of black nationalism—the belief that black people must establish a black nation-state for their survival." Blacks all over America, but especially in Harlem, debated whether African Americans' ultimate goal should be integration into a society and polity that may not have been perfect but at least had constitutional protections for minority groups like them. Should they work to improve the system? Or was the system so rotten at its core, so infected by white supremacy, that African Americans should withdraw completely and concentrate on creating their own institutions?

Baker had always agreed with the former approach, but now she was surrounded by people who made a learned and passionate case for the latter. She loved listening to and debating them, and their challenges initially served to strengthen her own beliefs. She had to learn to sharpen her own critical-thinking skills and read more widely and deeply to make her case more strongly, and she did. But Baker's Harlem colloquies eventually led her to either question or refine much of what she had been taught in North Carolina. Harlem's black socialists had more of an effect on Baker's thinking; she would come to identify as a socialist, but she never quite became an ideologue. Rather, Baker assimilated many of the tenets of Marxian thought and analysis into the cooperative egalitarianism of her North Carolina upbringing. (When she first heard Marx's principle "from each according to his ability, to each according to his needs," it sounded a lot like the way her family had lived on the farm.) And the more she saw of the hardships that the American way of life allowed for the people of Harlem, the more militantly she advocated radical alternatives.

Harlem, Baker said, "was the hotbed of—let's call it radical thinking. You had every spectrum of radical thinking. . . .The ignorant ones, like me, we had lots of opportunity to hear and to evaluate whether or not this was the kind of thing you wanted to get into. Boy, it was good, stimulating!" The freedom, the energy, the joie de vivre were intoxicating. "I went everywhere there was a discussion. . . . We had a lovely time!" she said. "All kinds of discussions were taking place. And so there was a rich cultural potential in terms of finding out things, if you didn't hesitate to go wherever there was something or to ask questions."

A child of the rural South who was beginning to think of herself as a citizen of the wider world, Baker devoured everything Harlem and New York had to offer. She knew she had arrived where she belonged, which is not to say that she found streets paved with gold. New York's economy was humming in 1927, but even valedictorians had to scramble to find work if they were black.

Baker commuted for a short time to work as a maid in suburban Westchester County, but she soon found work as a waitress at Judson House, across the street from Washington Square Park in Greenwich Village. Originally an expression of Judson Memorial Church's social gospel ministry, Judson House provided affordable short-term housing and a clinic that provided services to the women and children of the surrounding Lower Manhattan neighborhoods before the church sold the building to nearby New York University. By the time Baker worked there it was a dormitory with a dining room. She liked the job because Judson House was an easy commute on the elevated train line from her and Martha's new apartment on 143rd Street. Even better, it allowed her a break in the late mornings between breakfast and lunch service that she could fill as she wished. She might "run up" to the world-class New York Public Library on 42nd Street to read, or she might go for a walk in Washington Square Park, where she said she "liked to smell the fresh-turned earth . . . indulging my nostalgia for the land."

One morning Baker strolled through the park and struck up a conversation with a recent Jewish immigrant from the Soviet Union. He was eager to discuss Soviet communism and, Baker said, tried "to recruit me for one party or the other." She wasn't one to join a political party on a whim, but she was interested in what the man had to say about communism, socialism, and Marxist theory and ended up talking with him for what seemed like hours. The man "wasn't too keen about the Soviets," she recalled. "He was basically approving of the concept, but highly critical of the implementation of the concept as far as the Russian revolution was concerned." It was an important lesson for Baker: apparently one could appreciate the Marxian mode of analysis and accept Marx's ideas regarding social and economic organization without condoning the horrible things that were being done in Marx's name. The chance encounter encouraged Baker to begin reading Marx and other radicals on her own. According to a friend who met Baker in New York in the 1930s, "Ella Baker was a student of Marx and we used to debate that often."

Marx's ideas gained new currency in the United States after the shocking stock market crash of 1929 touched off a death spiral of underconsumption and unemployment, along with Americans' new levels of distrust of capitalism. Between 1929 and 1932 median family income in Harlem dropped 44 percent, and the neighborhood's unemployment rate was 1.5 to 3 times higher than that of New York as a whole. White investors owned roughly four-fifths of the neighborhood's business and real estate even before the Depression hit, so the catastrophe struck vulnerable African American renters and consumers especially hard.

Harlemites didn't sit back and accept these changes; they embarked on what Baker called a "social revolution." Communists and Socialists played a more prominent public role in the homegrown responses to the Depression in Harlem than they did in almost any other American community. Protest marches and street demonstrations were common occurrences. Racial self-help groups of every possible stripe proliferated, as did "Don't Buy Where You Can't Work" protest campaigns. Baker watched and learned from the protests, and, increasingly, she acted.

According to Baker, the lightbulb went off over her head one night during a conversation with a friend. "Look, Ella, a society can break down," she recalled the friend saying. "A social order can break down, and the individual is the victim of the breakdown, rather than the cause of it." "I began to see that there were certain social forces over which the individual had very little control," Baker said. "It was out of that context that I began to explore more in the area of ideology and the theory regarding social change," by which she meant socialism.

Baker began freelancing as a journalist, first for the *American West Indian News*, then for the *Negro National News*, for which she also worked as office manager. She worked as a stringer for her hometown *Norfolk Journal and Guide*, the Judkins News Service based in Harlem, and the *Pittsburgh Courier*, which was perhaps the most influential black newspaper of the day. Baker's interest in economic issues and her connection to George Schuyler, the publisher of the *Negro National News*, led her away from journalism and into the consumer cooperative movement.

In 1930 Schuyler founded the Young Negroes' Cooperative League (YNCL). It was "the only movement I know of among Negroes," he said, "that is actually offering some hope to our bewildered young brothers, sisters, cousins, nephews and nieces who eagerly come out of school with absolutely no hope of employment commensurate with their education." He might as well have been referring specifically to Baker, who joined as a charter member and quickly became the national organization's secretary-treasurer and the New York City Council's chair. Schuyler hired her as YNCL's national director in 1931. Schuyler was probably more responsible for Baker's Socialist education than any other single person. A World War I veteran, he had spent the 1920s working for *The Messenger*, a Socialist magazine run by A. Philip Randolph, the country's most important black labor leader. He remained close to Randolph even after the magazine folded and Schuyler had moved on to write a popular column for the *Pittsburgh Courier* and to publish the *Negro National News*.

With his wife, Josephine, a well-to-do, Texas-born white woman, Schuyler hosted one of Harlem's liveliest salons. At the Schuylers' apartment, Baker recalled, "You had access to people you wouldn't have been meeting, and that was always food for me. I didn't care so much about the socializing as the exchange of ideas."

Their personalities were as different as night and day—where Baker was a proper young lady who had been raised in the church, Schuyler was a bombastic atheist—but somehow they got along together famously. The pair settled into a productive working relationship at the YNCL, in which he served as the movement's charismatic, flamboyant spokesman and she did all of the necessary organizing work outside of the limelight. It was an organizational model with which Baker would become all too familiar in the course of her career.

Schuyler and Baker structured the YNCL as a network of locally organized cooperatives and buying clubs knitted together loosely by regional councils and the national office in Harlem. The YNCL's goal was simple: to "gain economic power through consumer cooperation." In theory, by consolidating members' buying power, cooperatives would drive down the costs of goods and services, keep more money in the members' pockets, and empower black consumers.

Schuyler contrasted the YNCL's approach with that of W. E. B. Du Bois, who at the time advised African Americans to organize cooperatives along black nationalist and classically Marxist lines that Schuyler considered undemocratic. Schuyler followed the Rochdale Principles, a set of governing ideals imported from the Rochdale Society of Equitable Pioneers in Great Britain. Voting in the YNCL proceeded along the one member–one vote, rather than the one share–one vote, principle, and all savings generated by YNCL activities had to be reinvested into given cooperatives or returned to members as dividends. In theory, at least, these arrangements sited power in the cooperative with the rank-and-file membership rather than the national headquarters. The YNCL also encouraged its members to form study groups to tackle the economic problems their cooperatives faced, and the members themselves insisted on allowing women to participate in YNCL activities as equals. Finally, while membership was restricted to African Americans between the ages of eighteen and thirty-five (older people who wanted to join could do so only if two-thirds of a local cooperative's membership voted to admit them), cooperatives were expected to work together with white co-operatives and wholesalers as much as possible, though they may have been organized separately.

In 1932 Baker embarked on a tour of the East Coast and Southeast to drum up new members. The YNCL's promotional materials promised that Baker would "awaken the Negro consumer to the ENORMOUS POWER that is his as a consumer; and it will act as an antidote to some of that hopelessness with which the inarticulate masses of Black Americans face the question, 'After the Depression, what?'" Not only did Baker make speeches before black groups—the YNCL made a particular effort to organize through and in cooperation with churches—she stayed in communities long enough to meet in small groups with local people to help them study the problems that faced them. Baker, the YNCL advertised, specialized in "organizing groups where there are none, pointing out from the experiences of others what plans to make and what steps to avoid." She learned through this experience how to be a community organizer.

The YNCL flourished for a time; membership doubled from 1931 to 1932, and it continued to grow, albeit at a slower rate, for the next few years. Several of the local cooperatives lasted and succeeded, even proved terrific investments. Some, including Harlem's Own Cooperative, Inc., of which Baker was an enthusiastic member from 1930 to 1940, became important community institutions that expanded their missions beyond those of buying clubs.

In retrospect, however, knowing what we now know about the depth and intensity of the country's economic problems from 1929 until its entry into World War II, the YNCL's plan was unworkable enough to be fantastical. No voluntary purchasing program was a match for the realities of double-digit unemployment, a collapsed banking system, and a cratered manufacturing sector, especially if it depended on the earning power of wage workers from a marginalized racial minority. It didn't help that the overwhelming majority of YNCL members had little or no experience running businesses; inevitably, local cooperatives succumbed to mismanagement.

Yet the cooperative movement did have many positive attributes: Baker treated it as an opportunity to educate and organize the black masses, and the members ran the cooperatives democratically. Anything that offered African

Americans education, organizing, and democracy was a positive good in Baker's book. The YNCL also provided Baker with significant opportunities for her own personal growth, as well as her first experience in mass, cross-class organizing and group-centered leadership. The YNCL was the most democratic, most youth-focused, and least male-supremacist organization she had ever been a part of. She would carry those particular ideals forward and emphasize them at every stop in her organizing career.

Living in Harlem allowed Baker to grow and develop in other ways, too. In the early 1930s the Harlem branches of the YWCA and the New York Public Library were her homes away from home. The YWCA had a cafeteria that served reasonably priced meals and had a vibrant speakers series that attracted women with ideas similar to Baker's. Pauli Murray, another remarkable African American woman who had been raised in North Carolina and made her way to New York in the late 1920s, described the atmosphere at the Harlem YWCA as "heady." Like Baker, she was drawn to the strong, intellectually daring women she met there. "None of these women would have called themselves feminists in the 1930s," Murray wrote, "but they were strong independent personalities who, because of their concerted efforts to rise above the limitations of race and sex, and to help younger women do the same, shared a sisterhood that foreshadowed the revival of the feminist movement in the 1960s."

The 135th Street Library, also known as the Harlem Branch Library and later to be renamed the Schomburg Center for Research in Black Culture, regularly hosted book club meetings and appearances by Harlem Renaissance poets and writers. According to historian David Levering Lewis, it provided "the intellectual pulse of Harlem." With librarian Ernestine Rose, Baker founded the library's first Negro History Club, and in 1933 she joined the branch's Adult Education Committee. The two clubs sponsored a lively assortment of programs that instigated discussion on historical topics and current events. (One of the most heated discussions led to a protest campaign: Baker and others demanded that the public library hire more African American librarians for the Harlem branch.) Baker especially enjoyed the programs that carried discussion and debate outside of the confines of the library and into the street.

Baker's social life revolved around the YWCA and public library programs, and she had little interest in, much less time for, dating. No one who knew her at the time would have considered Baker a romantic, but she did maintain a correspondence with an old beau from Shaw, T. J. Roberts, whom she called "Bob," after Baker moved to Harlem. He joined her in New York sometime in the early 1930s. (According to Baker's biographer Joanne

Grant, Roberts was born T. J. Robinson, but he changed his surname after arriving in New York.)

The library's programs took on added significance after the stock market crash of 1929. In the ensuing years, as more and more Harlem residents lost their jobs—the neighborhood's unemployment rate was estimated at a whopping 50 percent in 1932, the worst year of the Great Depression—and slipped into deep poverty, the library's free programs and classes became ever more valuable. The Harlem branch hired Baker in 1934 to coordinate community outreach programs. The library could not offer Baker a full-time salary, but she appears to have put forty hours a week, if not more, into the job. Building on her YNCL experience, she taught classes at the library in what might be called consumer economics and created the Young People's Forum, a program that brought young men and women together to discuss the issues of the day and to search for solutions to local, national, and world problems. Her supervisor at the library, Ernestine Rose, noticed that after "prominent speakers were brought into these meetings . . . it was Miss Baker's plan always to place emphasis on the increased participation by members themselves." As important as it was to Baker to bring young adults into the library and introduce them to the life of the mind, she was not content to have them sit and listen. They had to engage and commit. By all accounts, her program was immensely popular.

Baker also organized Mothers in the Park, a neighborhood group that met in Harlem's St. Nicholas and Colonial parks to discuss new developments in child development and parent education. It is unclear what Baker, an unmarried and childless woman who looked much younger than her early-thirties age suggested, could have contributed to the Mothers in the Park's discussions, but she remained true to her belief that knowledge was empowering for everyone, in every situation.

Baker continued to work as a freelance journalist. In November 1935 she and Marvel Jackson Cooke published one of Baker's two best-known pieces of writing, "The Bronx Slave Market," an exposé of the degrading conditions domestic day workers faced while finding work in the New York City borough, in the NAACP's journal *The Crisis*. Baker and Cooke, a clandestine member of the American Communist Party and a Harlem neighbor, were not close, but they did travel in similar social circles and had mutual friends before an editor at *The Crisis* asked Baker to collaborate with Cooke on the story. The two had a lot in common. They were born the same year and both arrived in Harlem within a year of one another. Marvel Jackson was born and raised in Minnesota. Her father was a graduate of the Ohio State University Law School but could not support his family as a black lawyer in

Minneapolis, so he became a Pullman porter and did well enough to buy a home in a previously all-white, upper-middle-class Minneapolis neighborhood. Her mother had worked as a teacher and cook on a Native American reservation before marriage.

Like Baker's, the roots of Cooke's radicalism were entirely homegrown. Her parents were great admirers of Eugene Debs, the railroad union leader and Socialist Party of America candidate for president in the 1904, 1908, 1912, and 1920 elections. Cooke recalled her father explaining his support for Debs in the 1920 race by saying, "I'm voting for him as a protest against the way things are going in this country. The bigger protest vote we can get in this country, whoever goes in will listen to this great group of people out here that don't agree." This strain of socialism was indigenous to American soil.

Marvel Jackson graduated from the University of Minnesota in 1925 and moved to Harlem shortly thereafter. She immediately found a job as W. E. B. Du Bois's assistant at *The Crisis*. (According to one source, Du Bois had once dated Jackson's mother; according to another, she spent much of her time at *The Crisis* deflecting Du Bois's romantic advances.) She soon found herself in the middle of the Harlem Renaissance covering the African American literature beat.

Baker and Cooke went undercover to research the story, posing as maids looking for work at street corners in the Bronx where desperate African American women were known to gather looking for day work and lower-middle-class white women were to known to hire them at shockingly low wages. (Though they were not the subjects of the article, Baker and Cooke also found even more desperate women at the corners who sold a different kind of physical labor to men.) Some of the women Baker and Cooke met at the corners had been housewives, but they were forced to find work when their husbands lost their jobs. Others had been employed full time by well-to-do whites on the Upper East Side or in Westchester County, but Depression economics had forced their employers to cut back, and now the women had to scrap for day work.

Baker and Cooke built the article around an interesting piece of socioeconomic analysis: the African American women gathered in the Bronx because the borough was full of a certain kind of household. "Paradoxically, the crash of 1929 brought to the domestic labor market a new employer class," they wrote. "The lower-middle-class housewife, who, having dreamed of the luxury of a maid, found opportunity staring her in the face in the form of Negro women pressed to the wall by poverty, starvation, and discrimination." The households shared another characteristic, and Baker and Cooke emphasized it, too: the members of the new class of employers were overwhelmingly Jewish. It was unlike Baker to define people by their ethnic or religious identities, but she and Cooke did in this article, which unfortunately played to anti-Semitic stereotypes.

Baker and Cooke pressed several points in the article. They argued that the labor market existed in the first place because the government's emergency relief efforts were inadequate, especially for this segment of the population. Organized labor, they emphasized, bore an equal responsibility—white men led the unions, and they needed to get past their racism and sexism to help these members of society who most needed their assistance. Now that the maids found themselves in this predicament, Baker and Cooke counseled, they needed to organize a union of their own. (Baker had worked with the Women's Day Workers and Industrial League unions in Harlem, both of which organized domestic workers.) The authors seem to have enjoyed working together on the story and remained lifelong mutual admirers, but they never again worked closely on a project. Interestingly, Cooke returned to the story in 1950 and published another exposé under the same title in the New York *Daily Compass*.

Depression-related budget cutbacks eliminated Baker's job at the 135th Street Library in 1936. With the help of her friend Lester Granger, who was then working as the secretary of the Committee on Negro Welfare for the Welfare Council of New York City and would later become the executive secretary of the National Urban League and one of the major, national-level, civil rights leaders of the 1940s to 1950s, she found her way to the Workers' Education Project (WEP), a division of the Works Progress Administration (WPA). President Franklin D. Roosevelt signed the legislation that created the WPA in May 1935, and not a moment too soon.

The WPA was arguably the signature program of the so-called Second New Deal of 1935 to 1938, and perhaps of the entire New Deal approach to government. The Roosevelt administration had succeeded in stanching the worst of the nation's economic bleeding in 1933 with a flurry of banking reforms and relief packages to the unemployed and suffering, but the Great Depression continued. Having won an overwhelming vote of confidence in the 1934 congressional off-year elections, Roosevelt and the Democrats embarked on another, more aggressive, and more creative round of "Relief, Recovery, and Reform" initiatives in 1935.

Among many other reforms, Congress passed and Roosevelt signed the Social Security Act, which for all intents and purposes created the social safety net as we know it in the United States, and the Wagner (or National Labor Relations) Act, which gave new protections to American workers to join labor unions and bargain collectively, during the Second New Deal. These have had long-lasting effects on the way Americans live, work, and vote, but the WPA may have been the most resonant symbol of how Roosevelt attacked the problem of the Great Depression and remade American government.

Previous New Deal efforts to alleviate the unemployment crisis had concentrated on creating construction-related jobs. (Roosevelt's critics denounced these as "make-work" jobs, but many of the results of these construction projects—be they civic auditoriums, airports, dams, parks, or college buildings—are still in heavy use.) The Public Works Administration, Civil Works Administration, Civilian Conservation Corps, and other "alphabet soup" agencies hired out-of-work men to build public works and infrastructure projects. The WPA did as well, but it also hired painters to paint public murals through its Federal Art Project. Its Federal Theatre Project hired out-of-work actors, musicians, playwrights, and technicians to put on free plays in public places. Its Federal Writers' Project hired unemployed journalists, historians, teachers, and folklorists to interview former slaves and publish state histories and travel guides, among many other projects. More important for Baker, the WPA was the first of the public works agencies to hire women in large numbers and the first to hire African Americans on an equal basis. Nearly as significant for her in particular, the WPA focused tightly on relieving urban unemployment; in the first two years of its existence the WPA spent one-seventh of its total budget, or roughly $1 billion, in New York City.

Baker's experience with the cooperative movement made her a natural fit for the WEP, which paired community groups with professionals and organizers whom the WEP trained to be adult educators. "We'd go around to settlement houses and conduct classes," Baker said. "For instance, those who were very knowledgeable about the history of working class organizations all the way back to the guild" would lead discussions on the history of the working classes and labor movements. "You'd conduct classes or discussions in the settlement houses, or if there were any unions that were still intact and wanted to have discussions on given issues," the WEP classes would meet in union halls.

WEP teachers taught classes on everything from American labor history and elementary economics to art appreciation and "Science and the Worker." State and local governments shared the costs of WPA projects throughout the country, and projects ranged from the apolitical to the nakedly partisan, depending on local officials' allegiances. At least in New York City, the WEP's work fell on the far partisan end of the spectrum. According to historian Susan Bernice Youngblood (now Susan Youngblood Ashmore), "The enterprise also served as the educational and cultural wing of the labor movement." Many of Baker's fellow teachers openly espoused socialist ideas and saw their WEP work as serving the needs of organized labor; others openly discussed their membership in the Communist Party. "You had every splinter of the CP [Communist Party]" in the WEP, Baker remembered. That "gave the project extra stimuli . . . and since I went everywhere, wherever there was a discussion, [I] picked things up," she said.

"Name it, and we'd have it," Baker said of the range of political opinions espoused by her coworkers. "Men and women. We were basically young. Some were older than others. . . . And many of these young people had grown up with families who were part of the Left." Once again, Baker found herself in the middle of a crowd of people from whom she could learn, and she lapped up the educational opportunities. "The good thing was that we could have dialogue. And basically (at least I found this fact, even though I made no claim to being knowledgeable) I think it was those who had the desire to search for knowledge, to search for at least some semblance of understanding, and were accepting," who were attracted to the WEP in the first place.

Baker began work as a WPA consumer educator in June 1936. For the first time, at the age of thirty-two, she had a steady paycheck and long-term prospects. "I've forgotten what the [pay] scale was," she later joked. "It may have been the highest pay I've ever gotten; I don't know." (It almost certainly was.) She moved out of the apartment she had until then shared with her "sister" Martha and into a nearby building on St. Nicholas Avenue at 133rd Street, still within a short walk to the Harlem Public Library. It was unusual, Baker admitted, "for a black woman from a nice, religious home" to live by herself in an apartment in Harlem, but she wouldn't be alone for long.

Soon after the move Baker wed T. J. Roberts, who was now working in and around the city as a traveling refrigeration mechanic, spending many nights on the road—although she forever after referred to the union as her "domestic arrangement" rather than a marriage. (A hopeless romantic she was not.) Baker kept her maiden name—"I have always been very happy that I didn't change my name. I didn't think that I *belonged* to any man," she said much later—although on a very small handful of occasions when dealing with apartment issues she did refer to herself in written correspondence as "Mrs. T. J. Roberts." Of course, these practices differed greatly from the norms of American life in the mid-twentieth century, but this was characteristic of the way Baker operated. The marriage was simply never a part of Baker's professional identity or the way she presented herself to the world.

WEP instruction was geared to be as practical as possible for its "students," all of whom were unemployed adults and some of whom may have been highly skilled in their previous occupations, whereas others were unskilled, non-native English speakers. "Instructors taught their subjects in an informal group discussion focusing on the immediate problems of the group members," Youngblood writes. "[WEP] teachers hoped this format would enable workers to relate the subject matter of their classes to their own experiences, making the courses readily applicable to the pressing problems of their daily lives." Baker surely considered the format useful, for she returned to it again and again as she and other civil rights activists searched for ways to empower members of the black working class long after the Great Depression had ended.

Baker taught and, beginning in 1937, supervised other instructors in the WEP's Consumer Education Division (CED), which was responsible for classes such as Consumer Education, Consumers' Problems, and The Cooperative Movement. She wanted the CED to serve "both the interest of the consumer himself [and "herself"; the division served more women than men], and the interest of the nation's progress." The nation, she believed, needed "a more enlightened, active, and dynamic worker-consumer republic." Baker hoped to provide "programmatic bases for the involvement of others," and she saw her role as that of facilitator. She created programs for the CED much like those she had created for the Harlem Public Library both as an employee and a volunteer because, she said, "I think people grow from talking to each other."

The CED's objective, she said, was not just to educate average workers as consumers but also to help them realize how much collective power they possessed. She especially wanted the CED to "lend some measure of direction to such groping restlessness . . . to paint a factual picture, however uncomplimentary it may be, of the plight of the worker-consumer under the present paradoxical state of Poverty amidst Plenty, and to arouse the consumer to his own potential forces for self protection and defense." Those were radical words coming from a federal employee, even in the context of the Great Depression.

In 1937 she described her own approach to teaching consumer education by writing that she wanted to "aid the consumer to a more intelligent understanding of the social and political economy of which he [or she] is a part. The approach is to be more informational and suggestive than dogmatic and conclusive, yet this aim is not education simply for its own sake, but education that leads to self-directed action." Again, she would stick closely in her civil rights work over the next several decades to the belief that education was not an end unto itself but a means toward the end of self-directed action.

Baker's work on behalf of the CED brought her into even closer association with Harlem's labor unions, social-gospel churches, and cooperative institutions. Baker worked on several projects with the Brotherhood of Sleeping Car Porters. The union's secretary-treasurer, Ashley L. Totten, gushed about her teaching and organizing style: "She . . . has always shown a marked interest in the social welfare program she has outlined for these men and their families. She has voluntarily served for us on several occasions and her splendid personality has won for her the admiration from all of the members."

Baker's experience as a WPA employee was formative. She drew on lessons she learned at the WEP in the midst of the 1930s "social revolution" for the rest of her working life. The foremost of these lessons were somewhat counterintuitive, for Baker did not put her faith in what today would be called "big government" solutions to social problems. Yes, she believed that government support, mainly in the form of job creation, was necessary for African Americans to bring themselves out of poverty and create social progress, and of course she wanted the federal government to provide equal protections to black citizens. Baker also appreciated government's role in breaking down segregation, having worked in an integrated environment for the first time at the WPA. She now had empirical evidence that, if given the chance, African Americans could do the same jobs as well as their white counterparts, and she never doubted that integration brought out the best in people of all races. That gave Baker an added impetus to challenge racial discrimination and segregation in all its forms.

But this employee of the biggest big-government agency of all placed her ultimate faith in the people. Baker's activism of later decades had much in common with her WPA work as she herself described it in 1937: she continued to promote "education that leads to self-directed action" and to "arouse the consumer to his own potential forces for self protection and defense," though she would have substituted "Negro citizen" for "consumer" after 1939. Baker believed that black Americans should look to themselves, not the federal government, for their own salvation.

A bloc of anti–New Deal conservatives from both parties gained new power following the 1938 elections, and they began chipping away at FDR's programs, beginning with the WPA. The WEP wound down beginning in 1939, and Baker's position was one of the first to be eliminated. She was back to the scuffling she had done before 1936, but now she needed steady employment more than she ever had. Roberts's work was intermittent, and Blake Baker had died in 1938, leaving Ella Baker with the primary responsibility for her mother's care in Littleton.

The Great Depression was hard on everyone, but it was especially hard on stubborn, college-educated women with strong political principles and class consciousness that kept them from working in certain occupations. Still unwilling to apply for jobs that were classified as "women's work"—teacher, social worker, and the like—Baker's options were that much more limited. She applied for jobs with the investigative staff of the New York Housing Authority, the American League for Peace and Democracy, as the organizer for the department of Negro Affairs, and even a janitorial service. In 1940, after several months without work, she applied for relief from a New York City charity. (She did not receive it.) Baker survived only because she had built up a strong social network. "Ella was always broke and always borrowing money from one friend or another," a friend of the time said.

Her old friend George Schuyler strongly suggested she apply for openings at the national office of the NAACP. "I had some qualms about it," Baker recalled, but "you don't shortchange a friend, you know; if somebody makes an effort for you, you go down" and apply. In fact, she was drawn to the work of the Association, and understandably so. By then she had a reputation as an active member of the New York branch and as the author of an article for *The Crisis*. She had helped plan and spoke before the NAACP's national conference in 1936. The national office seemed to be a good fit for her, and she applied for three separate jobs between 1938 and 1941. Her letters of recommendation detailed the skills she had already developed that would make her a perfect fit for the role of civil rights organizer.

In 1941 A. Philip Randolph took time away from planning a mass march on Washington to protest discrimination in defense industries to endorse Baker personally. Baker's supervisor from the 135th Street Public Library wrote, "Her work was particularly good in organizing and acting as adviser to a Young People's Forum. . . . Miss Baker successfully formed an active organization . . . I can especially recommend Miss Baker for work of this type." Her supervisor at the WPA wrote that Baker was "familiar with the activities of Negro organizations and has a sound philosophy of racial relationships. She brought to her work a high degree of intellectual capacity and integrity and was cooperative in all her relationships. She is tactful and considerate in her contacts with people."

She applied for the Association's position of assistant youth director twice, in 1938 and 1940, the second time at the Association's request. Baker impressed the staff, but the job went to a young man named Madison Jones instead. Executive secretary Walter White finally hired Baker as an assistant field secretary in February 1941 for a six-month trial period.

This was the job that would change Baker's life. She went to work full time as an advocate for the civil rights of African Americans at a time when both the NAACP and the United States were entering a period of great transformation. According to historian Patricia Sullivan, the NAACP field staff that she joined "led in expanding the base of the organization and, largely under the direction of Ella Baker, cultivated the militancy and expectations unleashed by the war, helping to shape the fuller contours of a southern movement." Baker was evolving, too, but when she began working for the NAACP she already had theories about how to organize a civil rights movement and some evidence to back up those theories. She would change the organization more than it changed her.

CHAPTER THREE

~

Give Light and the People Will Find a Way

By the time Ella Baker decided to devote herself to full-time, professional advocacy on behalf of the ideals of justice and equality and the interests of African Americans, the National Association for the Advancement of Colored People had established itself as the preeminent national civil rights advocacy organization. Founded in 1909, the Association had in three decades developed a sophisticated public relations machine that focused national attention on instances of racial injustice and a legal strategy that would eventually strike down Jim Crow state laws through the federal courts. "The need for this type of action was there. I don't think any of us will deny that there was . . . the need to fight through the courts," Baker said, but she believed that legalism by itself was ineffective. She had her own ideas about what the organization should be doing in addition to waging its legal assault on racial segregation.

The NAACP had settled on an organizational structure that sold individual memberships to chapters in communities throughout the country but consolidated power in its national office, and it had attracted to its ranks nearly every prominent African American who shared its goals. Baker arrived with a healthy amount of skepticism (the NAACP's program risked becoming "stale and uninteresting," she wrote in 1941) and fully formed ideas about the importance of mass organizing, but she initially attracted Walter White's attention as someone who "might develop into a money raiser," according to associate secretary Roy Wilkins. Baker saw the NAACP's individual members and branches as its greatest strength; she wanted to organize a mass movement through them. From her perspective, White was unable even to consider the branches as anything but a resource to be tapped on behalf of a national office that unilaterally set the Association's priorities and coordinated its campaigns.

The simple differences in organizing philosophy would later widen into a chasm, and although Baker's relationship with White remained cordial for the most part (indeed, he defended her vociferously when Baker ran afoul of a venerable branch president in 1941 to 1942), the differences between their respective goals for the NAACP were effectively irreconcilable from the very outset of Baker's employment. Baker had been to many NAACP annual meetings as a member but attended her first as an employee in July 1941, toward the conclusion of her six-month trial period. She took it upon herself to report back to the rest of the staff with her takeaway lessons. Baker recommended that the staff should work on fine-tuning organizational machinery and developing a conference format that would allow for more give-and-take between national staff and delegates from branches (the current, top-down convention format consisted of staffers giving speeches and delegates listening to them). She suggested giving delegates more of a voice in shaping the program and creating more space within the program for staff and delegates to share best practices in regard to common problems. These were bold recommendations coming from a woman whose job was not guaranteed beyond August. White ignored all of them.

Baker was thirty-seven when she began the assignment, and she had rich life experiences that she could draw on to great effect. Proper and put-together in appearance, she could also start a conversation with anyone—from a sharecropper to an insurance company executive—on their terms and at their level. Baker dove into the work of field organizing, which was in many ways the job she had been born to do. Between 1941 and 1943 she traveled widely throughout the South, and to a significant but lesser extent through the Mid-Atlantic and Northeastern states, selling memberships to the Association and strengthening local chapters. Along the way she began compiling what would become the most important address book in the history of the American civil rights movement.

There were many forceful personalities in the headquarters office during Baker's time there, at least four of whom conceived of drastically different missions for the Association. Baker wanted to channel the energies and resources of the NAACP's members into a mass movement. Walter White wanted to use his membership's resources to conduct national public relations campaigns and lobbying efforts and to bankroll antisegregation suits. Special counsel Thurgood Marshall was obviously most interested in having the Association bankroll the assault on Jim Crow through the courts, and in some ways his approach melded Baker's and White's visions. He needed strong branches in the South to help his legal staff develop strong cases and to support plaintiffs—and therefore supported Baker's approaches—but his work also required the sort of fund-raising operation White envisioned. Dr. Du Bois, a founding member of the NAACP and long its brightest intellectual light, had fallen out with White in 1934 and left New York but returned to the national office in 1944. He wanted the NAACP to play the role of think tank and attempted to position the Association as the voice of the international black diaspora. He quickly ran afoul of White again; the board of directors dismissed Du Bois from the NAACP staff for good in 1948. (By then he had come to agree with Baker. Under White's leadership, he later wrote, "The branches . . . have no . . . program except to raise money and defend cases of injustice. . . . The organization fears the processes of democracy and avoids discussion.")

There was some precedent in the national office for Baker's approach. Director of branches William Pickens had been on staff since World War I but was not a presence by the time Baker arrived. He, too, engaged in the kind of fieldwork with local people that would, he hoped, democratize the Association and build the foundation for a mass movement. When Baker began traveling the back roads of the South, drumming up support for the NAACP, She often found that Pickens was the only other national officer who had visited a given remote branch. She saw many photographs of Pickens displayed in prominent places at branch headquarters in town after town in the rural South, but never one of White. "Nobody from the national office had been there," she told Joanne Grant. "There were many places I went [where the branch members] didn't even know Walter was the executive. They had pictures of Pickens. They knew Bill Pickens, but they didn't know Walter." White and Pickens clashed for two decades, engaging in a personality-driven, internecine feud that forced others in the NAACP to choose sides. When Baker arrived at national headquarters preaching a creed that sounded Pickensian to White's ears, it raised his hackles.

Baker arrived at a critical period in the NAACP's history. With the United States preparing for what many considered to be an inevitable entry into World War II, the NAACP was at the forefront of efforts to desegregate hiring in defense industries and strike down Jim Crow in the armed forces. The *Pittsburgh Courier*, the nation's most widely circulated and influential black newspaper, launched the "Double Victory" campaign to defeat Adolf Hitler abroad and Jim Crow at home in 1942, but the concept long predated Pearl Harbor. Delegates to annual meetings of the

NAACP had been calling for the desegregation of the armed forces since at least 1937, and Walter White personally lobbied the White House to the same end long before the United States declared war on the Axis nations. In 1941 the Association backed labor leader A. Philip Randolph's threat to lead thousands of black Americans in a march on Washington to protest racial discrimination in the armed forces and defense industries.

The Association's wartime program followed the dictum "make every crisis an opportunity." As Baker put it in a February 1943 "N.A.A.C.P. Radio Hour" address delivered from a Washington, D.C., station, "Now more than ever, we who believe in the democratic way of life are challenged to make our American Democracy a Living and Vital Reality . . . to every man, woman, and child upon our shores. More than that: America must lead the way in making the world a saner place to live in; and in guaranteeing to all mankind the right to life, liberty and the pursuit of happiness."

Military triumph over the Axis forces, in Baker's view, would provide an incomplete victory if it did not accompany movement toward social and economic justice within America's borders. "We must prove our democratic way of life by battling against and destroying such undemocratic forces as bigotry, injustice, racial prejudice and discrimination," she said. "It is not enough to proclaim that we are a nation of free men because the nation was founded upon the principles of liberty, equality and freedom. We must see to [it] that every man is free to work and make a living in keeping with his ability; and that no one is denied the opportunity to an education because of class, creed or color." Quoting the journalist and Southern Agrarian Herbert Agar (an unlikely philosophical ally), Baker asserted, "Peace is not the absence of war; peace is the presence of justice."

Baker made her brief on behalf of African Americans, but she also argued that every American had something at stake in the country's treatment of its black citizens. "[W]herever democracy is strengthened by granting to Colored Americans a fuller measure of citizenship and manhood, all of the democratic forces throughout the world have been implemented," she said. "On the other hand, every infringement upon the rights of Negroes as citizens and men, weakens the cause of democracy everywhere." For that reason—here she closed the sale—"All persons who really believe in the democratic way of life; and who are ready and willing to accept the challenge that faces all Americans in this hour of national destiny, are urged to enlist in this [NAACP] membership campaign."

Total membership in the Association grew approximately ninefold during the war years; the number of branches tripled, with nearly three-fourths of the new chapters in the South. Double Victory ideology and the publicity

White and Marshall generated obviously had a great deal to do with the increase, but public relations and rhetoric could only open a door for the NAACP. It would require a tremendous amount of tedious, time-consuming groundwork to take advantage of the opportunities the war created. Making person-to-person connections and building movements based on relationships was Baker's specialty. She therefore deserves the lion's share of the credit for the Association's membership explosion. Her staff colleague E. Frederic Morrow considered Baker's wartime efforts "phenomenal."

There was only one way to put Baker's theories about organizing into practice: get into the field and work. So into the field she went. Baker's travel schedule was legendarily punishing. Between Labor Day and Thanksgiving Day in 1941 she spent all but four days in Virginia, Maryland, and upstate New York, addressing sixty-three meetings and groups and managing major membership drives in Norfolk, Baltimore, and Albany. The following year, between February and early July, she addressed 178 different groups (most of them mass meetings or church congregations) while visiting thirty-eight branches in Florida, Georgia, Alabama, North Carolina, and Virginia. On Sundays, while Walter White relaxed at home with his family in Manhattan, Baker visited five or more churches and made as many speeches, trying to drum up members. A 1942 dispatch from Pensacola, Florida, was typical of her daily reports: "I have spoken to six student groups (schools) and conferred with several individuals and one teacher group since ten o'clock this morning; and will meet with the [branch] executive committee at seven thirty and then address a mass meeting at eight. I go to Mobile tomorrow."

Local branch officials, especially those who were unused to attention, much less visits, from national officials, gushed in praise of Baker. Richmond branch president and Virginia state conference chairman J. R. Tinsley reported to national headquarters, "Never during her stay . . . did she slacken her pace. She was going from the time of her arrival until the time she left." Baker, he said, demonstrated the "outstanding quality of mixing with any group of people and trying to help solve their problems."

Baker's first reports back from the field indicate how well established her approach to organizing was at the time she began using it for the Association. In April 1941 she wrote from the field to tell Roy Wilkins, "We have as the chairman [of the Birmingham branch] the Rev. J. W. Goodgame, Jr., pastor of the Sixth Street Baptist Church. He is all preacher, but unlike most of them, he knows that it takes work to produce and he will work." Baker meant to emphasize her belief that the NAACP should organize the masses rather than elites, but her backhanded compliment betrayed her suspicion of African American ministers who, she thought, tended to value rhetoric over hard work. Over the years that suspicion would deepen and develop into full-blown anticlericalism.

Baker's travels exposed her to some of the worst indignities Jim Crow had to offer. "The travel was bum," she told a friend in a masterpiece of understatement. Racial segregation in rail travel was haphazard in the 1940s. African Americans were not treated as whites' social equals on trains in the North (for Baker's purposes, "the North" defined the area north and west of Washington, D.C.), but neither were they treated as lepers to be confined in inferior accommodations. In the Deep South, by law and by custom blacks could only sit in the car directly behind the locomotive and coal car, the smokiest, dirtiest, and least comfortable car on the train. Segregation was the law of the land in the Border South, but it was enforced mainly according to the whims of individual railroad employees and local officials. Navigating the system of laws and customs that governed Baker's territory while maintaining one's dignity was a full-time job in itself.

The system was arbitrarily enforced. If a given black passenger had a ticket for a Pullman berth, the small sleeper cabin that at least made overnight journeys bearable, she might be able to claim it without any trouble, but she might have to fight for it. If she patronized the dining car she would more likely than not have a curtain drawn around her table to create makeshift segregated seating. (For this reason, along with economic realities, most blacks brought their meals with them on trains. Oral histories with black travelers from the era inevitably include richly detailed descriptions of the meals that African American women carried onto the trains in picnic baskets and shoe boxes.) To make matters worse, wartime troop movement strained the American rail system to the breaking point. If rail employees had to inconvenience paying passengers to make room for troops, the burden was most likely to fall on blacks first. Even if a trip for an African American passenger went smoothly, he or she could expect it to be a demeaning one.

Ella Baker refused to be demeaned, and she refused to accommodate herself to a system that tried to treat her as less than a full human being. That said, the penalties for disobeying Jim Crow laws and customs could be harsh. In the worst incident from the era, Sgt. Isaac Woodard Jr., who had just returned from service in the Pacific Theater of World War II and was headed to meet family members in North Carolina, argued with the driver of a Greyhound bus while traveling through South Carolina. Police officers from the town of Batesburg removed Woodard from the bus and beat him so badly that he lost sight in both eyes. Baker knew of hundreds of similar examples, and she was principled but not foolhardy. She was at least as likely to find a way to avoid a Jim Crow situation as she was to confront the system head-on.

On the occasions when she found herself being treated separately and unequally, however, Baker did not back down. She talked back, forcefully, to passenger agents who treated her disrespectfully. She demanded that they honor her tickets on Pullman berths. When she had trouble in dining cars she filed official complaints with railroad companies. She did exactly that, with assistance from Thurgood Marshall, after separate May 1943 trips on the Seaboard Air Line Railroad. On the first, between Mobile, Alabama, and Jacksonville, Florida, she was able to sit down and eat in a temporary blacks-only section only after military policemen on board helped her by moving white troops from a table near the car's segregation curtain.

On the second trip, between Miami and New York City, Baker sat herself for lunch at a table that she believed to be available to black passengers according to the laws of Florida. The dining steward disagreed and asked her to leave; she refused to do so. At this point two military policemen physically unseated her, bruising her leg while removing her from the table. She shouted to her fellow diners, "This man is overstepping his authority!" and the MPs let her go. The train's conductor found Baker later that afternoon and lectured her: "You know it is against the law for white and colored to eat in the same restaurant in the State of Florida?" According to her complaint, Baker replied, "Yes, but it is also the law that dining car accommodations should be provided for all first class passengers." Their conversation went nowhere—the conductor refused to apologize to Baker for her treatment—though a steward did later serve her dinner at her seat.

The nature of Baker's job and the experience of heavy travel made her "fight for social justice waged through the NAACP . . . a personal as well as political crusade," as Barbara Ransby points out. She wanted Jim Crow to end and worked hard toward that goal, so even in the 1940s she lived her life as though segregation was unlawful and society could no longer expect African Americans to behave as second-class citizens. Decades after her work for the NAACP had ended Baker was still advising others interested in civil rights and social justice that if they wanted the world to change they had to start living and acting in ways that illustrated the changes they wanted to see on a larger scale. Activists who traveled with Baker in the early 1960s described behavior very much like that described in her complaint to the Seaboard Air Line Railroad Company: She did not go out of her way to seek confrontation, but she refused to compromise with Jim Crow. Politely, respectfully, but insistently, she demanded to be treated as a citizen and customer with equal rights.

Baker's organizing style required inordinate amounts of shoe leather and conversation. The NAACP's founders, most especially Dr. Du Bois, had intended to organize the black community's "Talented Tenth," its best-educated and most economically successful minority, who could then "uplift" the race's majority. Throughout the intervening three decades the NAACP had spent the vast majority of its organizing energies on the black middle and upper classes, but Baker took a different approach. In an early report she described her visits to "the mass-supported beer gardens, night clubs, etc., in Baltimore. . . . We went in, addressed the crowds and secured memberships and campaign workers." One club patron told her, "You certainly have some nerve coming in here, talking, but I'm going to join that doggone organization." This kind of organizing was rough and exhausting; Baker called it "spadework," comparing it to the backbreaking preparatory work that had to be done on a farm before planting. She had no idea at the time how apt her metaphor was.

The following year, on the heels of another marathon organizing trip, Baker suggested to associate director and *Crisis* editor Roy Wilkins her plan to "visit some of the pool-rooms, boot black parlors, bars and grilles, and tell of the Association, [and] secure individual memberships if possible; but take up a collection on the spot and sell [the] idea of having a *Crisis* made available to regular patrons of the 'business.'" Baker teasingly questioned whether Wilkins would want his magazine seen in such establishments or have memberships traveling through the mail addressed to "Joe's Bar and Grille," but her organizing philosophy stood: "This is but another offshoot from my desire to place the N.A.A.C.P. and its program on the lips of all the people . . . the uncouth MASSES included." The strategy diverged markedly from the NAACP's classical approach, to say the least, but Baker considered that proof that the classical approach was flawed. In the Association's ever-increasing membership rolls, she had empirical, experiential evidence that her way worked.

She encouraged branches to organize around issues that their local communities had already identified as problems in need of solution. Rather than pass down directives from NAACP headquarters, she asked local people about the problems that affected them and helped them develop campaigns around those issues—for instance, low teacher pay or police brutality—even if headquarters was more interested in raising money from the hinterlands to fund their national campaigns for federal antilynching legislation or class action lawsuits against segregated school systems.

She also built the movement relationship by personal relationship, never knowing where her web of personal contacts might lead. As membership in the NAACP skyrocketed in the 1940s, Baker did her best to personally deliver the charters to newly formed branches and present them to branch officers in public ceremonies. This added even more travel to an already packed schedule, but it was important to Baker to build personal warmth into what could otherwise be a sterile relationship between branches and headquarters. If she could make branch members feel that they *belonged* in the organization, the extra travel was worth it. If she could make them feel that they had something to offer the organization besides their dues money, all the better. In the future, when a branch officer faced pushback from local whites for his NAACP activities, maybe he would remember the woman from New York who had gone out of her way to deliver the branch charter personally. Perhaps that would give him the strength to continue in the struggle a while longer.

According to Worth Long, a Durham, North Carolina, native who attended several of the ceremonies as a boy because his mother was heavily involved in NAACP recruitment, Baker exhorted the audiences at these ceremonies to think of the creation of a branch as the beginning, not the conclusion, of their organizing efforts. His father, William Worth Long, presiding elder of the Durham district of the African Methodist Episcopalian Zion church, insisted that all his congregations hold NAACP registration drives. The lessons obviously took root with Long; he would later work closely with Baker as the staff director of the Student Nonviolent Coordinating Committee.

At the June 1941 annual meeting in Houston, Baker took it upon herself to open a discussion with delegates on the relationship between the national office and the branches. "The work of the National Office is one thing, but the work of the branches is in the final analysis the life blood of the Association," she told them. "The Association . . . is dependent on the branches for action." Baker—who had been on the job for less than four full months and had reason to worry about her job if she diverged too drastically from Walter White's position—encouraged delegates to think of themselves as branch members first and members of a national association second. They should organize around "something that can be done in your own community [such as] getting a new school building, registering people to vote, [or] getting bus transportation . . . work on it and get it done."

Neither would she allow branches outside of Dixie to think that "as long as they help support the National Office and some unfortunate person in Georgia they are doing their job." Baker was mortified by what she found on her 1941 visit to the Albany, New York, branch: The local high schools tracked students into three levels of training: college preparation, vocational education, and a third that did little more than mark attendance. "The majority of Negroes were being put in that last category," Baker found, which was bad enough. What was truly outrageous was that no one in the branch had thought to challenge the system: "They were always talking about the poor people down South. And so the question was, what do you do about the poor children right here?" The problem also extended to the border South. "I frequently would have people ask me as I came up from the deep South, up to Virginia and North Carolina, 'How are things down South?'" she said. "Which meant that to them that's where the problem was and they had not identified the problem in their own area." Baker advised branches in Albany, New York, Albany, Georgia, and in the cities and towns everywhere in between to "take the initiative in developing leadership in all social and economic problems and problems of discrimination, employment and the like which confront the Negro today."

Baker drew on everything she had learned in Harlem to build a philosophy of organizing, but her childhood experiences in the South formed her as an organizer. She was still a southerner at heart, and she dreamed of an indigenous *southern* people's movement that would strike down Jim Crow and replace it with a social system that more closely matched the ideals of egalitarian democracy. She thought of her work for the NAACP in these terms—she served not the Association that paid her salary so much as she did the idea of organizing for the benefit of her people.

Her reports from the South back to the national office may have contained a measure of wishful thinking. Taking the temperature of the southerners with whom she visited in 1942, she wrote, "The prevailing attitude is no longer one of hoping and waiting for the effects of national victories to trickle down to the South but it is increasingly one of working and fighting for victories against local injustices and discrimination." Wishful thinking or no, it was impossible to argue with the results in the form of raw membership numbers. Clearly Baker had found thousands of black southerners who were willing to step forward. And even if Baker's description of the South in 1942 was utopian, she worked harder than anyone else over the next three decades to make that vision a reality.

Walter White rewarded Baker's tireless efforts by promoting her to the position of director of branches in 1943. At least, that's how White spun the decision. William Pickens had taken a leave of absence from the post in 1941 to work for the U.S. Treasury Department, where he directed efforts to sell war bonds to African Americans and advocated for African American interests during the war from inside the government. Pickens continued to make public statements regarding blacks' contributions to the war effort that he considered pragmatic and wrongly assumed were in line with NAACP policy. The Association's official line was that there could be absolutely no cooperation with racial segregation—period, end of discussion—but Franklin Roosevelt's War Department made decisions that complicated that discussion during the mobilization for war.

In the years since World War I the American military had not just segregated black servicemen from whites, it had denied African Americans all but the most menial jobs. But in the days before the 1940 presidential election, Secretary of War Henry L. Stimson announced that he was bringing a retired black colonel in the army, Benjamin O. Davis Sr., back to duty and promoting him to the rank of general, making him the first African American in American history to earn the rank. Stimson also announced that the army would create new opportunities for African Americans in various fields, including a pilot training program to be built in central Alabama, the Tuskegee Army Flying School.

The flight training program offered a significant and brand new prospect for blacks, as it would train cadets in what was then considered the most technologically, mentally, and physically demanding specialty in the armed forces and a domain from which they had up to then been blocked completely. On that level, the multimillion-dollar facility represented a victory for African Americans. However, it was also entirely separate from similar, all-white training facilities already in existence, and it was no coincidence that the Army Air Corps chose a site for the program in the deepest South, where it was thought that blacks could most effectively be controlled. For that reason it touched off a spirited debate within the NAACP. Roy Wilkins mused in private, "If it comes to a choice between being trained in Alabama or not being trained at all, I would be for Alabama," even though that would require tacit acceptance of Jim Crow segregation. There were surely others within the NAACP who agreed with him, but the Association maintained a united public front opposing segregation in all cases. The NAACP advocated training black pilots, black tank drivers, black radio operators, and black specialists of every other conceivable stripe for the war effort, but it demanded that they be trained alongside whites in existing programs, according to the best of everyone's abilities. Unfortunately, the War Department made it crystal clear that it considered full racial integration a pipe dream at best. The official pronouncement from Army Chief of Staff Gen. George C. Marshall in 1941 was, "The Army is not a sociological laboratory." It should not be expected to solve "a social problem that has perplexed the American people throughout the history of this nation."

Pickens supported the creation of the Tuskegee program and another for black infantrymen at Fort Huachuca, Arizona, as half-a-loaf measures and encouraged African Americans to join him in cheering them on. He advocated a position that seemed to require blacks to place the fight for full equality on the back burner while they devoted their full attention to the war effort. In a January 1942 *New York Amsterdam Star-News* opinion column, Pickens pushed back against blacks who criticized the segregated training programs.

He argued, for example, that once the Tuskegee pilot cadets were given a chance, "these black boys are going to get into the air and prove their equality." His position may have been pragmatic, but it contradicted the NAACP's official line. Pickens made it clear that he personally abhorred Jim Crow but that he thought larger issues were at stake: "Segregation based on skin-color or eye-color is damned nonsense, of course, but this man's Army is not planning to break or to make segregation," he said. "[I]t is planning to win a war, in spite of segregation or of those who oppose segregation."

The assertions had merit, but they understandably made White and the board uncomfortable. At a February board of directors meeting a majority of members voted not to extend Pickens's leave of absence. He appealed the decision, asserting, "I have never 'advocated' racial segregation anywhere, in the Army or out of it. But I look with realism upon the dilemmas which face us in these times—these times which bristle with dilemmas: for Negroes, for labor, for pacifists, and for others." The issue divided the board, but while it simmered Pickens again stoked controversy.

Virginius Dabney, the racially moderate editor of the *Richmond Times-Dispatch*, editorialized that black Americans should keep any concerns they had about racial justice to themselves for the duration of the war effort. He blamed the NAACP for "interracial tensions" in general and for igniting "race riots" near army camps. For some reason Pickens took it upon himself to praise Dabney and criticize the line of thinking that blacks should fight for their country overseas and their own rights at home simultaneously—which was, after all, the NAACP's official position. In a letter that Dabney republished in his newspaper, Pickens argued that although it was true that blacks in America had gotten a raw deal, "only a fool . . . would exchange American democracy for European fascism. . . . We of all races are on one ship, the United States. If any enemy wants to sink that ship, even if we have been fighting all over it—only idiots would debate whose business it is to keep the ship afloat and sailing." He suggested that there were "some few traitors, and some very foolish persons" amid the majority of loyal black Americans, which seemed to endorse Dabney's criticism of the NAACP. The board of directors finally fired Pickens for good in June. White assumed the title of director of branches himself, though he appears to have paid little attention to the work, leaving it up to Baker's contemporary E. Frederic Morrow (to whom he gave the title coordinator of branches) as he had during Pickens's leave.

White elevated Baker to the post of director of branches a year later, and the manner in which he did so was of a piece with his management style. White did not announce a job opening and invite applications, nor, it appears, did he even canvass the staff and board members for their opinions on who might or might not have been a good fit in the role. (Baker did come to believe that her allies Thurgood Marshall and William Hastie lobbied White on her behalf.) On April 12 he informed the board of directors that Baker had accepted the appointment (perhaps, as Joanne Grant suggests, to forestall board member Alfred Baker Lewis's attempt to strip the title from White). Sometime between April 12 and April 15 he issued a press release, postdated April 16, announcing the appointment. On April 15 he wrote to Baker, who was working on a membership campaign in Alabama, to apprise her of her new position.

She received the news on April 17 and immediately fired off a reply: "Were I not more or less shock proof I would now be suffering from a severe case of hypertension caused by your letter." Baker thanked White and the board of directors for their "vote of confidence" in her abilities, but she thought it better if she returned to the national office to discuss the position with White before accepting it. "It is because of my desire to do any job as well as I possibly can that leads me to withhold commitment until I can have a full discussion on what directorship of branches involves," she assured him. (Baker later referred to her promotion as an action that "precipitated" her into the position.) White brushed aside her concerns and suggested that they talk when she returned to New York as planned; he knew very well that she could not refuse the promotion after he had announced that she accepted it without tremendous public embarrassment for everyone involved. Baker had proven herself to be a team player and a graceful personality, so he knew very well that she would do no such thing. (It is difficult to argue with Barbara Ransby's conclusion that White "viewed Baker as more of a pawn than a peer.") White promised to produce a memorandum detailing her new job responsibilities, but it apparently never materialized.

In fact, if White put any job description for Baker on paper, it does not survive in the archives. Baker would come to consider this an unforgivable case of mismanagement, but in 1943 she cheerily embarked on the work of filling what she considered a void in the Association's program. She listed several objectives for the department she now oversaw. "To increase the extent to which the present membership participates in national and local activities . . . To extend the membership base so as to have local branches include a larger proportion of the people in any given community . . . To transform the local branches from being centers of sporadic activity to becoming centers of sustained and dynamic community leadership." Progress toward these goals would by definition democratize and energize the Association, but it would just as necessarily bring Baker into direct competition with White.

The new role came with significant challenges. As the title implied, the director of branches was responsible for managing the national office's relationship with local chapters. Baker would also have to supervise a small clerical staff and the field secretaries—all of whom had been her equals on the organization chart just days before. She was, of course, responsible for imposing some kind of order on a membership that was in the process of tripling in size, but with every fiber of her being she wanted to break down bureaucratic barriers and democratize the Association, to unleash the power of the masses, and to offer support to a new generation of homegrown leaders in the chapters. To make matters even more difficult, she would have to navigate the Association's internal political waters as the highest-ranking woman in a crew of cocksure men. But if Baker worried about going up against the formidable bureaucratic warrior White or doubted the efficacy of her organizing philosophy, she kept those worries to herself. Instead she dove into her new mission.

Baker wanted individual branches to join in common cause with other groups pushing for change in their communities. She particularly wanted to build bridges between the NAACP and friendly trade unions—a goal that many in the civil rights movement over its long history shared but few accomplished. Du Bois had talked about it in the World War I era. In 1943 it appeared that A. Philip Randolph, leader of the Pullman porters' union, might be able to forge a coalition of African Americans and working people of other backgrounds to build a movement for both racial and economic equality. Rev. Martin Luther King Jr. worked toward similar ends two decades later. But the goal remained—and remains—elusive.

Soon after Baker took over as director of branches, Alvin C. White, an official with a Philadelphia railroad union, advised her to pursue a closer working relationship with the organized labor movement. Whether White helped shape Baker's vision or was simply preaching to the choir is up for debate, but he certainly captured the philosophy Baker was already developing. "Talking with Working People of various crafts[,] the argument is that your organization is Top-heavy with Professional People who do not know anything at all about the need of the common people," he warned. "Others say that you all use the N.A.A.C.P. to further yourselves in your professions.

Another is that you all are interested in making things better for the Big Fellow and forgetting about the Little Fellow."

These sentiments meshed with the beliefs Baker had already formed and encouraged her to press on, even though she was also developing similar misgivings about the organized labor movement. "I'm afraid it succumbed," she later said, "to a large extent to the failures of what I call the American weakness of being recognized and having arrived and taking on the characteristics and the values, even, of the foe." Nonetheless, White's concluding idea, "If you will pull the Little Fellow up you will not have to worry about the big fellow," may as well have been Baker's mantra. White encouraged Baker to forge a closer working relationship between the NAACP and the labor movement in her new position and endorsed her approach to fund-raising.

While still a field secretary, Baker had begun advocating a new organizational structure for the NAACP. She wanted the Association to create a new level of bureaucracy: state conferences of branches and regional suborganizations that would have opened up more leadership opportunities for NAACP members who distinguished themselves at the local level and decentralized policy-making power in the Association. Baker envisioned the state and regional conferences setting their own priorities and pressing for change on the state level. If the people of a given state identified low pay for African American teachers as the issue they most wanted to address, the state conference could organize NAACP members and other interested parties to lobby the state legislature, write letters to newspaper editors, and stage voter registration rallies around the issue. They could rely on the national office to provide expertise in together putting the campaign, but they would not have to wait for headquarters to issue marching orders. If a branch identified segregated seating on the city buses as an indignity it wanted to attack, the national office should provide the necessary resources and move, instead of trying to put together a national campaign.

If most civil rights problems were, as Baker believed, best attacked at the local level, local people needed new institutions, power centers that they could control to their advantage. She wanted to transform NAACP chapters into those kinds of institutions. In the NAACP as it existed, she believed that members could too easily become complacent and chapters moribund. Baker's ideal national organization would be highly structured, but power within it would be dispersed. It would demand total commitment from members, who would be able to act with some autonomy in return. As director of branches Baker initiated systemic changes that moved the NAACP tangibly toward becoming the Association of her dreams.

To train the leaders who would be responsible for changing their communities, Baker instituted a series of training sessions designed to instruct branch officials and active members in what Baker called the "NAACP Line," a means of building movements around local issues through community organizing and the techniques of what she plainly called "propaganda." Baker worried that too many branch leaders had to look to the national office for advice on how to respond to a local situation, whether it be police violence, the tracking of African American children into inferior schools, or access to the ballot. If she could teach them the NAACP Line on dealing with such problems, they could address the problems themselves, using methods of the branch's own devising. In the course of the training sessions she would also mention issues that the national office had already identified as priorities: school desegregation, equal access to GI Bill of Rights benefits, housing discrimination, and others, and encourage branch members to suggest programs of action that could bubble up from the grass roots rather than trickle down from the national office.

The NAACP sponsored the first of Baker's Leadership Training Conferences in New York City in December 1944. Additional conferences followed in Cleveland, Indianapolis, and Atlanta in the first half of 1945. Having developed a sophisticated and comprehensive set of ideas about community organizing over the previous decade, Baker now put those ideas into practice. She encouraged branches to pay the way of their most committed officers and members to the regional workshops, which she titled "Give Light and the People Will Find a Way." The program of the March 1945 session in Atlanta included discussion on the themes "Techniques and Strategies of Minority Group Action," "Developing a Program through Branch Committees," "Problems of Democracy in the South," and "Securing Civil Rights of Negroes." Baker took a long view of the civil rights struggle—she did not expect her efforts to bear fruit right away—but not even she could have dreamed how much these conferences did to build a foundation for the mass movement she hoped to achieve.

To take just one example, the Montgomery, Alabama, branch, which Baker had nurtured as a field secretary, sent two members to a 1946 "Give Light and the People Will Find a Way" conference in Atlanta. E. D. Nixon, a local labor organizer, was also the very capable Montgomery branch president. Rosa Parks, a local seamstress who volunteered her time as Montgomery's branch secretary, was "already a seasoned activist," according to historian Danielle McGuire. Together they had built the Montgomery branch into a vibrant community resource. By 1946 they had already organized multiple voter registration drives and initiated a press service that publicized instances of discrimination against black Alabamians. Nixon, a Pullman porter, had traveled widely, but this was Parks's first trip outside of Alabama. She was taken with Baker, whom she found "smart, funny and strong." They connected immediately as talented, strong-willed, freedom-fighting women who were used to being taken for granted even within the freedom struggle. Nixon and Parks put what they learned in Atlanta and at a subsequent workshop in Jacksonville, Florida, to good use after returning home to Montgomery; Baker and Parks remained personal friends, and Baker stayed with Rosa and Raymond Parks when her travels took her to Montgomery thereafter.

The training sessions provided a program that was built on Baker's hard-won experience as an organizer and, just as importantly, a healthy dose of inspiration to local people who stood ready to challenge Jim Crow. They promised to remake the Association in Baker's action-oriented image. But the approach also brought Baker into direct conflict with the (all-male) leadership of the organization, especially Walter White, who according to Baker viewed the branches as little more than an automatic teller machine for the home office. Baker and White might have been able to overcome the philosophical differences had she not also sided against White in intraoffice power struggles. Beginning in 1944 she waged a campaign to regularize the staff's job descriptions and salaries, which if implemented would have professionalized the office but also would have loosened White's tight control of personnel. He soured on Baker by 1945, having come to believe that she was disloyal to him personally. The executive secretary's correspondence with the director of branches became increasingly petty that year, but Baker did not back down or beg forgiveness. Every time White chided Baker for a reporting delay she reminded him how woefully short her department was of clerical staff.

In the end, the philosophical differences were too great to surmount. The constant bickering with White and others surely played a role in her departure, but Baker mostly despaired that the NAACP was not doing more to develop civil rights activists on the local level. She remained convinced that the grassroots approach to organizing she had begun to perfect held the most promise for black Americans, but Baker resigned the job she seemed to have been born to perform in May 1946. She offered three reasons for her departure: "I feel that the Association is falling far short of its present possibilities; that the full capacities of the staff have not been used in the past; and that there is little chance of mine being utilized in the immediate future." Baker also had personal reasons for leaving. Having taken on new family responsibilities, she could no longer maintain her exhaustive travel schedule, and her health had begun to falter in any case. Even so, these situations might have been better managed if Baker had been willing to continue to butt heads with Walter White, but she was not. The personal criticism she directed at the executive director was blistering, and entirely warranted.

"The manner in which I was appointed, or rather 'drafted' as Director of Branches indicated a thought pattern that does not lend itself to healthy staff relations," Baker told White. "At no time had we discussed the directorship" before the appointment, she reminded him. She stepped into the high-profile, high-pressure position in the first place feeling that her "right to an opinion in the matter was completely discounted," but she "accepted the appointment because there was no graceful alternative." Having agreed under duress to begin the assignment, she received no directives from the executive director on the program's management and little guidance as to what was expected of her. Baker had filled the void quite creditably with the regional leadership training conferences. White never fully supported the approach, however, because the original idea for the program had come from Baker and not the executive director or board of directors.

Baker again complained about her program's lack of clerical support, which truly was a hindrance considering how quickly the number of branches expanded during her tenure, but she saved her most pointed critiques for White's leadership style. Baker described a toxic office atmosphere, framing the relationship between White and the staff in much the same way she had described the relationship between the NAACP's main office and its branches. "An almost complete lack of appreciation for the collective thinking of the staff"—a number of whom were women, although apart from Baker all others in leadership positions were male—"seems to prevail," she wrote. "Most of us work better when we feel that we are an integral part of a well-coordinated program and when we can share and exchange thoughts with our co-workers." This was not idle criticism. Baker had devoted serious time and brainpower to the study of social movements, and she had in the NAACP's membership rolls empirical proof that her methods worked. Yet White did not take her ideas seriously.

"I came to the Association because I felt that I could make a contribution to the struggle for human justice and equality," Baker concluded. "I am leaving because I feel that there must be some way to do this without further jeopardizing one's integrity and sense of fair play." Baker would insist for the remainder of her working days that any group advocating democracy in the United States had to operate democratically. Philosophical differences—and the belief that Walter White was no democrat—clearly played a leading role in the break, but so did another obstacle that Baker would continue to face in the movement: male chauvinism. Robert Carter, a Legal Defense Fund attorney, observed, "Walter and Roy liked full control. Ella was an independent woman and none of them intimidated her. . . . She was too powerful for them to do anything about." Baker would have agreed with Carter's perception of the clash of personalities that forced her to leave the national office. "You see, I don't worship individuals," she later said. "I like people, but there was nobody I felt that you had to pay obeisance to three times a day."

The response from branch officials, especially from the South, in reaction to Baker's departure was overwhelming. J. L. LeFlore, executive secretary of the Mobile, Alabama, branch, wrote, "The entire Mobile Branch regrets to know that you will leave the N.A.A.C.P. official family . . . All of us here and people throughout the country to whom we have talked, and who know you, have nothing but statements of praise for the very fine work you have done for the Association. To us down here your leaving brings a feeling of deep regret. We have grown to love you." In her final letter to leaders in the field she concluded coolly, "We did not accomplish all that we had hoped for, but we tried to be of definite service to all branches both individually and collectively," but she also pledged to continue to support the Association. She refused to criticize White or the national office publicly, because to do so would "detract from discussion of program." Baker attended the 1946 national convention in Cincinnati as her last official act as a national officer of the NAACP and resisted a steady stream of requests from branch officials to take the podium to explain her resignation. When she left the national office Baker also left behind the last full-time job with a dependable salary and benefits and long-term prospects she would ever hold. She was forty-two years old.

Baker's investment in the NAACP continued to accumulate interest well into the future. Her wartime work helped lay a foundation for the Association's future successes. In the years since, the NAACP has been at its most influential during the periods in which it has been able to combine an aggressive national-level approach to public relations and broad legal assaults with the community-based activism of local branches. To Baker's dismay, the Association never in her lifetime rekindled the spark of the wartime years in which branches and individual members had been made to feel that their ideas truly mattered to someone in the national office, that they had more than their membership dues to offer the NAACP. (To add insult to injury, Gloster Current, the head of the Detroit branch whom White selected to replace Baker as national director of branches, struck Baker as an self-satisfied autocrat in White's mold.) After Baker departed, the nation's most important civil rights organization never took advantage of its most valuable resource, its people, to foment a mass movement. But the principle of Baker's organizing at the grass roots paid great dividends for civil rights organizations yet unborn.

Baker's life changed dramatically after she returned home from the annual conference in Cincinnati, and not just because she gave up her steady NAACP salary and benefits. She and Roberts adopted her nine-year-old niece Jacqueline Brockington, the daughter of Baker's sister, Maggie, and brought her home to 452 St. Nicholas Avenue. "My sister wasn't going to be very responsible" for anything or anyone but herself, Baker said, so Anna Baker had taken Jackie, as she was known, home to Littleton to live with her extended family just days after she was born in 1937. Curtis Baker, Ella's bachelor brother, helped raise Jackie in Littleton, but by 1946 Anna Baker was an eighty-year-old widow who no longer had the energy to take primary responsibility for the young girl. Ella Baker thought that her "sister" Martha, who had stronger maternal instincts and domestic skills, might have been the ideal choice to take over Jackie's care, but Martha succumbed to cancer in October 1945. So Mr. and Mrs. Bob Roberts's domestic arrangements became even more unorthodox.

Baker learned how to be a mother on the fly, beginning at the age of forty-two. Jackie's arrival forced Baker to pull back a bit professionally—"Not to the point of not having meetings," she laughed. (After all, dragging children to the parents' meetings was a family tradition. Baker recalled, "I was young when I became active in things and I became active in things largely because my mother was active in the field of religion.") Jackie concurred: "In order to be with her you had to go to meetings," she said, and Baker's contemporaries in New York remembered the sight of Jackie doing homework in the back of many a conference room or auditorium. With the help of a neighbor named Miss Lena who subscribed to the "it takes a village" school of child rearing, Baker and Roberts provided Jackie with a loving, supportive home life.

Baker enrolled Jackie in The School on the Hill, a nearby private school run by Quakers, because she was worried that the "unruliness" of New York public schools would provide too much of a culture shock for the girl used to the sheltered world of Littleton. Jackie had "gone to school in a small town kind of school. The teachers lived with Mama, and all the teachers knew Mama, and all of that kind of thing," Baker said. Adjusting to the switch from Littleton to Harlem would be difficult enough. Enrolling Jackie in The School on the Hill would absorb some of the culture shock, but it also placed Baker in the uncomfortable position of advocating for the desegregation of and increased support for the New York City public schools while she appeared to have determined that they weren't good enough for her own family.

After short stints working as a fund-raiser for the Urban League and the Salvation Army, Baker began directing fund-raising efforts for the Harlem branch of the New York Cancer Committee. Where her work for the

NAACP had been a vocation not unlike a religious calling, this was merely a job, a means to a paycheck. Then again, cancer had taken Martha far too young, so Baker could feel that her work served a higher purpose.

She remained popular with the rank and file at the branch level of the NAACP, particularly in the South, and she responded to several requests to speak at membership drives throughout the country. If anything, ending her affiliation with the national office gave Baker permission to speak her mind more forcefully. For example, in her Emancipation Day (New Year's Day) address that kicked off a membership drive in Bethel, Georgia, she bellowed, "The Negro must quit looking for a savior and work to save himself and wake up others. There is no salvation except through yourselves."

Now something of a freelance civil rights organizer, she continued working from her New York base toward the goal of creating a southern mass movement. In 1946 she began helping CORE and the Quaker direct-action group Fellowship of Reconciliation plan the visionary Journey of Reconciliation, an integrated bus trip through the Upper South and border states—a direct precursor to the much more well-known Freedom Rides of 1961. The Journey would test compliance with the U.S. Supreme Court's *Morgan v. Commonwealth of Virginia* decision of that year, which seemed to strike down Jim Crow in interstate bus travel for good. The organizers hoped that it might also give courage to black southerners along the route to challenge Jim Crow in their own ways.

Only after they had completed planning did the male leaders of the Journey tell Baker and her fellow organizers Pauli Murray and Natalie Mormon that the Journey of Reconciliation would be for men only. The decision stung Baker. "I guess it was decided that I was too frail to make such a journey," she said. "I had made a number of them alone, but I was too frail to make it with a group" of men. Between 1941 and 1946 she had logged more interstate miles and endured more Jim Crow indignities than all but a small handful of African Americans. Baker's travels on behalf of the Association had steeled her determination that African Americans had to put an end to Jim Crow, and the Journey was the most forceful means of bringing attention to the issue that anyone had yet devised. It promised to force the federal government into action against segregation in a way that no previous campaign had. It hurt to be told she could not participate.

The men who patronizingly prevented Baker, Murray, and Mormon from participating may have had a point; this would almost surely be physically dangerous work because they intended to publicize it ahead of time, and white racists had already proven how emotionally and violently they could respond to challenges to their "way of life." But the three women were adults capable of assessing the risks themselves and coming to their own conclusions. Baker had personally engaged in a great deal of direct action against segregated interstate travel (though without fanfare), and she had as much or more experience fighting Jim Crow as any of the men involved. Once again, the men in the movement took her less seriously because she was a woman.

In April 1947 sixteen Journey of Reconciliation volunteers, eight blacks and eight whites, traveled in racially (but not sexually) integrated teams from Washington, D.C., through Virginia, West Virginia, North Carolina, Tennessee, Kentucky, and Ohio. At six stops along the way local authorities made twelve arrests, and one participant, Bayard Rustin, ended up serving twenty-two days on a North Carolina chain gang. Although the Journey received only limited publicity, failed to launch the wave of organized nonviolent direct opposition to Jim Crow that Baker and the other organizers had hoped for, and did not spur the federal government to action, it did at least provide a blueprint from which a later generation of activists could work.

Concurrently, Baker dove into her work with the New York branch of the NAACP. She initially devoted most of her time to the branch's education committee and its youth council, which she served as adviser from 1947 to 1952, still attended national meetings, and kept in close touch with the local people throughout the South she had befriended and supported as a field secretary. She concocted a fund-raising plan for the branch that perfectly expressed what Baker's biographer Joanne Grant called "her constant efforts to involve ordinary people in social causes." In order to raise $25,000 the campaign would enlist hundreds of volunteers to collect $50 each. (If the campaign was successful enough that she could hire herself as a salaried employee to direct it, all the better.)

Baker also served on advisory boards for the New York City Welfare Council, the federal Office of Price Administration, and the Consumer Advisory Council of the President's Council of Economic Advisors, in addition to several New York–area consumer and cooperative groups. She appears to have lent her support to any and every group working for progressive change in New York City that asked for it in this period—up to and including the Citizens' Committee for the Integration of Negroes in the Brewery Industry. In 1951 she made a halfhearted run for a seat on the New York City Council. Baker surely could have been more effective had she channeled her energies into two or three, instead of twelve or fourteen, causes at a time. It is worth asking: Why couldn't she say no to more of the requests that came her way? And did Baker's commitment to building broad-based coalitions, to supporting anyone who fought racial injustice, whatever form it took, ultimately hinder her effectiveness?

In 1952 the members of the New York City branch of the NAACP elected Baker president, the first woman president in the branch's history. Over the previous decade she had developed strong opinions about how branches should be organized, what their priorities should be, and how they might best realize them. Now she had the opportunity to put those ideas into practice with one of the largest and best-resourced branches in the country. She would develop committees and delegate power to them, giving others the opportunity to develop their own leadership abilities. She would pursue partnerships with labor organizations and other progressive groups working for change throughout the city. She would charge ahead on issues that the rank and file of the branch membership identified as most important: ending police brutality and creating a public school system that provided a quality education to every child and respected the opinions of every family. The post offered a peerless platform for a woman who had put in hundreds of thousands of hours of service to her community, who had developed a program that she could now put in place, and who relished the chance to defy expectations of what a woman should and should not do.

Baker resigned the presidency the following year. Why she would have stepped back from branch leadership and thrown herself back into electoral politics is one of the great mysteries of Baker's public life, but she did just that, running against popular incumbent Earl Brown for a seat on the New York City Council as the nominee of the Liberal Party. (Baker never offered a detailed explanation for the move, but it later occurred to her that the branch vice president who stood to rise to the presidency once she resigned it had been particularly enthusiastic in encouraging her to run for office again.) Her platform called for more low-income housing, greater support for public schools and day care programs, and good-government reforms, none of which greatly distinguished her from Brown. He won the election by a margin of nearly six votes to one. Barbara Ransby suggests that "the value of the campaign lay not in a vain hope of victory but in the broad-based educational effort that running for office entailed." But it is not clear that even Baker had this optimistic a view of her candidacy. Never again would she run for office, seldom would she have anything positive to say about a politician, and only on one occasion would she advise community organizers to devote their attention to a quixotic electoral campaign.

Baker returned to the executive committee of the New York branch and dove back into the work of community organizing at which she excelled. Shortly after the U.S. Supreme Court declared segregated school systems unconstitutional in 1954, operating simultaneously on behalf of and independent from the NAACP branch, she developed an interracial parents' group that shocked New York City officials by demanding desegregation in *their* city. Up to then Northern liberals smugly assumed that segregated and unequal schools were a problem for southerners to deal with. In asserting that segregation and inequality were also a problem for the urban North, attacking the problem head-on, and organizing the masses the problem most affected, Baker practiced the lessons she had earlier preached to northern NAACP chapters.

Kenneth Clark, a City College of New York psychology professor whose famous doll studies (conducted with his wife and research partner, Mamie Phipps Clark) proving that Jim Crow damaged the self-esteem of black children ipso facto provided influential evidence in the *Brown* case, instigated the local movement with a speech at an Urban League dinner in 1954. In front of an audience that included recently inaugurated Mayor Robert F. Wagner Jr., members of the Board of Education, and other high officials, Clark declared that education for children of color in the city was "in a state of decline." The segregation of schoolchildren by race and the denial of equal educational opportunities for minority children was as much a problem in the urban North as it was in the Deep South, he said. The latter charge was guaranteed to strike a nerve, and it did. Soon after the Schools Superintendent William Jansen issued a statement blaming segregation on de facto housing patterns, not policy; he did not deny that schoolchildren were segregated by race in the city, but he characterized the situation as "normal" and "accidental."

The Intergroup Committee on Public Schools, which Baker led along with Clark, Judge Hubert Delany, and others, issued a report, "Children Apart," which showed conclusively that segregation existed in the city's public schools, was getting worse, and was leading to increasingly unequal outcomes for students of different ethnic groups. When another study commissioned by the nonpartisan Public Education Association confirmed the Intergroup Committee's findings, it forced the school board into action.

Baker's goal was not racial integration for its own sake. Rather, she saw segregated schools as symptoms of larger problems, the most critical of which was a system that made decisions that affected schoolchildren without the input of their parents. Parents who had little or no say in the development of school system policies were more likely to have their children shunted off into underfunded schools, and those schools were more likely to have higher concentrations of children of color. "Where there is separation," Baker said, "the schools are too often inadequate." It was a question of democracy: Did the New York public school system really intend to provide a first-rate education to *all* of its students? Did it respect and honor the wishes of *all* parents and allow them a real voice in making the decisions that affected their families?

Under the auspices of their grassroots group Parents in Action Against Educational Discrimination, Baker, the Clarks, and interested parents, most of them African American or Puerto Rican, pushed for greater parental involvement in school decisions via direct action. "They were supposed to be eliminating de facto segregation in the school system in New York," Baker said. "So for the summer of 1957 we had weekly meetings with parents in the different boroughs for getting them to deal with the question of their schools, what was happening to their children." Baker's point in organizing the group was, Charles Payne writes, "that the parents worked on the issues themselves rather than having the civil rights professionals work on their behalf."

The branch's rank and file clearly authorized the approach and participated in Parents in Action, but the national office of the NAACP encouraged branches to avoid actions that would alienate northern white liberals whose support the Association depended upon. The national office preferred to keep the country focused on the dramatic efforts of southern blacks to desegregate their communities' schools—especially the efforts of Baker's NAACP friend Daisy Bates to integrate the schools of Little Rock, Arkansas. Baker ignored those concerns. On September 26, 1957, two days after President Eisenhower sent the 101st Airborne into Little Rock to escort nine black students into Central High School, Baker led a raucous rally of five hundred black and Puerto Rican parents in front of New York City Hall. They denounced the practice of assigning less-experienced teachers to their children's schools, which tended to be overcrowded, and the school board's indifference to their concerns. After two hours Mayor Wagner finally agreed to meet with a delegation of twenty-one protestors. Speaking for the group, Baker demanded, "New York City, the world's leading city, should reflect the highest degree of democracy in its public school system."

At Wagner's direction the New York City Board of Education created a Commission on Integration; while she pushed on the board from the outside she also served voluntarily on its Subcommission on Zoning for two years beginning in 1956. The subcommittee's report called for a "clear, positive zoning policy to promote racially balanced schools" in the face of de facto segregation. Baker and one other subcommittee member thought the recommendations too watered down and offered their own more aggressive suggestions.

The hundreds of hours Baker put into the Commission on Integration were utterly wasted. Most of the "action" in New York's desegregation efforts over the next several decades amounted to punchless committee meetings and empty official rhetoric while the situation on the ground grew worse. In 1954, the year of the *Brown* decision, there was not a single New York public school with a black or Puerto Rican student population of greater than 90 percent. By 1960 there were thirty-eight such schools, and by 1963 the number had increased to sixty-one. On the eve of the passage of the 1964 Civil Rights Act, nearly a quarter of the public schools in the borough of Manhattan had a supermajority of minority students. Despite the efforts of Baker, Clark, and Parents in Action, the system assigned the least-experienced teachers to these schools, and the results were predictable.

Baker's grassroots organizing led to much greater change than did her work from within the system. The organizing might not have produced immediate results, but Baker was more interested in developing long-term, community-led initiatives than she was in producing immediate victories that could, after all, be blunted or overturned when public attention died down. New York parents' interest in community input into education policy hardly went away. If anything, the movement Baker had helped to launch only intensified over the coming decades; it reached critical mass in the late 1960s and 1970s, when the city's community control movement forced the public schools system to decentralize decision making.

Police brutality against people of color was the other major issue New York branch members had identified as the problem they wanted the branch's leaders to address. Black and Hispanic New Yorkers believed that police systematically treated them with disrespect. Going back to the World War I era, when the first waves of the so-called Great Migration brought southern blacks like Baker into the city in increasingly large numbers, relations between the races had been troubled. More often than not, the flashpoint was the treatment of people of color at the hands of white policemen. This was the case in 1943's Harlem Riot, in which a policeman shot a black soldier who had been trying to protect a black woman from the policeman; in response, outraged Harlemites did an estimated $5 million worth of damage to white-owned businesses. Over the course of two-and-a-half years in the early 1950s the branch documented more than one hundred cases in which New York policemen either violated the civil rights of or brutalized citizens of color.

The tipping point came in the summer of 1953, when police arrested truck driver Jacob Jackson; his wife, Geneva; and Samuel Crawford, another African American, for no discernible reason. Jacob Jackson and Samuel Crawford sustained horrific beatings at the station house, and Jackson required two operations on his badly damaged skull. The branch sponsored mass meetings that attracted hundreds of participants to demonstrate widespread frustration with the police force and pressed criminal charges and a civil suit against the officers involved, but to little avail. Branch leaders then got the wheels of the national NAACP's publicity machine in motion and appealed to the U.S. Justice Department.

Police officials were able to sidetrack investigations into systematic brutality against citizens of color by throwing out a red herring. The complaints, they charged, were merely the result of Communists trying to drive a wedge between the New York Police Department and the FBI. "No communist plot can explain away the fact that Jacob Jackson had to undergo two brain operations," Ella Baker responded. "Nor does it explain how other able-bodied persons have walked into police precincts, but had to be carried out as hospital cases."

The NAACP's inability to gain traction on the issue illustrated how deep the problem ran. The branch demanded the resignation of Police Commissioner George Monahan, but he emerged from the controversy as strong as ever. He did announce that police officers would undergo sensitivity training and that he would initiate a Civilian Complaint Review Board. But decades later people of color were still fighting New York City to bring the police department under some measure of civilian control.

It was true that American Communists opposed Jim Crow more ardently and did more to organize antiracist efforts than most, but the charge that they had infiltrated and begun to set policy for the NAACP was preposterous. (And, even if they had, that was a matter entirely separate from police brutality.) The NAACP branch's executive committee believed that it needed to be purer than Caesar's wife, however. Along with many other private clubs, public advocacy groups, universities, and governmental agencies on the federal, state, and local level, the branch decided to ferret out any Communists that might have burrowed in, lest someone else find them first and embarrass the branch.

In response to prodding from the national office, the branch's executive committee formed an Internal Security Committee (ISC) in 1957. Baker served on the committee from its inception and helped to write policies that expelled those "having any affiliation with communists" within the past fifteen years—a distressingly elastic classification that could conceivably have included Baker in the 1930s, though she was never a member of the American Communist Party—from the branch. Nominees for spots on the executive board had to provide a written statement listing all of their past and present affiliations, which the ISC then had to approve. Members of the ISC insisted that theirs was "not a 'witch hunt' but a 'watch dog' committee," but in the context of American politics in the 1950s this was a distinction without much difference.

Fortunately for Baker, no one seems to have remembered an August 1941 memorandum on NAACP organizing strategy that she cosigned with other members of the field staff—Daisy E. Lampkin, Madison S. Jones, and E. Frederic Morrow—either when it was written or when the ISC began its investigations. Morrow was officially listed as the memorandum's author, but Baker's fingerprints were all over it. (Assertions such as "[O]ne of the prime phases of the work of such an organization as the NAACP is a question of jobs, employment, labor and the economic condition of the masses" had the distinctive ring of Baker's voice.) The memorandum argued that the national office should be more responsive to branches and members, should decentralize and share its decision making, should hire regional administrators, and should allow the largest branches to hire executive staff rather than rely solely on volunteers.

Though they did not use the term, Baker and the other members of the field staff implied that the NAACP would be strongest if it organized "cells" of activists throughout the country who could respond to the national office's directives but would otherwise operate autonomously and energetically. "Communists are anathema to many people—but their methods of organization are unexcelled," they argued. "They have these community groups or units and work most effectively." Though they tempered their esteem for the Communist Party's organizing methods by pointing out, "we have other precedents [for organizational models] in lodges, the Catholic church, and other fraternal organizations," there was no walking back from the candid statement of admiration for a group that most Americans truly did consider "anathema." The memorandum hardly proved that Baker and the others were Communists in 1941, but in the midst of the Red Scare of the 1950s many other Americans' lives were made miserable because they had expressed appreciation for the Communists' methods in previous decades. Baker's career could have been ruined, perhaps permanently, had the memorandum resurfaced.

The ISC pressured a number of branch members to resign quietly and expelled one member, radical attorney and admitted Communist Party member Ben Davis Jr., publicly. Baker was herself anti-Communist by this point. Ironically, she came to this position not because she was a member of the herd that willingly trampled civil liberties in the name of national security, but because she believed communism hindered the free expression of ideas. At the time Baker justified her participation on the ISC as distasteful work that had to be done for the greater good of the NAACP, but she later admitted that cooperating with the national wave of anti-Communist hysteria had been a mistake.

A decade after giving up her position in the national office, Baker remained a committed member of the NAACP. She put the skills she had honed in the field to work on behalf of the New York branch, and the work she performed in various branch leadership positions attuned her to intra-movement politics in new ways. But working on committees that ferreted out Communists or marginally increased job opportunities for blacks in the beer industry was not an especially effective use of her time; Baker knew full well that this work did little to bring about the birth of a mass movement against Jim Crow. In her dreams, the movement would be peopled and led by black southerners, so she kept on the lookout for signs that such a movement might be aborning. She finally caught sight of those signs in the early 1950s, and by the end of the decade she had returned South to do whatever she could to assist the movement through its labor pains.

CHAPTER FOUR

The Hard Job of Getting Down and Helping People

The NAACP's decades-long legal assault against Jim Crow came to fruition in May 1954 when the U.S. Supreme Court announced its decision in the *Brown v. Board of Education* school segregation case. The decision seemed to open new doors for civil rights activists. At the very least, those interested in wiping out racial inequality now had the sanction of the highest court in the land and the symbolic weight of the federal government behind their cause. Robert F. Williams, the leader of the Monroe, North Carolina, branch of the NAACP, said, "I was sure that this was the beginning of a new era in American democracy." Baker, too, was overjoyed by the news, but her reaction was tempered by her understanding of how the American system of government operated. As she saw them, jurists' rulings were mere words on paper. Only the masses' determination to test the ruling and force the executive branch to enforce the verdict, she believed, could give the judgment meaning and power.

That would require the kind of mass movement Baker had long anticipated, but such a movement did not exist in May 1954, and a betting person would not have wagered that one was on the horizon. As southern states and local school boards surveyed the new landscape and tried to concoct plans that complied with the decision either fully or in name only, white segregationists organized themselves and saw to it that "their" schools would desegregate as slowly as possible—if at all. In Indianola, Mississippi, where a local doctor had taken charge of the NAACP branch and launched a voter registration drive, the white town fathers formed a new organization that they called the Citizens' Council. Members of the Citizens' Council—small business owners, bankers, and lawyers—defined racial segregation as a positive good for society and argued the point forcefully. They proudly defined themselves against the Ku Klux Klan; the Councils were to use economic means, not bullets and dynamite, to punish black dissidents. They had a simple goal: to make it as hard as possible to be a civil rights activist. While the rest of the country waited for the Supreme Court's 1955 implementation decision (*Brown II*, as it became known), the Citizens' Councils spread throughout the South. The original decision said nothing about how local districts should accomplish desegregation, but *Brown II* advised them to proceed with desegregation plans "with all deliberate speed."

As important as their development was, the Citizens' Councils were far from alone in organizing resistance to the *Brown* decision and federal efforts to enforce it. White moderates were curiously quiet as hard-core segregationists managed to turn outright resistance to the Supreme Court into something like a mainstream activity throughout the South. As Richard Kluger has documented, in Clarendon County, South Carolina, whites used every weapon in their arsenal to ruin J. A. Delaine, the plaintiff in one of the five suits that had been folded into the *Brown* case. They fired DeLaine, his wife, two of his sisters, and a niece from their jobs, dried up his credit, and burned down both DeLaine's house and the church he pastored. They shot into his house, and when he shot back they charged him with felonious assault with a deadly weapon. They literally ran him out of the state for trying to enroll his children in better schools. Hundreds of brave black men and women who wanted to give their children more opportunity shared DeLaine's experience.

In Mississippi, whites working under the aegis of the Citizens' Councils threatened local activists such as Gus Courts in Belzoni, Amzie Moore of the Delta town of Cleveland, Dr. Clinton Battle of Indianola, and Dr. T. R. M. Howard of Mound Bayou with financial ruin and physical harm if they didn't call off their voter registration drives and challenges to segregation. Courts, Battle, and Howard had to leave the state, but Moore—an NAACP branch leader with whom Baker had worked in the 1940s—stayed and fought. When the Yazoo City, Mississippi, branch of the NAACP found fifty-three African American parents willing to petition the local school board to admit their children into what were then all-white schools, the Citizens' Council took out a full-page ad in the local newspaper, printed broadsides, and posted them all over town. The publications listed the names and addresses of the signers, many of whom lost their jobs almost as soon as their names went public. Within days fifty-one of the fifty-three had removed their names from the petition, and more than a dozen of them eventually had to leave the state. Similar fates befell the parents in the nearby cities of Vicksburg and Jackson who were brave enough to challenge Jim Crow in their schools. Now that white Mississippians had proven how effective these campaigns could be, organized efforts to "defend" white schools from desegregation cropped up in every state of the former Confederacy. In community after community, blacks who stuck their necks out for the cause met with economic intimidation and violence.

Baker felt a visceral need to provide whatever assistance she could while the southern activists held on by their fingernails. If the segregationists could snuff out their activism with violence and economic terrorism, she rightly feared, the nascent movement would be set back at least a generation. With two other New Yorkers, Stanley Levison and Bayard Rustin, Baker began organizing a network of northern financial supporters that quickly coalesced into an organization they called In Friendship. Together they raised money through New York churches and labor unions for the material and legal aid that parents in Yazoo City and Clarendon County and hundreds of other southern communities suddenly needed simply to survive and live with some measure of dignity. Much of the work was ad hoc; when Baker heard of a need, she donated her time (which was precious—without a full-time job at the time, she strung together freelance consulting, fund-raising, and conference organizing work to make ends meet) to go out and raise money to help alleviate it. Charles Payne describes In Friendship's modus operandi as "find someone who is already working and support that person."

Baker, Levison, and Rustin were three unlikely peas in a pod. In previous decades all three had either expressed admiration for American Communists' organizing strategies (in Baker's case) or joined the American Communist Party (as Levison almost surely did) or the Young Communist League (of which Rustin was briefly a member). All three had worked for racial justice.

Baker had first worked with Levison, a wealthy New York–based lawyer and real estate investor, in the unsuccessful lobbying fight against the Cold War–era McCarran-Walter Act. The legislation, which Congress ultimately passed into law over President Truman's veto in 1952, allowed the United States to deport immigrants, even those who had become naturalized citizens, simply for having "Communist and Communist-front" affiliations. Communists and sympathizers such as Baker's former associate W. E. B. Du Bois and the popular black entertainer Paul Robeson were among the many American citizens whose lives the U.S. government made miserable under cover of the legislation; over the ensuing years the government also used the act's provisions to deny entry to prominent foreign leftist intellectuals. Baker's interest in the legislative fight may well have sprung from her guilt over her involvement in the effort to purge Communists from the NAACP. Levison had proved himself a successful fund-raiser for the American Jewish Congress, and he shared Baker's energy and intense interest in civil rights.

Baker had known and worked closely with Rustin at least since 1946, when they planned the Journey of Reconciliation. A committed Quaker pacifist, an acolyte of Gandhian nonviolent civil disobedience, a former member of the Young Communist League, and an open homosexual, Rustin was, to put it mildly, one of a kind. In the immediate postwar years he functioned, in the words of his biographer Jervis Anderson, "as a one-man civil disobedience movement." As it was with Baker, movement building was a way of life for Rustin, a lifelong vocation that took multiple forms. Like Baker, he set his sights on a southern-led mass movement in the late 1940s and early 1950s and did what he could to build a foundation for what he hoped might eventually emerge. Together they formed In Friendship with these goals in mind.

Baker called on New York City's major religious leaders, union officials, and leftist activists to support In Friendship. Once again she and Rustin leaned on A. Philip Randolph, who agreed to lend his prestige to the new organization by serving as chairman. Over the course of a little less than two years the group raised tens of thousands of dollars to aid the people In Friendship accurately defined as "race terror victims," southern activists facing economic retaliation. Here the new group followed the lead of the NAACP, which in 1955 deposited more than a quarter-million dollars at the black-owned Tri-State Bank in Memphis to back loans to southern activists who had been targeted by the Citizens' Councils. But the amount of money it would have taken to assist every single black activist the Councils were in a position to ruin would have cost many times that. At best, these efforts were drops in a bucket. No outside effort, no matter how coordinated, could have raised enough money to meet the need.

The best In Friendship could hope to do was to provide just enough of a bandage to limit the bleeding, make a few lives marginally better in the South, and build bridges among southern activists and between southerners and their northern allies until better opportunities presented themselves. To that end, Baker, working under the auspices of In Friendship, also provided technical assistance to southern civil rights campaigns, organized conferences that brought together activists from throughout the region, and embarked on public relations campaigns that publicized conditions in the South to the rest of the country. She served as a civil rights free agent whenever "called upon by the outstanding leaders of the civil rights struggle to perform specific tasks that need to be done, but which seem not to fall within the operational scope of other organizations," as she put it in a report for In Friendship. For

Baker, who was in the movement for the long haul, that was enough for the moment. But she still pined for a honest-to-goodness mass movement.

The indigenous southern movement Baker had hoped for all her adult life announced itself in December 1955. Rosa Parks, the secretary of the Montgomery, Alabama, branch of the NAACP who had connected with Baker a decade earlier, touched off what seemed to some observers a spontaneous display of frustration with Jim Crow when she refused to give up her seat on a Montgomery bus and was arrested for violating the city's segregated seating laws. Baker knew better.

The African Americans of Montgomery, more than any black community in any other city, were *organized*, and Parks's refusal to give up her seat was not out of character. In addition to the NAACP leadership training sessions she attended in 1946, Parks had more recently participated in a two-week workshop at the Highlander Folk School in Monteagle, Tennessee. Founded in 1932 as a training ground for labor organizers, Highlander was one of the few places in the South where blacks and whites could come together to discuss the problems that faced them as workers and as citizens in a racially integrated setting. In the 1950s Highlander developed into the premier training site in the South for desegregation activists. Ella Baker had found kindred spirits at Highlander, participated in dozens of its programs through the years, and maintained long professional and personal relationships with Myles Horton, Highlander's cofounder, and Septima Clark, its education director. Virginia Foster Durr, a white Montgomerian with a long history of work with interracial organizations in the South and with a friendly relationship with Rosa Parks, recommended Parks for a workshop titled "Racial Desegregation: Implementing the Supreme Court Decision." According to Baker biographer Joanne Grant, Baker led classes at the Highlander workshop and reconnected there with Parks, but the evidence for this claim is scant.

By her own admission, Parks was at first unsure what to make of the people at Highlander, all of whom addressed one another as "brother" and "sister," and who square-danced or played volleyball when they weren't engaged in hours-long discussions about the race problem. (They also sang a lot: among the many other things they did, Highlander people repurposed and popularized the organized labor song "We Shall Overcome" for the civil rights movement.) Parks recalled, "That was the first time in my life I had lived in an atmosphere of complete equality with members of the other race." For the first time in her life Parks saw, heard, and felt evidence that "this could be a unified society." At Highlander, she said, "We forgot about what color anybody was. . . . I experienced people of different races and backgrounds meeting together in workshops and living together in peace and harmony. I felt that I could express myself honestly, without any repercussions or antagonistic attitudes from other people."

Parks scribbled twenty-two pages of handwritten notes on yellow legal pads at Highlander; she took the educational seminars seriously, and she took the questions that were raised there to heart. But more than anything, Parks left Highlander with the sense that blacks and whites really could live together as equals. She now had a deep belief based on her experience in the Tennessee mountains that integration was a positive good for society, and she went home with a determination to do her part to end Jim Crow. Horton, Clark, and others at Highlander had helped her develop a vocabulary to describe the problems she saw in her community and an action plan for bringing down segregation. She returned to Montgomery resolved to do whatever she could—either as a member of her NAACP branch or as an individual—to kill Jim Crow.

Black Montgomerians had already identified segregated seating and disrespectful treatment on the city's buses as the one indignity they most wanted to end. A delegation of local black women told city officials as much in a February 1954 meeting, and the leader of the NAACP branch, E. D. Nixon, began looking for ways to test the constitutionality of the local ordinances that wrote Jim Crow into law. According to these statutes blacks were to sit in rows from the back forward and whites in rows from the front back; no black could sit in a row with a white, so the middle rows were available to black paying customers (who made up three-fourths of the city's ridership) only if they were unused by whites. To make matters worse, several bus drivers, all of whom were white in 1954, took special pleasure in mistreating their black passengers in any way possible. "Some bus drivers were meaner than others," Parks said. "Not all of them were hateful, but segregation itself is vicious, and to my mind there was no way you could make segregation decent or nice or acceptable."

Days after the U.S. Supreme Court announced its *Brown* decision in May, Parks's colleague Jo Ann Gibson Robinson, an English professor at Alabama State College, Montgomery's historically black institution, and head of the Women's Political Council, a counterpart to the all-white local chapter of the League of Women Voters, demanded that the city desegregate the buses or face a boycott from its black ridership. Robinson later admitted that the threat of a boycott did not at the time have widespread support from the city's black leaders, but she believed the issue could spur the entire community into unified action. Every bit of this organizing had gone on independent of leadership from national organizations. Lo-

cal people had identified the problem and begun to define so
entirely by themselves.

Parks, E. D. Nixon, and Jo Ann Robinson nearly had the test case they
had been searching for in March 1955 when Montgomery police arrested
Claudette Colvin, a high school junior and member of Parks's NAACP
Youth Council, for refusing to give up her seat in a middle row to a white
rider. Colvin said that Parks's advice—"Always do what is right"—rang in
her ears as the police led her away in handcuffs. A judge dropped the charge
of violating the city's segregation laws so that the NAACP branch could
not pursue the matter in federal courts, and the black community failed to
rally around Colvin, a brash-talking, unmarried young woman who was, as
it turned out, several months pregnant. "If the white press got ahold of that
information, they would have a field day," Parks accurately concluded. In
October, eighteen-year-old Mary Louise Smith was arrested for refusing to
give up her seat to a white passenger, but again local leadership failed to rally
behind her. Smith's father was a well-known alcoholic.

Montgomery's budding antisegregation movement needed "a plaintiff
who was more upstanding before we went ahead and invested any more
time, effort, and money," Parks said. She became that plaintiff in December
1955. On the first day of the month she finished a workday at the downtown
Montgomery Fair Department Store where she worked as a seamstress, did
some Christmas shopping, and boarded the Cleveland Avenue bus. It had
been a typical workday for Parks, which is to say that she worked more than
one job. She spent her morning coffee break trying to arrange a space for an
upcoming NAACP branch workshop and getting branch correspondence in
the mail, and she met Fred Gray, Claudette Colvin's attorney, for lunch to
plan strategy for her case. That afternoon Parks took a seat in a middle row
of the thirty-six-seat bus and settled in for the ride home to the Cleveland
Courts apartment building. At the bus's third stop several whites boarded,
and the driver, James F. Blake, told Parks, two women, and a man sharing her
row, "Move y'all, I want those two seats." Blake, a tobacco-chewing, pistol-
packing racist from central casting who was known in Montgomery's black
community as a "vicious bigot," had a history with Parks. He had physically
mistreated her on a bus in 1943, and she had vowed never again to pay the
fare on a bus he was driving; she also joined the NAACP shortly after the incident. She had apparently kept her pledge to avoid his buses until December
1, 1955, when she boarded the bus—"my bus," he insisted on calling it—with
her mind on other matters.

"Y'all better make it light on yourselves and let me have those seats,"
Blake repeated, and the three other African American patrons complied.

Parks sat. Blake made his way back and asked Parks, "Are you going to stand up?" Parks looked him in the eye, flatly said, "No," and told the bus driver he would have to call the police. He did just that. Officers F. B. Day and D. W. Mixon removed Parks from the bus without incident, took her to city hall to swear out and sign a warrant for her arrest, and then transported her to the city jail.

Baker considered the events in Montgomery, not the announcement of the *Brown* decision, as the exciting opening of a new chapter in the history of the American civil rights movement, not because Mrs. Parks had acted bravely in staring down Jim Crow and refusing to cooperate with it any longer, but because so many local African Americans joined her side. From the beginning—really, even before Parks's arrest, it was a mass movement. Parks, Nixon, Robinson, and handful of others had black Montgomery organized so tightly by the time of Parks's arrest that they were able to use the event as a springboard to mass, nonviolent, direct action. Parks had not intended to become the plaintiff in a test case, but when Blake demanded her seat—the seat for which she had paid full fare, same as the white passengers—she concluded on the spot, "There had to be a stopping place, and this seemed to have been the place for me to stop being pushed around and to find out what human rights I had, if any."

News of Parks's incarceration moved quickly through the Montgomery grapevine; no one was as surprised by the arrest of the well-respected, respectful Parks as E. D. Nixon. When his wife told him, "You won't believe it. The police got Rosa," Nixon was temporarily and uncharacteristically dumbstruck. "Holy mother of God" was all he could think to say that night, but he later allowed, "My God, look what segregation [has] put in my hands[:] The perfect plaintiff."

Parks was arrested late on Thursday afternoon. Late that night she and Nixon planned their next steps—they agreed to turn her arrest into a test case, taking it all the way to the U.S. Supreme Court if necessary, despite the economic and social hardships becoming such a publicized plaintiff would impose on Rosa and Raymond Parks. Nixon briefed attorney Fred Gray, who in turn contacted Jo Ann Robinson late the next evening. Robinson suggested they call for a boycott of the city's buses to begin the following Monday. She wrote herself a note: "The Women's Political Council will not wait for Mrs. Parks to consent to call for a boycott of city buses. On Friday, December 2, 1955, the women of Montgomery will call for a boycott to take place on Monday, December 5."

Boycotts are easy to declare, of course, but nearly impossible to pull off effectively. Robinson knew that as well as anyone, so she went to work. After midnight she assembled a small work crew—two women students and a business professor who had access to his department's mimeograph machine—at the Alabama State campus. Speaking for the three hundred members of the Women's Political Council, Robinson composed a short manifesto. It read:

Another Negro woman has been arrested and thrown in jail because she refused to get up out of her seat on the bus for a white person to sit down.

It is the second time since the Claudette Colbert case that a Negro woman has been arrested for the same thing. This has to be stopped.

Negroes have rights, too, for if Negroes did not ride the buses, they could not operate. Three-fourths of the riders are Negroes, yet we are arrested, or have to stand over empty seats. If we do not do something to stop these arrests, they will continue. The next time it may be you, or your daughter, or mother.

This woman's case will come up on Monday. We are, therefore, asking every Negro to stay off the buses Monday in protest of the arrest and trial. Don't ride the buses to work, to town, to school, or anywhere on Monday.

You can afford to stay out of school for one day if you have no other way to go except by bus.

You can also afford to stay out of town for one day. If you work, take a cab, or walk. But please, children and grown-ups, don't ride the bus at all on Monday. Please stay off of all buses Monday.

Robinson and her crew typed up the call for boycott, then printed and delivered an estimated 52,500 leaflets between midnight and 4:00 a.m. on Saturday, December 3. Black Montgomery awoke that morning to find the leaflets had been delivered to virtually every school, business, church, and home in the community. The people of the community would have to decide whether to honor the boycott, and anything short of unanimity would doom it to failure.

While Robinson planned and publicized the boycott, Nixon mobilized Montgomery's black preachers. As an organizing medium, the black church had no peer. No other institution—no black newspaper, social club, or any other entity—could match Montgomery's black churches' "grapevine," or communications infrastructure, and no one—not Robinson or even Nixon— spoke with more power and authority on issues that affected the black community than the preachers. In Montgomery, as elsewhere throughout the South, the churches were the community's most important institution, and they were also the most autonomous—which in theory made them the least vulnerable to white counterattack. There was no guarantee that the preachers would support the boycott, but if Nixon could convince them to throw their influence behind the effort it stood a good chance of success.

Nixon first called his own pastor, Rev. Ralph David Abernathy, whose First Baptist Church was the oldest and most imposing black Baptist church in town. Abernathy responded positively and promised to use his post as secretary of the town's Baptist Ministers Alliance to bring others on board. He suggested that Nixon follow up by enlisting Rev. H. H. Hubbard, the president of the Alliance, and a newcomer to Montgomery, the twenty-six-year-old pastor of Dexter Avenue Baptist Church, Rev. Martin Luther King Jr., in the effort. Nixon invited King on board, but the preacher replied, "Brother Nixon, let me think about it and call you back." That disappointed Nixon, but a pep talk from Abernathy subsequently brought King onto the team; he agreed to host a meeting of roughly fifty black leaders to discuss the boycott at Dexter Avenue that Friday evening. The assembled clergymen had to be convinced to support the boycott—which was still conceived as a one-day, one-off affair—but they did agree, and they did promote it in their Sunday sermons.

Community organizers such as Ella Baker and Jo Ann Robinson inevitably find that life gets in the way of political action. In the context of the mid-1950s South it was not difficult to find examples of the truism at work. An employer angrily questioned his employee about his signature on a petition requesting the desegregation of local schools, so the employee removed it. The local banker recommended that a homeowner give a second thought to the voter registration card he filled out yesterday—it would be a shame if the bank had to call in his home loan—so the homeowner rescinded it and told the civil rights workers to go away the next time they came by to encourage him to register. How could a domestic worker who supported the ideals of a bus boycott but could not afford to risk being late to work—her family depended on this job, and keeping her children fed was more important than anything else—do anything but shuffle onto the back of a bus? Robinson's idea for a bus boycott could not possibly work. That domestic worker in Montgomery earned an average wage of just $523 a year, so it wasn't like she could just buy a car to get to work. She and thousands like her simply depended on the bus system too greatly for a critical mass of them to give it up even for a day.

And yet the one-day boycott called for December 5 did work, to an almost magical degree. Nearly every single African American in Montgomery refused to ride the bus that morning, which meant that nearly everyone had to walk, in some cases for miles, or hastily arrange a carpool to get to work. "Here you have a situation historically unthought of and unpredicted," Baker later said, "where thousands of individuals, just black ordinary people, subjected themselves to inconveniences that were certainly beyond the

thinking of most folk. . . . [O]ld women and maids who ran the risk of losing their little income would walk [to work], if they got there, rather than
ride the buses." That was remarkable enough in the context of black Montgomerians' resistance to Jim Crow, but Baker peered deep into the boycott
and saw something even more significant. "Now this meant that you had a
momentum that had not been seen even in the work of the N.A.A.C.P. And
it was something that suggested a higher potential for wide-spread action
through the South," she said. King attributed the boycott's success to "the
zeitgeist," but Baker, Parks, Robinson, and the other women of Montgomery
knew better. It "was not a prairie fire, or a rising tide, or a gear that tumbled
in the cosmos," according to historian Danielle McGuire. It was "a women's
movement for dignity . . . the end of a drive chain that ran back into decades
of black women's activism" in Montgomery.   community bond

The number of regular people from every economic and social class, from
grade school dropouts to PhDs, who rallied around the issue of racial segregation on the Montgomery buses was unprecedented. First they gathered at
city hall, where Parks had to make her way through a crowd estimated at
five hundred people to appear before a municipal judge to answer the charge
of having violated Montgomery's segregation laws. The trial's outcome was
foregone. Attorney Fred Gray had already decided not to mount a defense
so that he could argue against the constitutionality of segregation on appeal.
Five minutes after gaveling the court to session, Judge John B. Scott found
Parks guilty and fined her $10 plus $4 in court fees. The crowd outside the
building was incensed by the verdict, but instead of stoking the rage, Nixon
and Abernathy encouraged the people to go home and cool off, then attend
a previously planned mass meeting to be held that evening at Holt Street
Baptist Church.

Nixon, Abernathy, and Rev. Edgar N. French then met over lunch to
plan out an agenda for the mass meeting and for the boycott more broadly.
They adopted what in retrospect looks like a ridiculously moderate set of demands, asking only that the bus company instruct all drivers to treat African
Americans with respect, hire African American drivers for routes on which
black riders were the majority, and institute a separate-but-truly-equal system
of seating on the buses. They approved the name Montgomery Improvement
Association (MIA) for the new group that would be necessary to manage the
boycott they hoped the community would agree to continue. At a second
meeting that afternoon Nixon attempted to sell the plan to a larger group
of black pastors, businessmen, and community leaders. When some of the
clergymen raised legitimate concerns about the retaliation they could expect
to face if they supported the boycott, Nixon lost his cool and accused them of

being "scared little boys." He thundered, "If we're going to be men, now's the time to be men." The gendered language he chose was interesting, because he had failed to invite the women who were responsible for the boycott in the first place. "The men took it over," Robinson said.

One of the pastors—King—spoke up on behalf of the others. "Brother Nixon, I'm not a coward. I don't want anybody to call me a coward," he said. Up to that moment nearly everyone had assumed that Nixon, or perhaps Abernathy, the pastor of the church Nixon attended, would assume leadership of the MIA. But Nixon and Abernathy had worked in Montgomery long enough to make enemies, and a sizable faction of those present at the meeting wanted someone else to serve as their spokesman. They jumped at the chance and nominated King, who was then elected by acclamation.

At first glance, King was a curious choice to act as the MIA's spokesman. Parks had met him for the first time that summer, soon after he arrived in Montgomery, when he delivered an address on the importance of the *Brown* decision at an NAACP branch meeting. "He looked like he might have been a student in college instead of a minister at a very prestigious church," Parks later said. Only twenty-five years old at the time, King had arrived in Montgomery with impressive credentials. The son and grandson of Baptist preachers who tended to well-to-do flocks on Atlanta's Auburn Avenue, King had graduated from Atlanta's Morehouse College and Crozer Theological Seminary in Philadelphia. He had also completed his coursework for a PhD in theology at Boston University and would receive his degree the following year.

When the other members of the MIA tapped him to serve as spokesman for the group, King had never so much as marched in a civil rights protest. But he had given a great deal of thought to how African Americans might use their churches as a force for social change, he had read at least superficially about Mohandas Gandhi's nonviolent campaigns against British imperialism, and he had established a reputation as a gifted public speaker. Perhaps he really was a better choice for the spokesman's role than he initially appeared.

King erased any doubts that night at the Holt Street Baptist Church mass meeting, when he delivered one of the greatest speeches in the entire history of American protest rhetoric. A thousand people filled the pews and aisles inside the church, and thousands more listened in via a hastily constructed public address system in the church basement and outside on the sidewalk. "We are here this evening for serious business," he assured the crowd. "We are here in a general sense because first and foremost, we are American citizens, and we are determined to acquire our citizenship to the fullness of its meaning. We are here also because of our deep-seated belief that democracy

Ella Baker, circa 1942. (Visual Materials from the National Association for the Advancement of Colored People Records, Library of Congress Prints and Photographs Division LC-USZ62-110575).

NOW!
MORE THAN EVER
YOUR FREEDOM DEPENDS ON YOU

"We must guard against divisions among ourselves
. . . . . We must be particularly vigilant against
racial discrimination in any of its ugly forms"

—*President Roosevelt in his address to the Congress
on the State of the Nation, January 6, 1942.*

Hear Miss Ella J. Baker
National Representative of the N. A. A. C. P.
Sunday, March 1st - 4 P. M.
McCABE M. E. CHURCH

CITY-WIDE MEMBERSHIP CAMPAIGN
February 22nd - March 6th
Campaign Headquarters:
Bethel Baptist Church, 10th St. and 3rd Ave. South

JOIN NOW!
THIS IS YOUR FIGHT, TOO!
ST. PETERSBURG BRANCH, N. A. A. C. P.

Ella Baker hosts the first NAACP "Give Light and the People Will Find a Way" regional leadership training conference in New York City, 1944. Baker is standing, far right, along with, l to r: Attorney Theodore Spaulding of Philadelphia; Alfred Baker Lewis of Greenwich, Connecticut; Walter White; Judge Charles E. Toney of New York; and Arthur B. Spingarn, president of the NAACP board of directors. (Visual materials from the National Association for the Advancement of Colored People Records Library of Congress Prints and Photographs Division LC-DIG-ds-01443.)

Baker attends the May 1962 Student Leadership Conference in Chapel Hill, N.C. (front row, far left). Other attendees include Carl Braden (second row, hands clasped around knees), Anne Braden (second row, in black dress), and Tom Hayden (right of window in dark jacket). Carl and Anne Braden Collection, Wisconsin Historical Society.

Baker addresses the MFDP State Convention, Jackson, Mississippi, 1964. (Take Stock)

Baker addresses a crowd in Atlantic City on behalf of the MFDP. (Take Stock)

Mississippi Freedom Democratic Party delegates and supporters singing at a rally on the Atlantic City Boardwalk outside of the Democratic National Convention, 1964. Fannie Lou Hamer holds the microphone, Baker is at far right, and SNCC's Eleanor Holmes Norton stands between them. (Take Stock)

Ella Baker speaking at an unidentified political gathering, circa 1970. (Photographs and Prints Division, Schomburg Center for Research in Black Culture, The New York Public Library, Astor, Lenox, and Tilden Foundations.)

transformed from thin paper to thick action is the greatest form of government on earth." Speaking in the tones and vocabularies of both the black church and the American civic tradition, King laid out the MIA's goals and inspired his listeners to continue the bus boycott, together. "This speech had evoked more response than any speech or sermon I ever delivered," King later wrote. "My heart was full. . . . The unity of purpose and *esprit de corps* of these people had been indescribably moving." The members of the MIA voted to continue the boycott. They were high on the boycott's one-day success, and few among them would have imagined that their protest would have to last 381 days, but it did.

This was a game-changer. Almost immediately Baker, Levison, and Rustin pivoted to transform In Friendship into a support group for the MIA. Night after night, the three of them "talked into the wee hours of the morning," Baker said, "in terms of, how do you develop a course that can enlarge upon the gains or the impact of the Montgomery bus boycott?" Levison and Rustin thrilled at the possibilities they saw in the well-spoken, charismatic spokesman of the movement, whom they hoped they might be able to mold into an American Gandhi. In contrast, Baker swooned at the numbers: five hundred African Americans at Mrs. Parks's trial, thousands at the mass meeting, nearly 100 percent compliance with the boycott. This was a mass movement! Black Montgomerians had identified a problem and developed their own indigenous, democratic institution to combat it. And it looked as if they had a strong chance of success.

In Friendship's first large fund-raising rally, a Madison Square Garden extravaganza, resulted in a direct $2,000 contribution to the MIA. The group later raised another $4,000 to send Rev. King to Africa and India so that he could attend the ceremonies surrounding Ghana's independence from the British empire and to study Gandhi's philosophy and methods in the hope that he might be able to apply them in Alabama.

As the bus boycott unfolded, the trio looked for ways not only to support the MIA but also to extend its methods to other southern communities. Baker said, "We began to talk about the need for developing in the South a mass force that would . . . become a counterbalance, let's call it, to the NAACP." Whatever form a new organization growing out of the Montgomery experience took, it would have to grow organically from the grass roots—a movement of, by, and for southern blacks. Ironically, Alabama officials made this easier by banning the NAACP from operating in the state in 1956. From that point on, there was no chance for the Association to co-opt the local energy of the Montgomery movement even if it had been inclined to try. Baker, Rustin, and Levison moved aggressively to fill the void.

"[H]ere you had a social phenomenon that had not taken place in the history of those of us who were around at that time," Baker said, "where hundreds of people and even thousands of people, ordinary people, had taken a position that put them in a very uncomfortable [position]—at least made life less comfortable for them—when they decided to walk rather than to ride the buses." By any definition, she said, this was "a mass action that anybody who looked at the social scene would have to appreciate and wonder. Those of us who believed that . . . only through mass action are we going to eliminate certain things, would have to think in terms of how does this get carried on." Carrying it on became her life's work.

However, Baker also saw a familiar (and distressing) pattern taking shape in the bus boycott. She had spent a lifetime in the church, where "in terms of things taking place"—actual work getting done—"[a]ll of the churches depended . . . on women, not men. Men didn't do the things that had to be done[,] and you had a large number of women who were involved in the bus boycott." That organizational model seemed to be replicating itself in the MIA. While the news media (and Rustin and Levinson, among many others) focused on the MIA's charismatic spokesman, Baker thrilled at the unanimity of black Montgomerians across economic classes. She marveled at the working-class women, who after putting in eight or more hours of domestic labor day after day energized the MIA's nighttime mass meetings and encouraged one another to carry on. "They were the people who kept the spirit going[,] [along with] the young people," Baker said. "I knew that the young people were the hope of any movement. It was just a normal thing to me." In contrast, she added, "The average Baptist minister didn't really know organization."

Nonetheless, Robinson and the organizers of the MIA kept the boycott going and kept black Montgomery almost completely unified. (The recognized "leaders" of the movement were all men, but women staffed the organization and managed its most complex aspect, the logistics of a volunteer carpool that replaced the buses.) They found the Chicago-based owners of the city bus line willing to negotiate, but local elected officials remained recalcitrant. The city fathers drew a line in the sand and refused to compromise on any aspect of Jim Crow segregation. Using an antiunion state law that forbade economic boycotts, local officials arrested eighty-nine members of the MIA. Someone bombed King's home. The Ku Klux Klan marched through Montgomery. Still, every day tens of thousands of black residents refused to ride the buses, at great personal sacrifice, and the MIA's mass meetings continued to attract thousands of enthusiastic supporters. In 1956 federal courts agreed with the protesters and decided that segregated seating systems inherently violated African Americans' constitutional rights. The city finally agreed to abide by the decisions, and on December 21, 1956, black citizens rode at the front of Montgomery buses for the first time.

There are few if any examples in American history in which communities of nearly fifty thousand people who share nothing but proximity and skin color can agree on *anything*, much less something that requires them to sacrifice so heavily, and maintain unanimity for any length of time. But that many black Montgomerians banded together in the bus boycott and maintained their unanimity for twelve months. It was a truly remarkable accomplishment. The spokesman and moral compass of the boycott, King had become at the age of twenty-seven arguably the preeminent proponent of racial justice and nonviolent protest, not just in the United States but throughout the world.

A mass movement—conceived, peopled, led, and nurtured almost entirely by native southerners—succeeded in bringing down at least a vestige of Jim Crow. King and the MIA struck gold, in part because they used nonviolence as both a tactic and a philosophy. It must be noted that Baker, along with the vast majority of African Americans and, for that matter, Americans of all races, did not share the philosophy of nonviolence. Comparing herself to Bayard Rustin many years later, Baker candidly admitted, "[Rustin] had a history of dedication to the concept of non-violence. I have no such history; I have no such commitment. Not historically or even now can I claim that, because that's not my way of functioning." She did come to appreciate its strategic usefulness, but Baker was slow to recognize how useful nonviolence was in building a movement culture in Montgomery. Rustin believed that the nonviolent movement in Montgomery gave MIA supporters "the feeling that they could be bigger and stronger and more courageous and more loving than they thought they could be." Moreover, as historian Adam Fairclough writes, "Nonviolence not only promoted unity and discipline among the blacks but also inhibited the employment of violence by the whites" of Montgomery.

Carrying on the work of the MIA, spreading the mass action gospel to other southern communities while there was still momentum to build on, became Baker's sole focus. "You needed a force in the South that was comparable to the N.A.A.C.P. in some respects," Baker said. The Association, she continued, "primarily dealt with legal action. Although it had a program of branch action it had not organized mass action that lent itself to demonstrations. So, if you think in terms of something in the South for mass action you'd start with the group that had been involved in something." That left the Montgomery movement, but even it had a critical flaw in Baker's mind:

MIA drew its strength from the masses, but black ministers had dominated it. As moving as their speeches were, she had little confidence that ministers could run an effective anti–Jim Crow organization. Baker believed that the nascent mass movement had to somehow take advantage of the black churches' networking capabilities without replicating the churches' organizational model of one charismatic leader and many members of the congregation. It was critical that movement supporters act quickly, she counseled. "After the Montgomery bus boycott success it became very obvious that there was need to move. You had the big boycott and then nothing," she said.

Baker dealt in the world of the possible, so instead of waiting for the perfect prospect to present itself she worked with the opportunities that existed. She, Rustin, and Levison encouraged King and the ministers throughout the South who identified with the MIA's brand of struggle to form a new civil rights group. The idea for a new organization was born, Baker said, out of the idea that "it would be good to have an organizational base in the South comparable, to some extent, to the NAACP. Because the NAACP was not activist in that direction. And these people who had come out of the bus boycott or its leadership ought to be involved in something worth more than just relying on the past." The Montgomery bus boycott showed that mass direct-action campaigns could work in the South. "There had been cooperative or interrelated action" in the South, Baker said, "but you still didn't have a viable base for political social action in the South out of the black community." A new organization would have to fill that void.

According to Baker (King would surely have told a different story), she herself brought up the idea of capitalizing on the boycott's momentum to "build something larger," and she took that idea to King. Why had he allowed the energy and momentum of the MIA to dissipate? "I irritated [King] with the question," Baker recalled. "His rationale was that after a big demonstration, there was a natural letdown and a need for people to sort of catch their breath. I didn't quite agree. . . . I don't think the leadership in Montgomery was prepared to capitalize [on what] . . . had come out of the Montgomery situation."

In any case, two months after the bus boycott concluded successfully with Montgomery having desegregated its buses, King and roughly sixty supporters met in Atlanta in January 1957 and decided to form what they called the Southern Christian Leadership Conference (SCLC). They included the word *Christian* in the new organization's name not only because it accurately reflected the group's membership but because, they hoped, it would deflect accusations that the group was influenced by godless Communists. To avoid open competition with the NAACP, they decided against selling individual memberships. The SCLC would organize primarily through church networks (which is not to say through congregations, from the bottom up), as a confederation of local movements and activist clusters.

Beyond that loose definition, what kind of organization the SCLC would become remained very much up in the air. Baker believed that the fix was in from the beginning. Because the founders were nearly all black ministers, the SCLC would follow a top-down church model. When he arrived at Dexter Avenue Baptist Church in 1954, King wrote, "The pastor's authority is not merely humanly conferred, but divinely sanctioned. . . . Leadership never ascends from the pew to the pulpit, but it invariably descends from the pulpit to the pew." As pastor he expected "to be respected and accepted as the central figure around which the policies and programs of the church revolve." SCLC would work the same way.

"Those of us who preferred an organization that was democratic and where the decision making was left with the people would think in one vein [that included] the organizing of active . . . chapters or units of people," Baker said. The "majority of the people who were called together [to create the SCLC] were ministers and the decision as to who was called together emanated, no doubt, from the background out of which . . . Martin came." She thought that he might lack "understanding . . . of the virtue of utilizing the mass surge that had developed there in Montgomery." Because ministers dominated the early stages of the SCLC, Baker recalled, "The nature of the organization became to a large extent a ministerial thing."

The Kings invited preachers who had already demonstrated an interest in civic engagement to the initial meetings of the SCLC, but "you have to reckon with the fact that most of the people involved had never had any experience in developing mass action," Baker insisted. "They functioned largely in the church vein; if you had a meeting and you preached to the people the people would go out and do what you said to do and come back. So it wasn't a question of opening it up. It was largely ministers and just about all ministers."

Baker's activism drew on another model of church-based activism, the work of the women's missionary societies that women like her mother had perfected early in the twentieth century. According to historian Evelyn Brooks Higginbotham, Anna Ross Baker's generation of African American churchwomen "encouraged an aggressive womanhood that felt personal responsibility to labor no less than men . . . their evangelical zeal fervently rejected a fragile, passive womanhood of the type preoccupied with fashion, novels, and self-indulgence." It manifested itself in community organizing campaigns of various stripes. Rejecting that organizational model, the SCLC settled into a more hierarchical and male-dominated church model.

Baker perceived that the ministers of the original iteration of the SCLC banded together with one another because they were comfortable in one another's presence. In the process they shut out the secular organizers—Baker, mainly—who wanted to generate mass action based on the Montgomery model: "You see, basically your ministers are not people who go in for decisions on the part of people. I don't know whether you realize it or not," she said. "And they had been looked upon as saviors." Baker didn't look upon *anyone* as a savior, and as an ultraegalitarian she approached a conversation with the belief that anyone's ideas could be challenged and perhaps improved upon. When that happened in the context of SCLC strategy sessions, "here they are faced with a suggestion that goes against the grain and with which they are not prepared to deal. So they come together" in defense of one another. They circled the wagons.

Baker's reservations about a minister-dominated organization were evident from the outset, but the SCLC offered the best hope for a southern-led mass movement, so she stayed involved. Besides, she said on more than one occasion, "I was never working for an organization. I have always tried to work for a cause. And that cause to me is bigger than any organization, bigger than any group of people, and it is the cause of humanity."

Good preachers are not necessarily good administrators. Although the SCLC's founders issued some impressive rhetoric in the earliest days of the organization, they had a tough time getting it up and running and actually doing anything. The SCLC clearly needed someone who could step in and do the tough work of setting up an office, setting an agenda, and keeping the organization on task. The SCLC especially needed someone to organize its planned Crusade for Citizenship, a one-day mass action the preachers planned to take place on February 12, 1958, Abraham Lincoln's birthday, in twenty different southern cities to demonstrate blacks' desire to vote and to insert the issue into national political conversations.

That person was Baker, who reluctantly hired on as the SCLC's first and only staff member in January 1958. Without consulting her, Rustin and Levison had first convinced King to hire her in much the same way that Walter White had promoted Baker at the NAACP. King, who seems to have considered the term *professional woman* an oxymoron, doubted a female could be effective in the role Levison and Rustin suggested. They promised King that they would raise the funds for Baker's salary in New York, so that she would cost SCLC nothing, and King agreed to the arrangement. Baker found the episode "a bit presumptuous" but swallowed her pride—again—for the good of the cause and agreed to go along. "[M]y ego isn't very pronounced," she insisted, but she also acknowledged that "not to ask me what to do but to designate me to do something without even consulting me" was disrespectful. Baker went to Atlanta intending to help SCLC set up an office and put the infrastructure in place for the Crusade, then return to New York. Yet even that seemingly well-defined, short-term task was a daunting and wide-open one; what was supposed to be a six-week-long trip turned into a multiyear southern sojourn.

The preachers of the SCLC had done just as Baker had predicted they would: They had talked a great deal about the Crusade for Citizenship, had announced it was coming, but had otherwise done nothing to actually plan a program or build the network that would be necessary to pull it off. SCLC planned a $200,000 budget for the Crusade but raised only about $50,000. "There had to be somebody to pull together the program and to make contact with these cities and the like," Baker said. But "when I came in, there was no office," so she worked out of her room in the Savoy Hotel on Auburn Avenue. "For the first couple of days . . . I had to function out of a telephone booth and . . . keep my notes in the pocketbook."

Baker found that she could not even count on the considerable resources of nearby Ebenezer Baptist Church, the home church of Rev. Martin Luther King Sr., to organize the Crusade. "I had to accommodate myself to whatever time the manager of that office felt that the mimeograph machine and other facilities could be available, usually after office hours," if at all, Baker remembered. She finally procured office space for SCLC near Ebenezer on Auburn Avenue.

The SCLC board of directors gave Baker few if any detailed instructions for the Crusade. "In fact, they spelled out nothing because there was nobody to spell out anything," she said. Having at least opened the office, Baker did what she had previously done when an organization disappointed her: She beat the bushes and built up a network of supporters through phone calls, letters, and face-to-face relationships in the field. Drawing on her contacts from the NAACP days and the local networks of SCLC members, she traveled the South, lining up speakers for February 12. This was no small order, because many of the most influential African Americans did not want to risk cooperating with an effort that could be seen as competition to the NAACP. She made hundreds of phone calls to arrange local meeting logistics, held mass meetings to drum up popular support for the Crusade, and convinced local journalists that the Crusade would be newsworthy enough to merit their attention. "I talked with New Orleans, Baton Rouge, Shreveport, Mobile, Tallahassee, Jacksonville, Nashville, Chattanooga, Knoxville, and Durham," she reported to King one day in February.

Baker dove into the work because she believed deeply in the specific cause as a means to the end of empowerment. "The voter registration [effort in general] was not just for the sake of getting people to register but to get them politicized to the extent that they would recognize that they could only fight the system if they had some political power," she later said. (Then again, she added, "It also helped to show the limitations of political power simply by the vote.") Due almost entirely to Baker's efforts, black activists in twenty cities in fourteen states held Crusade for Citizenship rallies on February 12 and generated considerable press coverage. Though the Crusade failed in its stated goal of doubling the number of registered black voters in the South and is little remembered today even by civil rights historians, it was much more successful than anyone in 1958 had a right to expect it would be. But just as Baker had feared, the Crusade was a one-time-only phenomenon in nearly all the communities it reached. She had not had enough time to develop indigenous leaders or to build sustainable networks in those cities, so her efforts sparked just enough energy to mobilize communities for a day, like the proverbial flash in the pan.

The Crusade at least gave the SCLC a focus—voter registration—and although the one-day event accomplished little in the way of mass mobilization or long-term results, it suggested a direction that the organization might head in if it wanted to achieve those larger aims. It barely made a dent in voter registration numbers, but Baker considered the event the beginning of a process, not an end in itself. The SCLC had announced that following the Crusade it would launch a ten-state voter registration drive. If the SCLC had followed through on those intentions historians today might be more impressed with the Crusade for Citizenship's accomplishments, but the organization opted not to hire the huge field staff the effort would have required. In fact, the SCLC hired no one else besides its one-woman whirlwind, and it only kept Baker on in a part-time role after February.

In order to take any kind of advantage of the little momentum the Crusade had generated, Baker would have to remain in the South a little longer. "I had anticipated being there for about six weeks," she said. "I gave myself four weeks to get the thing going and two weeks to clean it up. But they had no one." So she stayed in the South. Baker hit the road again, devoting the bulk of her time in 1958 and most of 1959 to two local movements affiliated with the SCLC that could take advantage of her expertise, the MIA and the United Christian Movement (UCM) of Shreveport, Louisiana.

Montgomery, as we have seen, was already organized. Baker helped the community document instances of discrimination against aspiring black voters through sworn affidavits, then organized them into a formal complaint for the U.S. Civil Rights Commission. The commission held the first public meeting in its short history in Montgomery, in December 1958. Baker also aided the UCM, which had previously organized a highly effective boycott of Shreveport's public trolley system, in a similar effort to document voter discrimination. That resulted in another formal complaint to the Civil Rights Commission, but the state of Louisiana and an unfriendly federal judge were able to postpone the commission's public hearings until 1960. (In the interim, the state actually removed ten thousand African American names from the voting rolls.) The publicity these campaigns and the resulting commission hearings generated were valuable, and the attention they brought to the issue of voter discrimination was necessary. But they did not match the goals SCLC had laid out for the Crusade. In any case, for Baker the campaigns were more like means to an end—and that end, again, was the activation of local black communities for long-term struggle.

As late as the spring of 1958 the SCLC still had not hired a full-time executive director. Baker believed that in some ways Bayard Rustin would have been the man (and she recognized that, due to the SCLC's dynamics, it almost had to be a man) for the job; she certainly respected Rustin's energy and his ideas about direct-action campaigns and community organizing, though she did not share his philosophical commitment to nonviolence. "But I knew Bayard's lifestyle did not fit Atlanta at that stage, because there was nowhere that he could function in his manner without exposure," she said, in another major understatement referencing Rustin's openly gay lifestyle. Besides, she added, "Bayard [wasn't] basically one to take on the nitty-gritty," the prosaic office work that had to get done behind the scenes to keep the organization moving.

Having seen the SCLC's board of directors in action, and knowing well her own set of personal strengths and drawbacks, Baker understood that she would be a bad fit in the position. "I had no ambition to be . . . executive director," she later told an interviewer. "If I had had any, I knew it was not to be. And why do I say that? Two reasons. One, I was a female . . . and non-minister. The other, I guess, [was] . . . the kind of personality differences that existed between me and the Rev. Dr. King. I was not a person to be enamored of anyone," she reiterated. "My philosophy was not one of nonviolence per se and I knew enough about organization (at least I thought I knew enough about organization) to be critical about some of the lack of procedures that obtained in SCLC." She therefore had to tiptoe around the SCLC's issues and its personalities. "Within the inner councils, whenever there was discussion, I did not try to force myself upon them, recognizing the sensitivities that existed. Now, I did not hesitate to voice my opinion and sometimes [in] the voicing of that opinion it was obvious that it was not a very comforting sort of presence that I presented," she admitted. Baker's description of the dynamics within SCLC and her appraisal of her own ambitions may have included a dose of self-serving justification after the fact, but in the main they illustrate her knowledge of self and comfort in her own skin.

Baker's accounts of her time at the SCLC could conceivably come across as so many sour grapes. But other women who rose to contemporary prominence in the organization described its culture in remarkably similar terms. Septima Clark, the remarkable South Carolina school teacher who created literacy and citizenship curricula at Highlander for black southerners who wanted to vote, and who later became the SCLC's education director, said, "Those men didn't have any faith in women, none whatsoever. They just thought that women were sex symbols and had no contributions to make." She recalled an occasion when she had asked King to do more to organize in the communities that invited him in to lead protests instead of just mobilizing them. "I sent a letter to Dr. King asking him not to lead all the marches himself, but instead to develop leaders who could lead their own marches. Dr. King read that letter before the [otherwise all-male] staff. It just tickled them; they just laughed."

Dorothy Cotton, who succeeded Clark as education director, recalled, "I did have a decision-making role, but I'm also very conscious of the male chauvinism that existed. . . . [Black preachers] are some of the most chauvinistic of all." But the women also described the sexism they faced in the most matter-of-fact terms possible. The preachers they worked with may have been sexists, but at the time so was every other segment of American society. Baker was so used to sexist behavior that she came to expect it even while she worked around it. Her real beef with the organization was its dependence on King's charismatic leadership at the expense of mass organizing, not rampant male chauvinism.

In any case, after Baker kicked off the Crusade the SCLC as an organization seemed to be stuck in neutral. It needed a program. "What was happening was nothing except what I was doing in the office," she said. King was already being pulled in so many directions that he could not consistently offer the sort of leadership the organization sorely needed from its chairman. Still the pastor of Dexter Avenue Baptist Church in Montgomery, he was in constant demand from other southern congregations. When he was not lobbying the White House and Congress for civil rights legislation, he was working with a ghostwriter on his book about the bus boycott, *Stride Toward Freedom*. Clearly he could not devote the time to SCLC that the organization needed.

The board of directors appointed an executive committee to hire an executive director. According to Baker, they "wanted a minister. I knew that. They couldn't have tolerated a woman." So she suggested Rev. John Tilley, a Baltimore pastor, for the post. Baker had met the much older Tilley at Shaw, where he studied theology while she was an undergraduate, and she was aware that he had worked closely with the Baltimore NAACP branch, one of the largest and most active in the country, and organized successful voter registration campaigns. Those credentials seemed to square nicely with the activist direction Baker hoped the SCLC was headed.

Again according to Baker, the executive committee "never got around to calling anybody, so Stanley [Levison] and I met Tilley here in New York. Tilley said he would be interested and then he went down to see them. He became the executive director [in May 1958] but he maintained his church connections in Baltimore, which meant he was in and out." Tilley apparently never mentioned to Baker at the initial meeting that he planned to keep his pastorship if he got the job with SCLC; if he had she would have demanded in no uncertain terms that he choose one or the other. But the committee offered Tilley the job without forcing him to choose. It is baffling that anyone in the higher reaches of the SCLC thought Tilley could succeed as the director of a serious, hard-charging civil rights organization headquartered in Atlanta while continuing his work as a full-time pastor in Baltimore, but the results were predictable: the SCLC wasn't hard charging at all during the year under Tilley's direction.

If they hadn't before, the SCLC's internal politics, lack of discipline, and organizational dysfunction by now made the NAACP's look like child's play to Baker. According to Adam Fairclough, the author of the first major organizational history of the SCLC, Baker "found the haphazard informality of the Southern black church exasperating," and the SCLC built its organizational structure and work culture on exactly that model. During the Tilley period, "Whatever was being done in terms of continuity had to be done by whoever was there, namely me," Baker said. Then again, until 1960 *everyone* of consequence in the SCLC, including Baker and King, worked part time. Baker split her time between Atlanta and New York, where she still kept an apartment, even though there was now less to draw her back home to Harlem. Jackie had graduated from high school and matured into an independent young adult by this point, and Baker's marriage ended quietly in divorce in 1958. She and Roberts had gone their separate ways almost since the beginning of their "arrangement," so the separation was not surprising. King resigned his position at Dexter Avenue Baptist Church in Montgomery only at the beginning of 1960, at which time he joined his father as pastor of Ebenezer Baptist Church in Atlanta and devoted more of his time to SCLC.

King made another momentous decision for SCLC in 1959. Upon his return from India, where he had met with associates of Gandhi and studied the philosophy and methods of nonviolent resistance, King learned that Tilley had made no progress whatsoever on extending the Crusade for Citizenship. King concluded that the project "has not had a dynamic program commensurate with the amount of money that it is spending," so he did something that was, according to historian Taylor Branch, "alien to his character and almost unique in his entire career": He demanded Tilley's resignation, leaving the SCLC again without an executive director. King wanted Baker to serve in the role—they hardly ever saw eye-to-eye on the most important issues facing the SCLC, but she knew the organization better than anyone else and at least she could be counted on to do *something*. But when he took the prospect to the board of directors, the ministers agreed to it only on the condition that Baker be given the title of *acting* executive director. They felt the organization needed another man, another preacher, at the helm, and they wanted to continue looking for one, but they allowed King to hire Baker in the interim role.

Baker agreed to take on the job she knew ill suited her, and she did so without illusions. The role in SCLC was "different from the role of director of such organizations as the NAACP, CORE, and so forth," she later said. "The executive director was more or less nominally under direction. The personality that had to be played up was Dr. King. [In] the other organizations . . . the executive director was the spokesman. But they couldn't tolerate having an old lady [in charge of the SCLC] . . . It was too much for the masculine and ministerial ego to have permitted that." After the fact, she claimed, "I had known . . . that there would be never be any role for me in a leadership capacity with SCLC. Why? First, I'm a woman. Also, I'm not a minister. . . . The basic attitude of men and especially ministers, as to . . . the role of women in their church setups is that of taking orders, not providing leadership."

By this point Baker had concluded that the SCLC as a whole was all but irredeemable, but she also knew from experience that there was no such thing as a perfect civil rights organization. Despite their faults, King and the SCLC still offered her the best possibility of activating southern communities. The SCLC's mission was to create a network of local movements (a la the MIA) that could then be supported (critics would have said "directed") by a central authority (which critics derided as a cult of personality around Martin Luther King Jr.) as they built regional direct-action campaigns against Jim Crow. Baker believed that the "cult of personality" criticism had weight, and she pushed back against the culture she saw developing within the organization. But she continued to put her faith in the masses, and until something better came along, SCLC offered the best opportunity to foment a mass southern movement. The men in charge of SCLC had squandered the opportunity they had been handed in Montgomery, but perhaps Baker could help them do better if they somehow caught lightning in a bottle again.

That hope did not last long. If Baker's efforts had gone unappreciated on her first time around the block with SCLC, the board members picked up where they had left off when she signed back on, first by insisting on adding "acting" to her title and second by paying Baker less than they had paid Tilley—less, in fact, than they paid her to launch the Crusade for Citizenship. One suspects that this would have been more of an issue were Baker not already so accustomed to such treatment that she was beyond caring about it. Rather than complain about the obvious inequity, she set off on the herculean tasks of creating programs for SCLC and developing a better working environment for its staff (which, as late as 1960, included only herself and two clerical workers). She arranged the SCLC newsletter and planned the organization's conventions and board meetings and wrote up reports to King and various SCLC committees. "I knew I didn't have any significant role in the minds of those who constituted the organization," she said. "I'm sure that basically the assumption is, or was, and perhaps the assumption still prevails in the minds of those who remember my being there, that I was just there to carry out the orders of Dr. King[.]" If she had any of her own ideas about how to run a civil rights organization, the board of directors expected Baker to keep them to herself and follow King's lead.

Nonetheless, Baker did not pull punches as she tried to cajole the SCLC into action. "I was difficult. I wasn't an easy pushover," she admitted. In an October 1959 memorandum she chided everyone in the organization for having failed to take advantage of the opportunities presented by the Crusade for Citizenship: "The word CRUSADE connotes for me a vigorous movement, with high purpose and involving masses of people." SCLC clearly had not created that kind of a movement, in her judgment. The organization, she said, ought to be identifying and supporting indigenous leaders, especially in the Deep South, harnessing the power of women, creating programs to fight functional illiteracy among southern blacks, making more of a push for voter registration, and developing more direct-action campaigns.

King and the board thought that the organization needed to do more to garner headlines through forceful, direct-action assaults on the segregated order. Baker agreed, though she was infinitely more interested in action for the sake of movement building than for the sake of news generation. To that end, Baker encouraged the board to hire Rev. James Lawson, a Methodist minister who had studied deeply in the Christian pacifist and Gandhian direct action traditions and who had begun training a cadre of college students to demonstrate against segregation in Nashville, Tennessee. Baker wanted Lawson to train nonviolent protest "action teams" throughout the South on behalf of SCLC.

Baker believed at her core that for the organization to become more relevant it would have to engage in more long-term community organizing and institution building. To that end she pushed SCLC to partner with the Highlander Folk School to create literacy and citizenship education courses that would ideally kill several birds with one stone. Literacy education was a goal in its own right: obviously, literate African Americans would live healthier, more secure lives. Better-educated blacks were also harder for southern officials to keep off the voting rolls, which made literacy a civil rights issue. Although King and the board agreed with the principle, they did little to translate their thoughts into action until 1961, when Highlander began to founder in the face of white resistance. Baker had resigned from SCLC by then, but before she left she finally convinced the board that northern philanthropic foundations were more likely to donate money for education and voter registration than for direct-action campaigns. SCLC hired Septima Clark to replicate the programs she had pioneered at Highlander as SCLC's education director.

Clark and a new arrival to SCLC, Rev. Andrew Young, built the new Citizenship Education Program (CEP) into SCLC's most important institution. According to Taylor Branch, Clark "specialized in teaching illiterate adults to read[,] and barely literate ones to become teachers" and leaders in their own right. "The basic purpose of the Citizenship Schools is discovering community leaders," she said. At Dorchester, a former school on the Georgia coast that had been donated by the National Council of Churches, she trained thousands of black southerners to pass literacy requirements so that they could register to vote. In the process she identified, encouraged, and trained dozens of new local civil rights leaders. Bringing Clark from Highlander to SCLC may have been Baker's greatest contribution to the organization.

As acting executive director Baker continued her travels through the Deep South, offering what assistance she could to the local movements she considered most promising. She spent an inordinate amount of time in Shreveport, where she wanted to see the work she had helped begin with the Crusade for Citizenship through to completion, and in Birmingham, where she formed an especially close bond with Rev. Fred Shuttlesworth and his wife, Ruby. Rev. Shuttlesworth led the Alabama Christian Movement for Human Rights (ACMHR) and was a founding member of SCLC, which he pushed from the inside to attack Jim Crow more aggressively. The civil rights movement's leadership in Alabama and across the South was "much less dynamic and imaginative than it ought to be," he complained to King in 1959. "When the flowery speeches have been made, we still have the hard job of getting down and helping people. . . . We [the SCLC] must move now, or else [be] hard put in the not too distant future, to justify our existence." This was music to Baker's ears, and it helps to explain why she devoted so much of her time to helping the Shuttlesworths organize Birmingham.

Tellingly, the Shuttlesworths invited Baker, and not another preacher, to give the keynote speech to the ACMHR's third anniversary celebration in June 1959. Baker biographer Barbara Ransby considered the address, which Baker titled "Nothing Too Dear to Pay for Freedom," "one of the most militant speeches of her career." A comprehensive statement of Baker's political beliefs, it did not lack for rhetorical firepower, and it illustrated her willingness to buck the SCLC's official positions, beginning with the organization's commitment to philosophical nonviolence. "What is the basic right of the individual to defend himself?" she asked—rhetorically, perhaps, but she was after all in the city that would come to be known as "Bombingham," where hard-core white segregationists used unprecedented amounts of violence against black activists. Self-defense was very much on the minds of Baker's listeners, that night and every night. "Guideposts to first-class citizenship call for the utilization of all resources at the group's command," Baker said, which, Ransby points out, sounds a lot like Malcolm X's "by any means necessary."

But Baker made it clear that although she might disagree with some of SCLC's philosophical underpinnings, she stood foursquare with the preachers on the subject of forceful assertion of their rights. The real enemy in the African American community, she warned, was "the accommodating type of Negro leader who says what he thinks local southern officials want to hear." African Americans, she said, faced an array of problems and needed to fight on several fronts. "The leader, self-styled or otherwise designated, who is quick to limit the Negro's drive for civil rights to some one phase, such as voter registration, and who pointedly avoids mention of desegregation of schools, buses, housing, public facilities, etc., is as dangerous as those white persons who lump together the NAACP and the White Citizens Councils as 'two extremes.' Both are misrepresenting the facts and therefore befuddling the issues," she boomed. Baker concluded the speech with a reminder that, despite how far the cause had come in the past decade, much remained to be done. Legal victories such as *Brown* would be implemented at full force "only if people make use of every right won, and continue a determined battle against segregation wherever and whenever it exists."

She continued that work at SCLC. As Baker worked to professionalize SCLC's operations, she also asked for institutional soul searching. Her SCLC memoranda include such observations as "Have we been so busy doing the things that *had* to be done that we failed to do what *should* be done?" and "Have we really come to grips with what it takes to do the job for which SCLC was organized; and are we willing to pay the price?" Was SCLC even necessary, Baker asked, if it wasn't engaged in long-term community organizing? The organization struggled to find its footing in the late 1950s. By 1959 Baker had begun to doubt that the group, at least under its present leadership, would ever develop a program for change, but she continued to support SCLC's efforts to gain national prominence. In January 1960, with Carl Braden of the Southern Conference Educational Fund (SCEF), she organized a "Voluntary Civil Rights Commission" to hold public hearings in Washington. SCLC, SCEF, and others had tried in vain to get the U.S. Civil Rights Commission to investigate their claims that African Americans faced systematic discrimination and harassment when they tried to register to vote. The Voluntary Commission was meant to shame the real commission into action.

The following month Fred Shuttlesworth happened to be preaching at a revival in High Point, North Carolina, when students from North Carolina A&T College in the nearby city of Greensboro sat down at the seats of a Woolworth's lunch counter designated for whites only and refused to leave until they were served. Shuttlesworth drove over to Greensboro to see the so-called sit-ins himself, then phoned Baker excitedly to provide an eyewitness report. "You must tell Martin that we must get with this," he said. Shuttlesworth predicted that the sit-ins would "shake up the world"—and he was right. College students in cities throughout the South used the Greensboro tactic, and a new movement spread like wildfire. Baker thought what the students were doing was "more productive than anything that had happened in [her] life." That spring she worked on a plan to bring the students together at a regional conference to discuss their common concerns and to explore new directions for their movement.

By then Baker was a lame duck on the way out of SCLC. She had helped the executive board find and convince Rev. Wyatt Tee Walker of Petersburg, Virginia, to take over as executive director. He accepted the position in early 1960 and planned to begin work in August. Never one to place loyalty to an organization over principle, Baker now had even less inclination to corral the students on behalf of SCLC.

Baker's tenure at the SCLC was unsatisfying on multiple levels—"more frustrating than fruitful," in Ransby's words—but it also brought her back into the game. Baker spent her tenure at SCLC demanding that the organization do more to create an active program, and in 1960 the students proved she had been right to do so. The sit-ins expressed the students' frustration with what they perceived as the NAACP's and SCLC's cautiousness as much as they expressed the students' unwillingness to cooperate with Jim Crow. To the organization's credit, SCLC did begin to heed Baker's advice by developing voter registration campaigns and engaging in increasingly militant direct-action efforts, if only after she left. Baker's insistence that SCLC needed to do more institution building led directly to the creation of its most important long-term project, the CEP.

She did not leave SCLC embittered. A cynic might say that Baker had such low expectations for SCLC all along that the organization could not have disappointed her. There is a grain of truth in the suggestion, but no more. SCLC might not have lived up to the potential she saw in it while Baker was associated with it, but the organization did mature and grow during the period. Moreover, Fred and Ruby Shuttlesworth, Ralph David Abernathy, Wyatt Tee Walker, and many others Baker had met through SCLC remained lifelong friends. When Baker died in 1986, Abernathy offered the opening prayer and Walker read scripture at her funeral service in Harlem.

Baker's relationship with King was complex, but students of the movement should not read more into Baker's statement, "I did not just subscribe to a theory just because it came out of the mouth of the leader," than is necessary. Baker respected King and liked him personally. With countless others, she thrilled at his ability to move crowds and to communicate the goals of the civil rights movement, especially to Americans outside of the South who might not otherwise have stopped to think about why the movement was even necessary. She might not have thought that the ability to deliver a moving speech was the most important trait a civil rights activist could develop, but Baker respected King's intellect greatly and believed that the work he did was critical. She just didn't think he should be worshipped for it, and told him so.

Baker told a story that illustrated their differing approaches to movement building, in more ways than one. In 1958 the MIA put on an Institute on Nonviolence for its third anniversary celebration. It provided a good opportunity to look back to the bus boycott for lessons the SCLC could use moving forward, but the institute's organizers took a different tack, dedicating the largest block of time to "A Testimonial to Dr. King's Leadership." The program featured six formal speeches from fellow preachers who did nothing but praise King. There was no mention of Jo Ann Robinson, E. D. Nixon, or Rosa Parks, much less the thousands of foot soldiers who made the MIA viable in the first place, and local people noticed. Nixon told a friend, "When people give all recognition to one because of his academic training and forge[t] other[s] who do not have that kind of training but are making a worthwhile contribution," it stung, and it made people like him less likely to devote their time and talents to the SCLC or any other civil rights organization in the future.

Baker considered the conference program emblematic not only of the budding movement's misguided hero worship but also of what she believed was a deeper problem: the stunning ability of African American ministers, and the institution of the black church as a whole, to waste breath and resources on insignificant, surface-deep issues when there was real, fundamental work to be done. Why not devote that time in the program to voter registration training? Baker asked King point-blank why he would permit his friends to organize an entire conference around his personality. "Well, I don't want to. The people want to do this," King answered guiltily in Baker's telling of the story. He did not want to disappoint them, so he allowed it to go on.

That wasn't good enough for Baker, obviously, but she blamed the people who all but worshipped King as much as she blamed the minister who, she believed, proved all too willing to accept and play the role of savior whether or not he sought it. The dynamic was unhealthy and old-fashioned, she thought. One observer of a Montgomery mass meeting reported that women in the pews had responded to King by gushing, "He's next to Jesus himself!" and "He's my darling!" Baker wanted the SCLC to teach those women how to become leaders for their own communities, but instead the organization encouraged them to swoon over King. Baker had enough respect for King that she offered this criticism to his face. And if Baker believed that King's ego too often got in the way of organizing a real program for change, then she recognized him as an imperfect, three-dimensional human being with feet of clay in a way that his worshippers did not.

Both King and Baker had been raised in the church, and much of the conflict between them developed from what they had done after having had that formative experience. Baker developed her own political philosophy in working-class New York and sharpened it through thousands of hours' worth of respectful argument with people across the political spectrum. She relished a good discussion on the issues of the day, if not an argument—in part because it helped her hone her own beliefs and practices, but also because she approached each conversation with genuine interest in her interlocutor and the understanding that she might be able to learn something from him or her. In contrast, King had arrived in Montgomery with stellar academic credentials and the expectation that he would do the talking and his congregation would do the listening.

Baker was still a Christian and a churchgoer (even though she had relocated to Atlanta, she remained a member of Friendship Baptist Church in Harlem), but by now she had developed an intense anticlerical streak. She believed that King had risen so far and so fast in Montgomery that his inner circle—in Baker's words, "a complete embankment of ministers who feel they've been called by God for leadership . . . and who had not had the discipline of thinking and real dialogue, especially dialogue that differed with them"—insulated him from criticism. "I was dealing with ministers whose only sense of relationship to women in organization was that of the church," she said. "And the role of women in the southern church—and maybe all of the churches but certainly the southern churches—was that of doing the things that the minister said he wanted to have done. It was not one in which they were credited with having creativity and initiative and capacity to carry out things—to create programs and to carry them out. Certainly that was not my concept of functioning."

Baker also admitted frankly that her personality played a role in the conflict. "I was not the kind of person that made special effort to be ingratiating. I didn't try to insult but I did not hesitate to be positive about the things with which I agreed or disagreed," she said. "I might be quiet but if there was discussion and I was supposed to be able to participate, I participated at the level of my thinking." American feminists now claim Baker as a patron saint of the modern women's movement because she refused to conform to society's expectations of how she should behave. "I wasn't a fashionplate," she said. "I make no bones about not being a fashionplate."

In any case, their two opposing "concepts of functioning" made it all but impossible for Baker and King to work effectively together. "I think I could make a generalization that Martin suffered from self-protectiveness that frequently goes with one who has been accorded high place in the public image," Baker suggested. "I don't care how much reading you do, if you haven't had the interchange of dialogue and confrontation with others you can be frightened by someone who comes [in] and is in a position to confront you."

There is, of course, another side to this story. King is not often described, even by other critics, as having been easily frightened, and his closest confidantes portray a man who constantly self-criticized, sought others' opinions on how he could work more efficiently and effectively, and agonized over the effects of his actions. Levison, for instance, described King as "an intensely guilt-ridden man. . . . If he had been less humble, he could have lived with this great acclaim, but as it was, he always thought of ways in which he could somehow live up to it." Rustin remembered King as someone who was "always struggling to make sure that he was trying to do the right thing in the right way." King's unquestioned skills as a communicator would also seem to indicate that he was more skilled at "dialogue and confrontation" than Baker gave him credit for. In any case, King chafed at Baker's criticism, and how could he not have? But the record proves that he respected her as well. Why else would he have encouraged the executive committee to hire Baker as executive director in 1958? In any case, as the chairman of an organization he had a right to expect the executive director and staff of that organization to execute his decisions, and Baker proved unwilling to do that, at least without debate.

The Montgomery bus boycott had given Baker hope that a new day was dawning in the South. The mass movement could conceivably have spread immediately throughout the region and led to massive change, but SCLC failed to deliver on that promise for a simple reason: Social movements need constant feeding and care to succeed, and the ministers of the SCLC either did not know how to organize or did not have the patience necessary to parent a grassroots movement. As historian Tomiko Brown-Nagin has written about organizing in another context, "Movements require structure and organization, unifying themes, concrete goals, effective symbols, tools for engagement with the public, and methods to influence policymakers." SCLC had not mastered all of these variables of successful movement building yet, but as an organization it was beginning to improve by 1960, and it would make even greater strides in the years to come.

The ministers would have to make those strides without Baker. Given a choice, she always put her faith in young people—and now she had a choice to make. "I knew that the young people were the hope of any movement. It was just a normal thing to me," she said. She had already decided to leave SCLC, which had only recently seemed like the best alternative to the NAACP, a possible incubator for the mass southern movement she had dreamed of nurturing. In 1960 she found young people, college students, with whom she was willing to place those dreams. The students would not disappoint her.

~

CHAPTER FIVE

Bigger Than a Hamburger

On February 1, 1960, Ezell Blair Jr., Franklin McCain, Joseph McNeil, and David Richmond, freshmen at the historically black Agricultural and Technical College of North Carolina (now North Carolina A&T State University), bought school supplies at a Woolworth's five-and-dime store in downtown Greensboro, North Carolina, then sat down at the store's lunch counter and ordered coffee. Because they sat in a section of the lunch counter designated for whites only, the waitress on duty refused them service and the store manager asked them to exit the store, but the four young men refused to leave until they were served. They kept their seats until the store closed that night, and they came back the next day with more than twenty friends. The day after that more than eighty students joined them, along with aggressive white onlookers and policemen. The four initially sat down on behalf of no organization, but they had gotten interested in civil rights activism as teenagers, when they joined the Greensboro NAACP branch's youth group. Randolph Blackwell, a stalwart member of the branch, had started the youth group in 1943 at the suggestion of NAACP field secretary Ella Baker.

Their protest against racial segregation in public accommodations was simple and dramatic, and it caught the nation's attention. Speaking in nearby Durham just a few days later, Martin Luther King Jr. quoted the French novelist Victor Hugo: "There is nothing in all the world more powerful than an idea whose time has come." "You students of North Carolina," King said, "have captured this dynamic idea in a marvelous manner." No one but the students had planned the sit-ins, and no one else knew to expect them. They therefore directly challenged not only Jim Crow but also existing civil rights institutions such as the NAACP and SCLC that were not, they thought, opposing the system with enough urgency. Almost by themselves, the students shook anyone who was willing to think about the sit-ins' full implications out of their complacency. Did Americans believe that they lived in a democratic meritocracy? "The sit-in movement and the subsequent developments which grew out of it began to punch holes, very deep holes[,] into that concept," Baker said. "More people began to see that what passed as the perfect image of the American democracy was not that perfect, especially for black people. It also began to raise the question of just where did the woman fit into the movement"—and into society.

Within days more than three hundred students were staging sit-ins in Greensboro, where the protests spread to other downtown businesses, and hundreds of others were replicating the tactic in other southern cities. Within weeks thousands of students were protesting in dozens of cities and towns, without any sort of organization more official than the grapevine and local activist cells. Soon students north of the Mason-Dixon line were picketing Woolworth's and other national chain stores whose franchises in the South segregated customers. An estimated fifty thousand young people participated in sit-ins between February and April.

The movement spread from city to city "like a fever," according to one protester. "Everyone wanted to go. We were so happy." Typically, students at one college heard about sit-ins from friends or family members on another campus where they had taken place and decided that if they could do it there, why, we could sit-in here, too. After a conversation or two with friends on their own campus, they would choose a business that practiced segregated service and sit-in. It was that simple. Julian Bond, who was then a student at Morehouse College, described how the sit-ins came to Atlanta:

> In February of 1960 I was just an ordinary college student. I was sitting in the drug store near the Morehouse campus one afternoon when a fellow I knew only slightly came up to me. His name is Lonnie King. He showed me a copy of the *Atlanta Daily World*—must have been about February 3, 1960—that reported on the sit-in demonstrations in Greensboro which had just begun on the first of February of that year. He asked me if I'd seen it, and I said I had. He asked me what I thought of it, and I said I thought it was a good thing to have begun. Then he asked me if something like that ought not to be done in Atlanta. I replied that it would probably be done in time. He said, "Why don't we make it happen?"

Lonnie King and Bond immediately began asking their fellow students to join them in planning demonstrations. Within weeks, their group had coordinated sit-ins at stores in the Atlanta downtown business district; formed an indigenous and autonomous civil rights organization, the Atlanta Committee on Appeal for Human Rights; and issued a set of demands.

Local officials throughout the South struggled to respond to the sit-ins; they could not contain the wildfire the Greensboro students sparked, and they worried that the backlash would hurt business, if not stoke an all-out race war. A bomb threat closed down the Greensboro Woolworth's, and the students agreed to suspend the protests during a two-week cooling off period. Much worse violence met the students in other cities over the coming months and years. In Alabama sit-in leaders had their phones tapped, and participants had to confront police officers armed with rifles, shotguns, and tear gas. In Chattanooga, Tennessee, whites threw plates at the protesters and actually used a bullwhip on a black student, touching off two days of rioting. In Nashville, counterdemonstrators stubbed out their cigarettes in the protesters' backs. Segregationists in Jackson, Mississippi, smeared ketchup and mustard into the hair and clothes of protesters, threatened them with knives and nooses, and then brutally beat them for several minutes while the store manager looked on and declined to call the police. In Houston, Texas, angry whites ripped a black student off his stool, kidnapped him, carved KKK in his chest, and left him hanging from a tree by his knees.

There was no grand plan; the students made it up as they went along. The growing movement attracted young people who knew they hated to be Jim Crowed but hadn't previously known what they could do about it. Here was a tactic that would allow them to express their displeasure, grind the system to a halt, and bring publicity to their cause. The students clearly were acting on an idea whose time had come, and Victor Hugo had it right: There was nothing more powerful. Many of the students were amazed to realize the power they suddenly possessed—a power no greater or less than their faith in the American dream, their principles, their willingness to sacrifice their bodies on behalf of those beliefs if necessary, and their swelling numbers. For many the sit-in was a tactic. For a few others, students who had already studied Gandhian direct action intensely, it was an expression of a new way of living. These young men and women would devote their lives to antiracist, nonviolent direct action. Just as Fred Shuttlesworth had predicted they would, these students shook up the world.

As the Montgomery bus boycott had before it, the sit-in movement offered new hope to activists such as Baker who wanted to initiate a mass movement.

Baker leaped at the chance; the prospect of a youth-centered mass movement excited her even more than the bus boycott had. Believing that the students needed to meet one another, to organize and discuss their collective next step, she carved out $800 from SCLC's tight budget for what she called a South-wide Youth Leadership Conference. She arranged space for the students to meet at Shaw University and called them together over the Easter weekend in April 1960.

King and the executive committee of the SCLC fully supported the move—mainly because they agreed with Baker that the students deserved their support and encouragement, but partly because they hoped that the students would choose to organize themselves into a youth wing of the SCLC. (CORE and NAACP apparently had similar wishes, though less likelihood of bringing them to any sort of fruition. Baker had other ideas.) King and Baker together issued the invitation, which clearly reflected Baker's thinking: "The courageous, dedicated, and thoughtful leadership manifested by hundreds of Negro students on college campuses, in large cities and small towns, and the overwhelming support by thousands of others, present new challenges for the future. This great potential for social change now calls for evaluation in terms of where do we go from here."

Baker expected roughly one hundred students, perhaps 150, to attend. Instead, closer to three hundred activists and observers showed up at Shaw. The students came from more than fifty-six colleges and high schools in twelve states and the District of Columbia; several others from northern and border states, and at least a dozen white southern students, attended. Observers represented organizations as diverse as SCLC, CORE, the Fellowship of Reconciliation, Students for a Democratic Society, the National Student Christian Foundation, and the National Student Association in Raleigh. If SCLC seriously expected to rope in the students, Baker and another minister affiliated with SCLC, James Lawson of Nashville, ruined the plan. Baker fought tooth-and-nail to allow the students the space to make their own decisions on their own terms, and even to make their own mistakes so that they might learn from them. Lawson, an "extreme communalist" who had been leading workshops on nonviolent resistance for several months before the Nashville students first sat-in, was, if anything, more adamant than Baker that the students should organize independent of existing organizations and without internal status distinctions.

Baker did not act disingenuously here. Yes, she used SCLC funds to support the conference, but she also warned King and Abernathy beforehand that she believed the conference should be "youth centered." Any adults who attended, King included, should, she told them, "serve in an advisory capacity, and should mutually agree to 'speak only when asked to do so.'" King, Abernathy, and the SCLC executive committee could certainly disagree with this approach, but they had to have known what they were getting from Baker by this point. If they honestly expected her to prioritize the organization's interests ahead of those of the long-term movement as she understood them, they had not been paying much attention to her over the years.

It is also possible that reports of SCLC's intentions to hijack the student movement have been overblown, by Baker most of all. She claimed that behind closed doors King, Abernathy, and Walker were part of an effort to "capture" the sit-in movement, but King gave no public indication that he wanted SCLC to colonize the students. In a press statement released at the beginning of the conference, he emphasized "the need for some type of continuing organization," because "those who oppose justice are well organized. To win out the student movement must be [just as well] organized. . . . The youth must take the freedom struggle into every community in the South without exception." He situated their movement in world-historical terms. "This is an era of offensive on the part of oppressed people," he said. "All peoples deprived of dignity and freedom are on the march on every continent throughout the world. The student sit-in movement represents just such an offensive in the history of the Negro peoples' struggle for freedom."

While the students gathered at Shaw, King addressed a mass meeting at Raleigh Memorial Auditorium, where he described the student movement as "a revolt against those Negroes in the middle class who have indulged themselves in big cars and ranch-style homes rather than in joining a movement for freedom." Northern reporters interpreted the remark as a slap at the NAACP, but King might as well have been criticizing leaders in his own organization. In any case, these are not the words of a man trying to capture a movement. As Barbara Ransby notes, Baker was by this point prepared to believe the worst about the ministers of SCLC. She also knew that if the students chose to affiliate with SCLC, which she would serve for only a few more weeks after the Raleigh meeting, she would be shut out of what might be the last, best hope for mass civil rights organizing.

So Baker did her best to arrange the leadership conference in a way most likely to allow the students to work independently of SCLC, but not necessarily independently of *her*. This was a balancing act, and Baker indulged in at least a small measure of self-interest as she put together the program and steered the students through the meeting. "Baker saw some forms of intervention and influence as empowering and supportive of the students, and others as meddling and self-serving," Ransby writes. Baker may have swallowed her pride on multiple occasions on behalf of the movement, but she was not a saint. Perhaps she was as likely to indulge in double standards as any other mortal. Then again, she could also be forgiven for her suspicions. After two full decades of working against the grain in the movement's major organizations, her distrust of the NAACP, SCLC, and others was well earned.

Baker drew on that experience in planning the conference. She had seen movements come and go, opportunities wasted, more attempts to find shortcuts to avoid long-term organizing than she could count. So she organized the conference around a program (titled "Where Do We Go from Here?") designed to help the students avoid the missteps that had taken the other civil rights organizations off course. What she most admired about the students—and what truly gave her hope for their movement—was the decentralization of their efforts, their failure so far to fall under the spell of a charismatic leader.

Baker gave over the podium to James Lawson for the first night's keynote. Lawson had studied Gandhian nonviolence as deeply as anyone else in America and practiced it more than most. He had been imprisoned as a conscientious objector to the Korean War, and he had advised King since the Montgomery bus boycott. In the late 1950s, while studying at Vanderbilt University Divinity School, he had set out to "make Nashville a laboratory for demonstrating nonviolence." Between 1958 and 1960 he led hundreds of workshops on behalf of the Fellowship of Reconciliation that trained a cadre of students from Vanderbilt, Fisk University, Meharry Medical School, and the American Baptist Theological Seminary in nonviolent direct action. Lawson had almost single-handedly shaped Nashville into the center of student activism before the sit-in movement even began.

The students who did not know Lawson before he rose to speak soon learned what made him so compelling to his colleagues in Nashville. He elevated the sit-ins to a higher plane of being. "Love is the central motif of nonviolence," he told the students. "Love is the force by which God binds man to Himself and man to man. Such love goes to the extreme; it remains loving and forgiving even in the midst of hostility. It matches the capacity of evil to inflict suffering with an even more enduring capacity to absorb evil, all the while persisting in love." The students manifested that love by sitting in, he told them, by refusing to respond violently to the violence used against them, and by returning to the lunch counters day after day.

But Lawson also injected pragmatic politics and interorganizational conflict into his speech. He called the sit-ins "a judgment upon middle-class conventional, halfway efforts to deal with radical social evil." He denounced the NAACP as "too conservative," mocked its strategy of seeking justice through court cases, and damned the organization for ignoring "our greatest resource: a people no longer the victims of racial evil, who can act in a disciplined manner to implement the Constitution." This was music to the students' ears, and to Baker's, but it drove a wedge between the students and the most important civil rights organization of their time. In fact, although she might have agreed with him completely, Baker had to clean up after Lawson. "There is no fight" between the students and the NAACP, she told reporters in Raleigh, just a "difference in emphasis." Not that her efforts did much good; Lawson's speech helped set up a less-than-constructive working relationship between the two groups that would worsen over the decade.

At thirty-three years old, Martin Luther King was little older than the students, but he was already a celebrity to them. He used his address to praise the students' dramatic turn away from gradualist tactics and to define their movement in world-historical terms. He urged the students to study and, if possible, devote their lives to nonviolence, to organize volunteers who were willing to go to jail for a cause they believed in, and to take their protest into every corner of the South in order to force the federal government to act on their behalf. As historian Clayborne Carson points out, those remarks "outlined much of the future strategy of the student movement." It was a thrill for most of the students simply to be in King's presence and to hear his soaring rhetoric in person. But King was somehow larger than life; they could not connect with him in the same way they connected with Lawson, or in the same way they were beginning to connect with Baker.

As the conference organizer responsible for the nitty-gritty of meal arrangements, space considerations, and speakers' time allotments, Baker had the power to mold the conference in unseen ways. She insisted that not only did the students need independence and space from adults to form their own organization if they so chose—and she strongly suggested that they should—but also that the southern students needed independence from their more classically educated northern counterparts. As a southerner transplanted in New York, Baker knew well that the northern students had more experience in leadership roles and in debate societies. She worried that they might, however unintentionally, cow the less-worldly southern students into subservient roles much as middle- and upper-class northerners had come to wield outsized influence in the NAACP. "Many schools and communities, especially in the South, have not provided adequate experience for young Negroes to assume initiative and think and act independently," she said. The northerners were "more experienced than the southerners, and their ability to articulate themselves would have been intimidating to the southerners," she thought. This "accentuated the need for guarding the student movement," the *southern* student movement especially, so that's what Baker did.

Baker also kept the press out of the students' strategy sessions so that they could freely speak their minds without resorting to grand rhetoric and, if necessary, make and learn from their own mistakes without too many repercussions from the outside world. "The chief emphasis I tried to make was their right to make their own decision," she said. "I have always felt that if there is any time in our existence that you have a right to make mistakes it should be when you're young, [be]cause you have some time to live down some of the mistakes, or to offset them."

Baker apparently did not save her own keynote address, but she published its major points in *The Southern Patriot*, the SCEF newsletter, the following month. SCEF was perhaps the premier racially integrated organization devoted to antiracist action in the South; critics on the right also considered it a Communist front group, if not an outright puppet of Moscow. It was closely aligned with Highlander and headed by Baker's close personal friends Anne and Carl Braden, both of whom had to run a gauntlet of anti-Communist witch hunts throughout their activist careers. Hoping to explain to a larger audience connected to SCEF, most of it white, what the sit-in movement was about, Baker quoted a publication from the student movement at tiny Barber-Scotia College in North Carolina: "We want the world to know that we no longer accept the inferior position of second-class citizenship. We are willing to go to jail, be ridiculed, spat upon and even suffer physical violence to obtain First Class Citizenship."

She insisted that the students were concerned with social change on a grand, even a global, scale. "This feeling that they have a destined date with freedom . . . was not limited to a drive for personal freedom, or even freedom for the Negro in the South. Repeatedly it was emphasized that the movement was concerned with the moral implications of racial discrimination for the 'whole world' and the 'Human Race.'" Lest anyone mistake Baker's perspective on existing civil rights groups, especially the one that still employed her, she concluded, "This inclination toward group-centered leadership, rather than toward a leader-centered group pattern of organization, was refreshing indeed to those of the older group who bear the scars of the battle, the frustrations and the disillusionment that come when the prophetic leader turns out to have heavy feet of clay." Tellingly, she titled her address and the article that resulted from it "Bigger Than a Hamburger": The issue of segregated seating at lunch counters was but an entry point for the student movement. "There were those who saw from the beginning that it was part of the struggle for full dignity as a human being," she later said. The students were after bigger game, and they responded so positively to her message, at least in part, because she told them something they already knew about themselves but had not quite been able to put into words on their own.

Baker was fifty-six years old. Some of the students must have had grand-mothers around that age. Properly dressed and impeccably mannered, she was (at least upon first impression) far less charismatic than the ministers who shared the stage with her. One might not have predicted that she would be the one to connect with and move the students, but when she addressed the gathering they responded to her as though there was an electric charge in the room. "I had no difficulty relating to the young people," Baker recalled. "We were able to communicate." One observer at the conference remem-bered, "She spoke simply but powerfully. It was as if she was speaking right to you about such large and important issues. She was much more effective than the men."

The students marveled at Baker in part because she dared to challenge the celebrity King in public if she disagreed with one of his ideas—not disre-spectfully, but forcefully. They might have noticed Baker's name and title if they had looked closely at the conference invitation, but it is safe to say that not one of them had an inkling of Baker's history in the movement. They came to admire her all the more for her passion and stamina for organizing and her long institutional memory. John Lewis, a student at American Bap-tist Theological Seminary who had been active in the Nashville sit-ins, met Baker for the first time in Raleigh. He immediately noticed that while Baker was three decades older than the students, "in terms of ideas and philosophy and commitment she was one of the youngest persons in the movement." Baker would have considered that the highest possible compliment. "My generation didn't have the nerve to do this," she observed, "but they did."

The students impressed her in turn by demanding their independence. They refused to be corralled by SCLC, and many even resisted forming their own new, regionwide organization. With some justification—the Atlanta and Nashville groups, among others, had already forced local elites to the negotiating table without any outside help—they preferred to maintain the autonomy of their local organizations. "They know the value of spontaneity and local initiative and don't want to lose it," Anne Braden reported. They also picked up and ran with Baker's "Bigger Than a Hamburger" philosophy. Baker proudly told another reporter that the students "are seeking to rid America of the scourge of racial segregation and discrimination—not only at the lunch counters but in every aspect of life."

Braden became another important mentor for the students. If Baker was the "mother of SNCC," historian Catherine Fosl writes, Braden was "at least an adoring aunt," another elder whom the young activists could emulate. Though she was twenty years younger than her close friend, Braden was in many ways the white version of Baker—a journalist, southern through and through, militantly antiracist, committed to the ideals of participatory democracy, and utterly uninterested in whatever opinions men in positions of power had about what women should and should not do. Baker and Braden both appreciated a good bourbon, and they debriefed with a bottle after many a strategy meeting in the 1960s.

The students assembled in Raleigh voted to form only a temporary coordinating body. They chose the name Student Nonviolent Coordinating Committee (SNCC, pronounced "snick") and elected as their chairman Marion Barry, a graduate student from Fisk University in Nashville. The organization's name and the statement of purpose the students adopted ("We affirm the philosophical or religious ideal of nonviolence as the foundation of our purpose, the presupposition of our faith, and the manner of our action.") clearly reflected Lawson's influence. Baker made it clear that she did not subscribe to philosophical nonviolence, but in every other way SNCC bore her imprint. Even years later Charles ("Chuck") McDew, the second chairman of SNCC, found it difficult to discern where Baker's ideas stopped and SNCC's started. "She made us in her image," he said.

After the Raleigh meeting a group of eleven students met in Atlanta and voted to make SNCC permanent. Though they had no operating funds, they voted to hire a coordinator. They also agreed to send representatives to that summer's Democratic and Republican national conventions. Each party's platform committee allowed the SNCC representatives to speak, and although the students' statements earned no traction whatsoever, they did at least put on record their concern with issues beyond desegregation. At the very least, SNCC made it known that the students expected to be taken seriously.

Baker set up SNCC's headquarters in a corner of the SCLC office on Auburn Avenue in Atlanta. She hired Jane Stembridge, a white southerner who was then studying at Union Theological Seminary in Virginia, as SNCC's executive director, as its only staff member. Constance "Connie" Curry, a recent graduate of Agnes Scott College who was then employed as the director of the Atlanta-based Southern Student Human Relations Project of the National Student Association, served as an adviser to SNCC and assisted Baker and Stembridge with day-to-day operations. Absent the help of Baker and Curry—and, perhaps more to the point, the resources they siphoned from their employers for SNCC's use—it is easy to imagine that SNCC might have died in infancy. Stembridge worked faithfully as a one-woman clearinghouse for information about the local student movements, crafting press releases about sit-ins throughout the country and writing a newsletter for the students, *The Student Voice*. Shuttling between New York and Atlanta, Baker nurtured SNCC's operations, organized a fund-raising drive for families in Tennessee that had been harassed for attempting to register to vote, and prepared to hand over her duties at SCLC to Wyatt Tee Walker on August 1.

In the summer of 1960, as Baker and Stembridge planned for an upcoming meeting for the new organization—by some definitions, the founding conference for SNCC, because the Raleigh conference concluded having established only the temporary version of the organization, and there were only eleven participants at the meeting in which SNCC was made permanent—they realized that no one would be there to represent the rural South. Enter Robert P. "Bob" Moses, a brilliant twenty-six-year-old math teacher at New York's prestigious Horace Mann School and arguably the most unlikely civil rights hero of the entire era. Moses had recently earned a master's degree in philosophy at Harvard, and he might have remained in academia had his mother not died in 1959. He returned to New York to help support his family, but the student movement drew his attention farther south. "The sit-ins hit me powerfully, in the soul as well as the brain," he said. Moses traveled to Newport News, Virginia, over his school's spring break, ostensibly to visit an uncle but really to participate in a sit-in. The experience left him with "a feeling of great release." He had finally found "a way to personally take on prejudice and racism—to engage."

Moses was excited to attend a Wyatt Tee Walker speech in New York that spring, but he found what the preacher had to say puzzling. "We all need to get behind one leader," Walker declared, and Moses made a point of finding Walker afterward to ask him to explain exactly what he had meant by that. "Don't you think we need a lot of leaders?" Moses asked the incoming executive director of SCLC, and he got little more than a "quizzical look" in return. Moses didn't know it yet, but he was cut from exactly the same cloth as Baker. (He soon realized that his family had been members of one of the Harlem cooperatives that Baker organized in the early 1930s; he and his brothers even delivered the co-op's milk to the other members to earn pocket money. Maybe Baker put something in the milk.) Unfazed, he began volunteering for the Friends of SCLC office in New York, where he met Rustin and Levison. They encouraged him to put his talents to work in SCLC's Atlanta office but apparently failed to tell anyone there to expect him. So Moses arrived unannounced.

Moses found Stembridge stuffing envelopes in the Auburn Avenue office. Without asking permission he sat down and joined her. Stembridge had no idea what to think of Moses, but they got to know one another a bit, and she introduced him to leaders in the Atlanta student movement. SCLC was all but inactive in Atlanta, so Moses joined the students' picket line protesting discriminatory hiring at an A&P supermarket—again, without asking permission and without much of an introduction. "We thought he was a Communist because he was from New York," Julian Bond later said. The students knew that authorities inserted agents provocateurs into protest movements in order to spy on and bring them down. Might Moses be one?

They were still trying to figure out Moses when he was noticed at a demonstration in front of Rich's Department Store in downtown Atlanta that was sponsored by SCEF. Now the students were doubly suspicious: a red-baiting U.S. Senate committee had accused SCEF of harboring Communists in its ranks, and the students proved surprisingly susceptible to such Cold War agitprop. Maybe Moses was a Communist infiltrator after all. They wondered, how had Moses even heard about this protest? "I told them I had heard of the demonstration while attending a mathematics lecture on the 'Ramifications of Gödel's Theorem' at Atlanta University," he said. Understandably, that did little to assuage their suspicions, and they asked Rev. King to investigate Moses himself.

King called Moses into his study at Ebenezer Baptist Church and impressed upon him the importance of keeping SCLC's reputation as pure as the driven snow. In a news article on the demonstration Moses was identified as an SCLC staffer, and King could not afford to have his people getting mixed up with others who might be *perceived* as Communists, especially in the midst of a major fund-raising campaign. Moses was satisfied that King was worried solely about perceptions, not whether Moses or SCEF members or anyone else doing antiracist work really were Bolsheviks. Nonetheless, it was a one-way conversation.

In contrast, Baker took it upon herself to talk *with* Moses, to get to know him as an equal. "She asked me about my upbringing, my thoughts on Harlem, my entrance into the movement. . . . I felt that this first conversation had seemed important enough to her that she had made time for it; it was not something that she had just squeezed into her busy schedule." Baker's intelligence impressed Moses, but so did her frankness and even more so her genuine curiosity about him. He learned, "If you really want to do something with somebody else, really want to work with that person, the first thing you have to do is make a personal connection. You have to find out who it is you're working with." Moses freely admitted that initiating those kinds of connections was not his strong suit; he was more comfortable reading existentialist philosophy or puzzling over mathematical theorems. Yet he was able to internalize Baker's lesson, and in a short time he became arguably the most effective community organizer of his generation.

Working closely with Baker and Stembridge, Moses slipped over from the SCLC side of the office to SNCC's. They gave him an assignment: to drum up interest in SNCC on the part of rural southern activists who might be interested in attending the fall meeting. Baker gave Moses a list full of her contacts from two decades' worth of work for the NAACP and SCLC and sent him out into the field. Because SNCC had no resources, he had to buy his own bus ticket. Moses met with Baker's contacts in Alabama, Mississippi, and Louisiana, and he began to lay the groundwork for the grassroots organizing campaigns that would distinguish SNCC from its fellow civil rights organizations. He connected especially deeply with Amzie Moore, an activist in Mississippi with whom Baker had worked in the NAACP and had supported through In Friendship.

Moses returned to his teaching position at Horace Mann that fall. Baker severed her ties with the SCLC and left for New York to attend Jacqueline's September wedding and rest for a bit (she suffered from respiratory problems, and her eyes were beginning to give her trouble), although she shortly returned to Atlanta to put the final touches on plans for the SNCC meeting. She left the SCLC on good terms, in part because she respected Walker and expected him to flourish as executive director in ways that she never could have. "My successor, the Reverend Wyatt Tee Walker, is a young man of vision, and I am confident that with him the program of the Conference will expand to meet the challenges that we face in the months and years ahead," she wrote to friends in the organization upon her exit. Walker already had activist experience and promise, but the main qualities he possessed that might allow him to succeed where Baker had failed were his profession and his gender. Perhaps Walker could even shake SCLC out of its doldrums, develop a program, and instill a more democratic culture. Baker had pinned her hopes on less over the years.

Under Baker's supervision the students put together an invitation to the October conference and set its agenda. SNCC, they proclaimed, would be "action-oriented." They were "convinced that truth comes from being involved and not from observation and speculation. We are further convinced that only mass action is strong enough to force all of America to assume responsibility and that nonviolent direct action alone is strong enough to enable all of America to understand the responsibility she must assume." They also encouraged their fellow students to "look beyond the South, into the Pentagon, into Europe, and into Russia," an indication that they had internalized Baker's suggestion that their movement was about issues much larger than the desegregation of lunch counters, and that they were developing their own original, coherent ideology.

Attendance at the Atlanta meeting was only about a third of the size of the meeting in Raleigh. The spring's widespread sit-in fervor had diminished slightly; those who remained committed to SNCC were diehards. This time the observers included representatives from SCEF, NSA, Students for a Democratic Society (SDS), and the Highlander School, but also members of the American Socialist Party and the Young People's Socialist League. Baker and Stembridge had secured funding for the conference from labor unions that had been burned in the past by association with far leftists, and the union leaders made sure that the leftists could not wield too much influence on the students. They insisted, for instance, that Bayard Rustin not be allowed a place on the program.

Again the students heard from Martin Luther King Jr. and James Lawson. Again Lawson upstaged King, castigating the students for having squandered the sit-in movement's "finest hour" by allowing those who had been arrested in the protests to be released from jail on bail. "Instead of letting the adults scurry around getting bail," he roared, "we should have insisted that they scurry about to end the system which had put us in jail. If history offers us such an opportunity again, let us be prepared to seize it." In the following years "jail no bail" would become a rallying cry for SNCC, but also for SCLC, as the organizations searched for effective techniques of creative nonviolence. By filling the jails, they hoped, they could disrupt business as usual in southern communities and force the whites who held power to the negotiating table.

The conference agenda was ambitious and would require much deep thought and intense discussion, but participants later described the conference as "a joyous occasion." The far-flung students were beginning to forge intimate bonds with one another, forming a version of the "beloved community" most of them had only read about, and those bonds seemed especially intense among the women involved. Sandra "Casey" Cason, a white student from the University of Texas who had participated in sit-ins in Austin, attended the conference and met Baker, along with Stembridge and Curry, for the first time. Cason vividly remembered the sight of the three women sitting at the registration desk, greeting each student as they arrived. "I've always traced much of the character of SNCC, as well as my own sense of who I was within it, to that first impression of the organization as an integrated group of women," Cason said. "The SNCC of which I was a part was nurturing, familial, supportive, honest and penetrating, radical and pragmatic. I think of it as womanist. I see Ella in all of that."

At this meeting the students had to construct and ratify a constitution, settle on organizational and staff structures, and, in a much more general sense, determine SNCC's purpose and future direction. Could they transform their protest movement against segregated public accommodations into a mass movement for social reform over the long haul? Each of these agenda items required long discussion, so the students settled into what would become the hallmark of SNCC meetings: long sessions in which everyone had their say. Baker settled into her own habit in such situations: intensive listening interrupted every so often by questions. She made a point to offer opinions only if asked. When the students did ask, of course, she had a deep well of experience to draw from when she answered.

If the students wanted America to change, Baker taught them, then they had to change. They had to live the change they wanted to see on a larger scale. If they wanted to transform America into an egalitarian and integrated democracy, they had to think, behave, and live in egalitarian, integrated, and ultrademocratic ways. Ultrademocratic behavior in this context entailed interminably long discussions. SNCC's institutional culture insisted that everyone got to have her or his say, and decisions had to be arrived at by consensus. That translated to literally round-the-clock meetings. Baker's breathing ailment made her sensitive to cigarette smoke, and in this era there was no stigma against smoking in public, so the meetings themselves were physically challenging for her. (Hours into a typical SNCC meeting, it looked as if a smoke bomb had gone off.) The students remembered her sitting in these meetings for hours at a time, just observing, occasionally asking a question meant to refocus discussion. SNCC's Courtland Cox said, "The most vivid memory I have of Ella Baker is of her sitting in on these SNCC meetings that ran for days—you didn't measure them in hours, they ran days—with a [hospital] mask over her nose, listening patiently to words and discussions she must have heard a thousand times."

If they could not recall the exact particulars of what Miss Baker said in a given meeting, the men and women of SNCC at least remembered her style. Above all, they remembered her asking nondirective questions: "Usually she preferred to answer [a question] with another question and then another, forcing us to refine our thinking and to struggle toward an answer for ourselves," one said. Chuck McDew recalled Baker's unique ability to "pick out a kernel that was a good idea" from a mound of something else. "Somebody may have spoken for eight hours. Seven hours and fifty-three minutes was utter bullshit, but seven minutes was good. She taught us to glean out the seven minutes." That was a movement-building tactic that worked on several levels. If the students could learn to concentrate on the productive kernel and separate out the rest in their meetings with one another, they would be better prepared to facilitate meetings with others outside their group, so that they could work with allies toward common goals.

Many years later, the people who sat with Baker in these meetings still considered the lessons they learned from her to have been among the most important in their lives. Mary King of SNCC recalled,

> At a very important period in my life, Miss Baker tempered my natural tenacity and determination with flexibility and made me suspicious of dogmatism. . . . She taught me one of the most important lessons I have learned in life: There are many legitimate and effective avenues for social change and there is no single right way. She helped me see that the profound changes we were seeking in the social order could not be won without multiple strategies. She encouraged me to avoid being doctrinaire. "Ask questions, Mary," she would say.

Between the fall of 1960 and the following spring, the students settled on an organizational structure with a coordinating committee composed of one representative from each of sixteen southern and border states and the District of Columbia. Members authorized the coordinating committee and staff to begin raising money and to continue publishing *The Student Voice*. Most importantly, they voted to hire field secretaries—organizers who would work with local groups much as Baker had early in her NAACP career, only for longer periods in given communities, at a typical salary of $10 a week before taxes.

The students had by now established that they wanted their own autonomous civil rights organization, and now SNCC's most committed members reiterated that the organization had staying power. Yet there were already cracks forming in SNCC's foundation. In part because 1960 was a presidential election year, SNCC's most vocal members became more overtly political, more willing to insert the organization into national partisan arguments over not just civil rights but other domestic and even international issues. The students who rallied around Lawson's statement of purpose, which defined the student movement against segregation in terms of a religious crusade, were less likely to respond to political messages. The group still had not decided definitively whether SNCC was to be a coordinating body whose primary mission was to facilitate communication among local groups or a body that initiated its own larger-scale and longer-term civil rights campaigns, though the decision to hire field secretaries certainly moved the organization in the latter direction.

The crack widened over the coming months. Baker had followed events in Fayette County, Tennessee, closely since 1959 and had established a relationship with local activists there. At the beginning of 1961, at Baker's suggestion, SNCC's newly hired executive secretary Ed King, a student from historically black Kentucky State College, traveled to Fayette County to meet with residents of "Freedom Tent City," an encampment of black share-croppers who had been thrown off their land for registering to vote. King's charge was to see if SNCC might be able to play a role in supporting and empowering the sharecroppers. He pledged SNCC's support, which put the committee on the road toward voter registration as a major impetus. Fayette County presented a proving ground for the students, a chance to develop and give meaning to their theories—which is to say, Baker's teachings. They began by publicizing the sharecroppers' plight through *The Student Voice* and involved themselves directly by organizing food and clothing drives for the people of Freedom Tent City.

It is easy to find Baker's fingerprints on these responses. The food and clothing drive was straight from the In Friendship playbook. Other black media sources reported on Fayette County, but only one, *The Student Voice*, took the sharecroppers seriously as leaders of their own movement who might have a perspective worth sharing with the wider world. (In contrast, Gloster Current, Baker's successor as director of branches of the NAACP, emphasized that Fayette County authorities had denied the franchise to African American teachers, ministers, and small businessmen—respectable people.) *The Student Voice* portrayed a situation in which an inadequate pub-lic education system had left rural blacks—in Fayette County, they made up roughly two-thirds of the total population—without the skills necessary to do anything but menial farmwork and in which the local political economy concentrated power in the hands of the few. As soon as members of the desperately poor African American majority attempted to assert themselves, using rights they were guaranteed under the U.S. Constitution, after all, powerful whites struck back viciously. The portrayal was, of course, entirely accurate, and the narrative repeated itself in community after community in the coming years.

Baker herself visited Fayette County in January 1961 and reported on con-ditions for SCEF's *The Southern Patriot*. Like the students, she refused to con-descend to the sharecroppers, whom she admired greatly; she thought they were as rich in wisdom and courage as they were poor in economic attain-ment and formal education. If anything, she found it even more difficult to disguise her outrage at the living conditions she found at Freedom Tent City and her disappointment that the federal government still had done noth-ing to enforce the sharecroppers' civil rights. "[I]n the wealthiest country in the world, in the jet-propelled atomic age of 1961," she wrote, American citizens simply deserved much better. Yet she also displayed a characteristic optimism. Because the sharecroppers had taken it upon themselves to solve their own problems instead of waiting for federal assistance that might never arrive, she reported, "A new dawn of freedom is breaking through the age-old social, economic and political discrimination that blighted the lives of both whites and Negroes in the South."

A steady stream of SNCC-affiliated students and other like-minded young adults made the journey to Fayette County to work with the local movement. One of them, thirty-three-year-old James Forman, a former schoolteacher from Chicago, so impressed the SNCC representatives that they convinced Baker to quietly move Ed King out of the executive secretary position (she arranged for a scholarship so that he could return to college) to make room for Forman in the fall of 1961. While there the students began developing a program entirely in line with Baker's theories about community organizing, and from the program came a philosophy best expressed in the unofficial motto they adopted along the way: Let the People Decide. SNCC staff would move into communities to help the local people help themselves; their job was to empower local people to make their own decisions, not impose decisions on them. The Fayette County project provided at least a rough blueprint for the programs that SNCC would undertake throughout the rural South over the next several years.

The approach also widened the cracks that had developed in SNCC's foundation, so much so that by the summer of 1961 the group had a full-fledged schism on its hands. While one group of SNCC students was organizing in Fayette County, others found themselves at the center of the Freedom Rides, another dramatic display of nonviolent resistance to segregation that was at least as consequential as the 1960 sit-ins.

The Freedom Rides began as a CORE project, although one that included participants who were also members of SNCC. It was a direct heir of the Journey of Reconciliation, the 1947 effort that Baker had helped plan and had been forced to abandon at the last moment. Designed to test compliance with U.S. Supreme Court and Interstate Commerce Commission rulings, the plan for the initial May 1961 Freedom Ride was simple: A racially mixed group of thirteen volunteers boarded buses in Washington, D.C., headed for New Orleans. They would sit as they pleased on the buses, and they would not abide by local segregation ordinances that separated the races in waiting rooms, bathrooms, and other facilities at bus stations along the way. If arrested they would challenge the constitutionality of those laws in court.

The first group of Freedom Riders, which included John Lewis, a SNCC member from the Nashville movement who would soon rise to the chairmanship of the organization, faced little trouble in Virginia and North Carolina. However, one volunteer was arrested in Charlotte for occupying a shoeshine stand that had been designated for whites only (they called it the South's first "shoe-in"), and virulent white racists in the mill town of Rock Hill, South Carolina, attacked Lewis and other Freedom Riders as they sat on the white side of the bus station's segregated waiting room. There were more arrests in South Carolina, but for the most part the Ride continued without incident through Georgia.

That changed as the buses rolled into Alabama, where local lawmen colluded with the Ku Klux Klan to put an end to the Freedom Rides. On May 14 the Freedom Riders split up and boarded two separate buses headed for Birmingham. Klansmen slashed the tires of a Greyhound bus as it waited to resume its journey following a stopover in the city of Anniston, Alabama, which forced an emergency stop outside of town. There a mob of roughly fifty people firebombed the bus, trapping inside fourteen passengers (five of whom had nothing whatsoever to do with the Freedom Ride; they just needed to get to Birmingham). The gasping passengers escaped only when the mob retreated from what they thought was an exploding fuel tank. That none of them died was a matter of pure luck—or, as many of them interpreted it, divine grace.

The second group of Freedom Riders fared not much better. Alabama Klansmen purchased tickets and boarded a Trailways bus with them in Atlanta. They verbally, and then physically, assaulted Freedom Riders and uninvolved African American passengers throughout the four-hour trip. When the bus arrived in Birmingham their Klan brethren formed a "welcoming committee" that beat the Freedom Riders with every kind of weapon imaginable. Screaming, "You damn Communists, why don't you go back to Russia? You're a shame to the white race," they unleashed a bloodbath in the Birmingham bus station. Local policemen watched and did nothing, and although one of the Klansmen had informed the Federal Bureau of Investigation of the group's plans from start to finish, the bureau made no effort to protect the Freedom Riders either. Again, the Freedom Riders were lucky to escape with their lives.

National newspaper, radio, and television reporters witnessed everything. CBS News correspondent Howard K. Smith said, "They . . . just about slaughtered those kids." Smith had been stationed in Germany in the 1930s, where he witnessed the rise of the Nazis. The experience at the Birmingham bus station reminded him of Kristallnacht. Within a day graphic reports, photographs, and film footage of the heinous response to the Freedom Rides reached every corner of the country, and many Americans outside of the

South who might not otherwise have had an interest in the civil rights of African Americans found the backlash unthinkable and absolutely unacceptable. Civil rights groups and fellow travelers now attempted to leverage President John F. Kennedy and his brother Robert, the U.S. Attorney General, into offering federal protection to the Freedom Riders and throwing the weight of the federal government behind the cause of desegregation more generally.

The Kennedys asked for a cooling-off period. Understandably shaken by the violence, CORE's leadership agreed. Rather than continue the bus tour through Alabama into Mississippi and Louisiana, two states where segregationist hardliners might provide an even worse welcome, most of the original group opted to fly to New Orleans. That seemed to end the Freedom Rides' chapter, but to the young people of the Nashville movement who had been the driving force in the early days of SNCC, the decision seemed exactly the wrong one to make. Diane Nash, who was distinguishing herself as a forceful voice within the student movement, told CORE director James Farmer that she and several others were talking about traveling to Birmingham to pick up where CORE had left off. "You realize it may be suicide," he responded, but that did not seem to faze Nash. "We fully realize that, but we can't let them stop us with violence. If we do, the movement is dead. Every time we start something, they'll just answer with violence." This had been Baker's impetus for founding In Friendship.

A new coordinating committee assembled in Birmingham to plan the Freedom Rides' resumption. Baker influenced the group from a familiar position, behind the scenes. She offered a three-page written critique of what had gone wrong so far and what the new committee could do to improve. For starters, she advised, the committee would have to do a better job of crafting a media strategy. The national reaction to the violence in Alabama pointed out how useful public opinion from outside of the South could be in putting pressure on federal officials who had the power to protect the protesters' constitutional rights and to force state and local entities to desegregate. The Freedom Rides needed to do more to capture and focus this attention. Baker also criticized the committee's tactics in negotiating with Robert F. Kennedy to secure the release of jailed Freedom Riders. Why not take advantage of the opportunity to demand his "action in the enforcement of existing laws and regulations," which already outlawed racial segregation in interstate travel, instead?

Reflecting her realpolitik understanding of interorganizational jockeying for position, Baker urged the SNCC representatives on the coordinating committee to protect SNCC's interests. CORE, the SCLC, and NAACP were raising money from donors who had been energized by the Freedom Rides. SNCC needed its cut, too, even more so now that SNCC members were at the front lines of the battle. Fittingly, Baker shifted gears and closed her critique by making sure that the coordinators were looking after the students who were sacrificing their valuable time and their bodies for the cause. After all, she wrote, they were "spending the longest periods in jail [and] will be in need of money for maintaining themselves and for scholarships next school term. Where will this come from?"

She was in daily contact with Diane Nash. Twenty-three years old at the time, Nash was suddenly the de facto director of the Freedom Rides, responsible for decisions that she knew could place her friends and colleagues in grave physical danger. She was confronting governors and negotiating with the most powerful officials in the White House and U.S. Department of Justice. Having access to Baker's experience, wisdom, and understanding of how politics worked at the highest levels was invaluable, but what she especially appreciated was Baker's ability to look after her psychological health. Baker helped Nash form strategy, but in each of these sessions she also asked after Nash's well-being. "Ella would pick me up and dust me off emotionally," Nash said.

The Freedom Rides took on new life. Buses rolled on from Birmingham, first into Montgomery, where the Riders were again attacked by a segregationist mob, and then into Jackson, Mississippi, where they were arrested and sentenced to long terms at the Hinds County jail and the notorious Parchman State Penitentiary. Baker wrote to one of the Freedom Riders and SNCC stalwarts who had been arrested in Jackson, Ruby Doris Smith, in the Hinds County facility. "I simply want to let you know that my thoughts and prayers are with you as you bear witness to your beliefs that racial segregation, wherever it is found, is both unchristian and undemocratic," Baker said. "I hope that your present experience has not been too trying for you." She assured Smith that her efforts were not in vain: SNCC was working tirelessly to publicize the Freedom Riders' plight, and Baker was "confident that more and more people will be making known their desire to travel as American citizens." Baker closed by expressing her "continued pride in the courage you have manifested on more than one occasion." Such expressions carried multiple SNCC workers through exceptionally trying times.

Dozens of SNCC members and other Freedom Riders eventually ended up at Parchman; Baker helped to coordinate legal aid and relief efforts. Additional Freedom Rides—now on airplanes and trains in addition to the buses—challenged segregated facilities throughout the Deep South and border states, and they brought a much wider and deeper level of national attention to the desegregation movement. In all, historian Raymond Arsenault calculates, 436 men and women between the ages of thirteen and sixty-one participated in at least fifteen Freedom Ride campaigns involving dozens of separate Rides in 1961. Under Nash's leadership, the Freedom Rides exponentially increased pressure on the Kennedy administration to support the cause of civil rights. They also had the effect of galvanizing the direct-action movement. As one Freedom Rider put it, "There were a lot of little movements going into Parchman, but one big one coming out."

While the Freedom Riders made their way through the Jim Crow Deep South, Bob Moses had returned to the region with a different goal. With local activist C. C. Bryant, he set up a SNCC voter registration project in the southwest Mississippi town of McComb. Amzie Moore, Bryant, and other activists on the ground had convinced him that of all the problems that black Mississippians faced, the key was political powerlessness. Without the vote, powerful whites could and would keep blacks poor, uneducated, and segregated into inferior spaces forever. They knew that the ballot was no panacea, but with it African Americans might at least have the chance to improve their communities. They gave their campaign the name "Move on Mississippi."

The idea for a voter registration campaign in McComb came from the grass roots, and it was not exactly novel; the state NAACP apparatus had attempted multiple registration drives over the previous two decades. Rather than impose his own ideas or his organization's theories on the community, Moses listened to Bryant and others in McComb, helped them come up with a plan, and went to work to help them realize it.

"What we did in essence was to try to do for the community people that we were working with what Ella had already done for us," he said. Moses's organizing is the stuff of legend among students of the civil rights movement today, but there was nothing glamorous about it. For weeks he did nothing but ride around with two retired rail workers who had long been active in their community and talk to men and women the age of his parents and grandparents whom his hosts thought might be amenable to a voter registration drive. He slept and ate with the Bryant family and did his best to gain the trust of McComb's African American community, from recognized leaders to otherwise unheralded common people who might have something to contribute to the movement. The work was tedious and promised few if any short-term benefits, but it was exactly the kind of community organizing that Baker believed would create long-term positive change.

Moses and his hosts raised enough funds in the community to bring in two additional SNCC field secretaries, Reginald Robinson and John Hardy, about a month after his arrival, and he soon recruited two local youth, Hollis Watkins and Curtis Hayes, who would become SNCC field secretaries themselves. Several other SNCC organizers, including Charles Sherrod and Chuck McDew, had joined Moses in McComb by August, when the project began holding mass meetings and teaching voter registration classes.

Whites in McComb reacted to the voter registration campaign much as other southern whites reacted to the Freedom Rides; that is, with horrific amounts of violence intended to smother the newborn local movement in its crib. Moses would have agreed with Nash's belief that to allow violence to stop or even slow down a movement would be to admit ultimate defeat, so he soldiered on. When alone with his thoughts, he also worried that he might have helped start something terrible for local blacks that he could not help them out of. If anything, however, the whites' violent response convinced Moses that SNCC was on to something. Organizing a community around the issue of voter registration on the Fayette County grassroots model could lead to real and lasting change, a more democratic and more egalitarian society. By the end of the summer he and many others within SNCC had caught the community-organizing bug and were even more determined to continue moving the organization in that direction.

Nash and a cohort within SNCC were just as determined to make SNCC a nonviolent, direct-action organization. SNCC had been born out of the sit-ins and had found its mission, they believed, in the Freedom Rides. If the organization was to continue to develop into a national force capable of truly changing American society, it would have to coordinate similarly daring campaigns in which hundreds, perhaps thousands, of young Americans would put their lives on the line and fill the nation's jails if necessary to protest Jim Crow. By the end of the summer, SNCC was in danger of separating into two wings, one centered around the voter registration/nonviolence-as-a-tactic approach and the other centered around nonviolent direct action/ nonviolence-as-a-way-of-life.

Baker arranged for SNCC's scheduled summer meeting to take place at the safe space of Highlander for the students to discuss SNCC's direction. Those who had worked in Mississippi were convinced that without the vote southern blacks would never be able to lift themselves out of their all-but-helpless position. The ballot by itself would never solve their problems, but political power was the sine qua non of self-empowerment. Nash and the Nashville circle were equally convinced by their own experience that direct action was the only way to build the beloved community. They wanted to transcend electoral politics, not immerse themselves in it.

The question of finances complicated the argument. SNCC had always operated on a shoestring, but now northern philanthropic groups were offering to support voter registration efforts that could sustain the organization for the foreseeable future. The Taconic Foundation, Field Foundation, and Stern Family Fund had recently funded the Southern Regional Council's Voter Education Project (VEP) to the tune of $870,000, with the idea that the VEP would disburse the funds to the NAACP, Urban League, SCLC, CORE, and SNCC to spend on local registration campaigns. SNCC was uniquely situated to recruit and train volunteer voter registration workers and send them into southern communities. In reality, only young people were free enough to drop everything for months at a time to move into a community to set up such projects, and the other major civil rights organizations had neither the inclination to build such programs nor the access to the young people needed to staff them.

The northern foundations dangled the carrot of hundreds of thousands of dollars' worth of funding before SNCC with the assent of the Kennedy administration. Attorney General Robert F. Kennedy was weary of the daily damage control the Freedom Rides had required, and he frankly wanted the students to go away for a while. If the philanthropists' dollars could somehow channel the students' energy into registering voters who were likely to vote for his party, all the better. Members of Nash's circle had come to distrust the Kennedys deeply, and they rightfully saw this as a naked attempt to co-opt their movement. The administration may have talked a good game, but in the behind-the-scenes negotiations that accompanied the Freedom Rides, Kennedy officials had proven to be unsteady allies, at best, to the civil rights activists. If the Kennedys wanted SNCC to accept this money and dive into voter registration work, this was more reason for the Nash circle to oppose it. With some justification, John Lewis worried that the "voter registration push by the government was a trick to take the steam out of the movement, to slow it down."

The divide is difficult to understand in retrospect; it seems almost artificial. (Nash herself had come up with the idea of leading nonviolent resistance classes in McComb and coined the phrase "Move on Mississippi." The voter registration campaign evolved in part from that effort.) But it was heartfelt and genuine at the time, and discussions at the Highlander meeting were heated. SNCC came very close to dividing formally into two separate organizations. Then Ella Baker did something unusual: she butted in, insisting that the community organizing and direct-action approaches were not mutually exclusive. In any case, Baker told the students, SNCC had too much important work to do to consider a division. She characteristically sat back and listened to the students at SNCC meetings, but this time she spoke with urgency. "I opposed the split as serving the purpose of the enemy," she said. If Baker felt that strongly about something, the students decided, she must be right. No one rose to challenge her.

Baker convinced the two camps to organize informally into two wings of the same organization. SNCC could pursue both community organizing and direct action, she counseled, and retain its soul in the bargain. She knew full well that any sustained voter registration campaign in the Deep South would necessarily entail direct action; that was precisely why groups such as the NAACP and SCLC had not embarked on one already. If the nonviolent direct-action group craved confrontation with the forces of racism, they would find more of it than they bargained for in voter registration work.

Baker may have been even more right than she knew at the time. Not only were voter registration and nonviolent direct action not inherently contradictory, but also they could sustain one another. The African American community of Jackson, Mississippi, had just provided a perfect example in its response to the Freedom Rides. Jackson women initially organized their own local, independent movement, Womanpower Unlimited, to collect money, clothing, and personal items for the dozens of Freedom Riders who were arrested and jailed in Jackson. Womanpower eventually developed voter registration, education, and peace activism programs. What appeared to have been from one vantage point a one-time-only mobilization, the arrival of Freedom Riders in Jackson, appeared from another vantage point to have been a flashpoint for community organizing that could create a lasting, autonomous institution. Indeed, Womanpower was a powerful force within the Mississippi movement for most of the next decade.

While the students were charting their own course and the women of Jackson were organizing on their own, Baker was herself performing the sort of support duty that may seem to have little to do with civil rights organizing but in reality was absolutely necessary to allow local people to continue being activists. The McComb movement attracted several headstrong high school students who insisted on attacking Jim Crow head-on, against the wishes of older local activists and Moses. In August 1961 they sat-in at the Greyhound bus station and were arrested. Authorities threw the book at the young people's leaders, including fifteen-year-old Brenda Travis. Travis spent two months in jail, was released on probation, and then was immediately rearrested after leading another public protest.

After several months in Mississippi's Colored Girls Industrial School, a euphemistically named reform facility for so-called juvenile delinquents, Travis was set to be released again to a family that could not care for her, in a community that largely resented her activism. What to do? SNCC and Baker could not very well encourage local people to become activists only to look the other way when whites retaliated. So when Travis won her release in 1962, Baker signed the papers to become her legal guardian. She called it "accepting a responsibility that [she] had not looked for but consequently [could] not refuse to accept." She arranged for Travis to enroll at the Palmer Institute, a boarding school for African Americans in Sedalia, North Carolina; Travis spent the next several months trying to leave. For a time she lived with Baker in Harlem, and Baker admitted in a letter to a friend that the ordeal was exhausting her. But she took care of Travis until it made sense for the girl to return to McComb. Travis later said that Baker "changed the direction of my life." Community organizing can take many forms. Among the most important things Baker did through such actions was to demonstrate conclusively that black southerners who wanted to push for their rights as citizens *had* a community whose support they could depend on.

The students did agree to the formation of two wings within SNCC, but they put the division behind them almost immediately. They did so in part because the division on paper never described reality in the first place: the direct action proponents also wanted to develop grassroots programs, and the voter registration proponents did not shy away from nonviolent direct confrontation. The students' shared vision overwhelmed anything that divided them. As they worked toward realizing the vision they forgot about this particular point of contention, but as a vibrant organization with confident and strong-willed members, SNCC continued to debate tactics, strategies, and ideologies.

Little more than a year after founding SNCC, the students were finding their way, learning from their mistakes, and building programs through group-centered leadership. What had been born as a "coordinating committee" of detached student groups was by the end of 1961 a disciplined, fully staffed civil rights organization with its own ideology and its own program of action. "I don't think there was an ideology that . . . was comparable to the Marxist-Leninist concept of a changed society," Baker said. "The nearest to an ideology would be, let's call it, the Christian philosophy and that tied in with the philosophy of Ghandian non-violence, non-violent mass action. That was the nearest to it." The students led themselves, but all of the answers they came up with were responses to Baker's questions. Quietly, indirectly, Ella Baker shaped SNCC into the democratic, grassroots, program-oriented civil rights organization the NAACP and SCLC could never be.

CHAPTER SIX

⁓

We Who Believe in Freedom Cannot Rest

Having left SCLC and holding no official position other than member of the executive committee in SNCC (she never held a paid position in the organization), Baker operated again in the early 1960s as a free agent for the civil rights movement, cultivating connections with several different organizations. The lifestyle was anything but glamorous. Baker found it challenging to string together enough freelance work in this period simply to survive while she devoted every last free minute to SNCC. (She joked with her friend Vincent Harding that if she ever got around to writing her autobiography she would title it "Making a Life, Instead of Making a Living.") Between the summer of 1960 and early 1962 she directed the Special Project in Human Relations (SPHR), an interracial college student project, for the YWCA from an office just down the street from SNCC's and SCLC's offices in Atlanta. A grant from the Field Foundation funded the SPHR. As project director, Baker had carte blanche to go around the South creating spaces for college students to discuss "human relations" and "citizenship"—code words for civil rights—in integrated settings.

A half century later, the notion that it would be necessary to plan out structured, small-group conversations between African American and white college students, or that the students would get anything meaningful out of the conversations, may seem quaint, but it was radical in the context of the Deep South of the early 1960s. Baker explained the planning that went into these meetings, which were often arranged in secret, in a report on her trip to Tuskegee Institute in April 1961. True to her belief that social change involved thousands of actors and came about over a long period of time, she emphasized the small victories that could accrue from the meetings.

Given the political atmosphere—only a month later vicious racists attacked the Freedom Riders in nearby Montgomery—simply bringing together white students from Auburn University and blacks from Tuskegee Institute at the Tuskegee campus was physically dangerous and mentally and emotionally taxing work. In addition, Baker's work schedule was reminiscent of her days on the road for the NAACP. In one day she had breakfast at 6:30 with Tuskegee student leaders, lunch with the secretary of the Tuskegee Civic Association (the major local civil and voting rights group), a two-hour afternoon meeting with the Auburn and Tuskegee students, and several meetings interspersed in between with the wife of the university president, members of the local YMCA and YWCA, and others.

Baker was pleased to find that small groups of students from Auburn and Tuskegee had met previously at ecumenical Christian gatherings and had continued to meet informally in interracial groups to discuss matters of race relations. The most productive idea to emerge from this particular gathering, it seemed, stemmed from an Auburn student's resentful statement that the larger culture of white supremacy placed him in a position of "not being able to do anything." An adviser from the Tuskegee YWCA suggested that even people who couldn't walk around carrying "a big banner" for integration could at least carry "a little banner, even a tiny one." Perhaps it was enough to simply begin to change one or two whites' minds about segregation, and even baby steps could lead toward mutual progress. Everyone involved except for the Auburn group's adult adviser, a minister, responded to the ideal of carrying "little banners," Baker reported. The minister thought it impossible for whites even to carry tiny banners in Alabama.

Baker assured the students that there was a role to play for everyone in the social justice movement; not everyone had to sit-in at a lunch counter or risk their lives to register black voters in the Deep South. The students apparently responded positively. "You were superb!" her hostess wrote after the meeting ended. "In these times it is so important to have issues stated clearly, responsibilities clarified, and techniques made bold. The youngsters need all the encouragement and guidance we can muster." Baker never wavered from the belief that the movement should remain big enough to include any whites, or anyone else, who were friendly enough and that they would accept whatever contributions they could make, no matter how small.

Baker's travels to campuses throughout the South allowed her to scout out potential activists whom she could add to the SNCC network. Among these was Casey Hayden (formerly Cason), a recent graduate of the University of

Texas who had herself gravitated to civil rights work through her involve-ment in the campus YWCA. "Through the Y, I was grounded in a demo-cratic manner of work, exposed to and educated about race, and a participant in direct action—though not in civil disobedience—by the time the sit-ins exploded the racial status quo of the country in 1960," she wrote. Baker hired Hayden as one of her "campus travelers," an organizer of the interracial meet-ings. "In my travels I met many young white people trapped in the cage of race for whom these workshops were a way out," she remembered. The SPHR and other projects like it "continued parallel to the [civil rights] movement (or as an integral part of it, depending on your perspective)," Hayden wrote, "right on through the sixties: real meetings of people across racial barriers, fostering healing and relationships that transcended race. This work under-mined and defeated segregation on the personal level, just as bringing down the legal barriers would defeat it politically." Hayden's experience with the SPHR only intensified her commitment to SNCC.

According to Mary King, a white New Yorker who replaced Hayden on the SPHR, Baker devised a work plan for her that bordered on direct action:

> I would be . . . traveling from city to city with a young black woman [Roberta (Bobbi) Yancy, a Pittsburgh native] who had also recently graduated from col-lege. They wanted to pair two recent graduates as an integrated team for the human-relations project. Our formal purpose, they explained, would be to as-sess the extent of academic freedom in southern colleges, continuing the work that Casey had done; the other purposes for the project would become clear shortly. . . . This project, although modestly described in the formal wording of the proposal to appease the officers of the philanthropic foundation funding it, was intended to break down some of the barriers erected by the system of segregation in southern universities.
>
> The project was not to be one of direct action, they stipulated, yet, in those days, two young professional women, one white and one black, traveling to-gether by bus, train, and airplane in the South for any purpose, represented a head-on conflict with legalized segregation.

King found the atmosphere at most of the college campuses she and Yancy visited "oppressive" and the travel "more difficult than even the perceptive Ella Baker had anticipated," but there were enough glimmers of hope to al-low her to think it was possible to defeat Jim Crow through organization. She, too, found her way to SNCC, first as a volunteer and later as a staff member.

SNCC continued its rise, and the students found themselves in seats of power alongside the leaders of more established civil rights organizations, high officials of the government, and popular culture celebrities. Baker continued to insist that the students had to make their own decisions, but that did not prevent her from making strong suggestions or framing the questions she thought they needed to answer. Most members of SNCC remember Baker sitting off to the side of their legendarily exhausting staff meetings, always attentive but nearly always silent and always dressed professionally. "Ella was usually quiet so that you became aware of her immense influence and wisdom gradually," SNCC's Bob Zellner remembered. Her style in the large meetings was to ask questions, many of which were so broad as to be unanswerable but worth discussion anyway, that she wanted the students to consider.

Baker's habit was to ask the students, "Why are we here? What do we hope to accomplish?" Her close friend Anne Braden described Baker's approach in these situations: "She wanted to know what people thought, but mainly she wanted them to think." She could also say a great deal without saying much. Martha Prescod Norman Noonan, a member of SNCC and SDS, recalled that by the time she attended her first SNCC meeting, a 1962 joint meeting with SDS, the members of both organizations "treated . . . Miss Baker's ideas like gospel."

In 1961, under Baker's guidance, SNCC found its community-organizing stride in McComb and fanned out from there throughout southwest Mississippi, Jackson, and the Delta region of the state, in its northwest corner. Jane Stembridge, who moved to work in SNCC's Greenwood, Mississippi, project following her close association with Baker in the Atlanta office, described SNCC's working philosophy in Mississippi, which was in fact Baker's. "The field staff saw itself as playing a very crucial but temporary role in this whole thing," Stembridge said. "Go into a community. As soon as local leadership begins to emerge, get out of the community so that the leadership will take hold and people will not continue to turn to you for guidance. You work yourself out of a job rather than trying to maintain yourself in a position or your organization." As Baker said, strong people don't need strong leaders.

In October 1961 SNCC sent two field secretaries, Charles Sherrod and Cordell Reagon, both of whom were veterans of the Freedom Rides and of SNCC's project in McComb, into Albany, Georgia, where they hoped to help local people launch a mass movement. They would soon be joined by Charles Jones, another SNCC veteran of the Freedom Rides and voter registration work. Within a month the SNCC group, the local NAACP Youth Council, and several other community groups had formed a broad coalition called the Albany Movement that included local blacks from across social classes.

Due in large part to the SNCC field secretaries' prodding, what began as the Albany Movement's call for desegregated transportation facilities in the city soon developed into a wide-ranging, Bakerite program demanding fair employment, equal treatment in the local justice system, total desegregation, and mass voter registration. As it attracted people from across social classes, the Albany Movement was becoming the kind of mass movement Baker had been trying to foment all her adult life.

A sleepy, small, south Georgia city of roughly sixty thousand people where African Americans made up about two-fifths of the total population, Albany had a larger and more comfortable black middle class than most southern cities of its size because it was the home of Albany State College, a historically black institution with a conservative administration. According to Clayborne Carson, Albany had "a history of generally peaceful if unequal relations" between whites and blacks. The whites who held power in Albany did not intend to ease constraints on their black neighbors, much less share power with them, but then they had never had to deal with anyone like Cordell Reagon or Charles Sherrod before.

Reagon was only eighteen years old when he got to Albany. He had suspended his studies at Tennessee State University to work full time for SNCC. He had already been arrested and spent time in Mississippi jails for his part in the Freedom Rides, and he had literally risked his life to register black voters in McComb, so there was little Georgia authorities could do to scare him off. Indeed, his personal style reflected his lack of fear and struck some in Albany as flamboyant, even foolhardy. Charles Sherrod provided something of a contrast personality-wise, but he was equally devoted to direct action and could be as audacious as he needed to be to draw attention to injustice. The oldest of six children raised by a single mother in the slums of Petersburg, Virginia, Sherrod had gone to work at a young age to help support his family. He also continued his studies, working, as he put it, "as hard as any two men getting through" Virginia Union University, where he was a religion major. He earned his second bachelor's degree from Virginia Union, in Divinity, shortly before moving to Albany. By then he was a thoughtful, gifted organizer who had been fully formed in the Baker mold.

Sherrod had been attracted to SNCC in the first place because he felt deeply that the sit-ins and other direct-action campaigns allowed him to live out his understanding of "the radical implications of Christianity." He was determined, he said, "to go ahead in a new way—maybe not the way the whites have shown . . . We are *not* the puppets of the white man. We want a different world where *we* can speak, where *we* can communicate." Creating that world was, of course, easier said than done, as Sherrod well knew. When he, Reagon, and Jones began organizing in Albany, they discovered that "people were afraid, really afraid." Their first order of business, Sherrod said, was to remove "the mental block in the minds of those who wanted to move but were unable for fear that we were not who we said we were."

They had to prove to the African American community of Albany that they were there for the long haul, and that they could work with different segments of the community rather than just a traditionally defined leadership class. "You don't achieve anything with the preachers, teachers and business-men until you work with the common people first," Reagon said, echoing Baker's early-1940s dispatches from the field to NAACP headquarters. Sher-rod organized in "churches, social meetings, on the streets, in the pool halls, lunch rooms and night clubs." He told anyone who would listen "how it feels to be . . . in jail for the cause . . . that there were worse chains than jail and prison. We referred to the system that imprisons men's minds and robs them of creativity. We mocked the system that teaches men to be good Negroes instead of good men."

In early November they led a sit-in at the city's Trailways bus station to test compliance with the Interstate Commerce Commission ruling that out-lawed racial discrimination in interstate transportation terminals, a direct result of the Freedom Rides. The station was in a black neighborhood, and the protest attracted a large crowd of African American onlookers. Sherrod saw in the eyes of the crowd "the expression of years of resentment—for police brutality, for poor housing, for disenfranchisement, for inferior educa-tion, for the whole damnable system." This was a protest against Jim Crow segregation, but Sherrod followed in Ella Baker's footsteps by making it "bigger than a hamburger." As planned, the group dispersed when threat-ened with arrest, but activists returned to the station later in the month. The day before Thanksgiving three high school students, members of the NAACP Youth Council, were arrested for refusing to leave the section of the waiting room designated for whites. They accepted bail and went home to their families, but Chief of Police Laurie Pritchett arrested another small group of Albany State students later in the day. Denied bail, they spent the holiday in jail.

The arrests captured the attention of all of Albany's black community in a way that previous incidents had not. The Albany Movement convinced the leaders of prestigious Mount Zion Baptist Church to host a mass meeting that drew a huge and energetic crowd. The high school and college students described their arrests and experiences in jail. Reagon and two local students, Rutha Harris (who had grown up in Albany, gone off to Florida A&M for college, and returned to Albany to be part of the movement) and Bernice

Johnson (who attended Albany State), led the audience in singing "freedom songs," some of which were updated slave spirituals and some of which were songs from the labor movement that had been repurposed for the black freedom struggle.

Full-throated singing of freedom songs would become the hallmark of the Albany Movement. "When I opened my mouth and began to sing" that night, Bernice Johnson said, "there was a force and power within myself I had never heard before. Somehow this music . . . released a kind of power and required a level of concentrated energy I did not know I had." Hundreds of attendees at the mass meeting could have said the same; the freedom songs unleashed depths of emotion that the veteran organizers Reagon and Sherrod had never seen before. "By the end of the evening the emotional surge in the Mount Zion sanctuary had surpassed Reagon and Sherrod's wildest expectations," Raymond Arsenault writes, "spiritualizing the Albany Movement before their very eyes." Reagon, Harris, and Johnson formed the Albany Singers and then the Freedom Singers, a group that toured the country singing freedom songs to raise money for SNCC. (Later, Bernice Johnson, who had by then married and divorced Reagon, formed the popular a capella group Sweet Honey in the Rock, which introduced the songs and the traditions from which they sprang to even wider audiences.)

Alas, the movement spirit that the Freedom Singers released in Albany could not contain movement rivalries. The national office of the NAACP instructed its local chapter not to work with SNCC through the Albany Movement. Only weeks after the SNCC field secretaries arrived, a contingent of the Albany Movement invited Dr. King and the SCLC to town to address a mass meeting. King biographer Adam Fairclough writes, "King arrived in the southwest Georgia town having promised to make a speech. But he stayed to lead a march, was arrested and jailed, and found himself embroiled in a remarkable protest movement."

Vincent Harding, a movement historian who was active in SCLC and other organizations in campaigns throughout the South, recalled one image above all others from the time he spent in Albany. As a group of ministers—all male—jockeyed at the front of Shiloh Baptist Church for position on a mass meeting program the night of King's arrival, Ella Baker sat at a table in the back of the church, working. As a long line of local people who had been arrested or otherwise punished for attempting to register to vote or for protesting Jim Crow filed by, Baker made a list of what they needed to survive. One woman's son was in jail without toiletries, another's landlord had threatened to evict her if she kept attending those meetings: Couldn't Baker find a way to help them? Speeches are important, but it was that kind of unheralded grunt work, invariably performed by women such as Baker, that sustained the civil rights movement.

King delivered his speech at Shiloh Baptist Church on December 15 and found *himself* moved by the movement spirit in Albany—the strongest he had felt since Montgomery, he said—so he agreed to lead a protest march the next day. King was one of 257 arrested by police chief Laurie Pritchett, and he announced that he was prepared to spend Christmas in jail. His SCLC lieutenants attempted to capitalize on the incident, raising funds to be used on what they expected would be a campaign every bit as dramatic and drawn out as the Montgomery bus boycott. Instead, the factionalized Albany Movement agreed to call off protests in exchange for the release of the 257 prisoners. A confused King left jail after only a night. The Albany Movement was disintegrating into factions, but King continued to enjoy the widespread support of the black community.

The students in the Albany Movement, whose base of support was much more narrow, took to mocking King, quite unfairly, as "De Lawd," a self-important blowhard worshipped by the ignorant masses. Fairclough blames Baker for the rift, believing that the former SCLC executive director "egged on" the SNCC field secretaries and the young people they influenced. Nearly everyone associated with SCLC shared the belief, blaming Baker for the organizational rivalries that destroyed the Albany Movement in the short term. Baker, of course, would have disagreed strongly with that assessment. She left the SCLC precisely because she had been unable to convince the organization to organize a campaign like the Albany Movement. Now, under her tutelage the students had organized a legitimate mass movement in southwest Georgia. No sooner did they have it up and running than (from their perspective and Baker's) the SCLC barged in and demanded that King call the shots. If Baker really did fan the flames of organizational discord (which is by no means a settled question), she did so by raising legitimate critiques of SCLC, based on her own long experience with the organization and her set of ideas on organizing.

It is indisputable that Baker encouraged the students and local people in Albany (and elsewhere) not to get caught up in hero worship when they should have been building community institutions. It is almost certain that she encouraged the Albany Movement to distance itself from King and the SCLC after having invited them in. But any effort to blame Baker for what various civil rights historians have termed a "defeat," a "fiasco," and "a debacle that verged on farce" misses the point entirely, and in more ways than one.

The party responsible for the Albany Movement's failure in 1961 to 1962 was not any one of its factions but its major adversary, Pritchett. The chief of police and the town's ruling elite seemed to have been caught off guard when the SNCC-orchestrated direct-action campaign kicked off that fall, but they regrouped quickly. Pritchett went so far as to read *Stride Toward Freedom*, King's book about the Montgomery bus boycott, to better understand nonviolent tactics. He consulted with public officials in other southern cities that had been able to blunt black activism, trained his officers to remain (mostly) cool and calm in the face of protests, and contracted with neighboring towns and counties for additional jail space so that the Albany Movement could not force Albany officials to the negotiating table by filling his jails. His strategy worked splendidly.

Pritchett's coup de grace came in August 1962, when King returned to Albany to stand trial for the previous December's arrest. Found guilty and sentenced to a $178 fine or forty-five days in jail, King went to jail and vowed to stay there and serve his sentence while the Albany Movement intensified public protests. But Pritchett worked out a plan with Albany's mayor: King was more valuable to the movement in jail, where he would attract the sympathy of local blacks who would then be more willing to protest and draw the attention of national media outlets, so they arranged to spring him from jail. Mayor Asa Kelly anonymously paid the $178 fine, and King had no choice but to leave jail a free man. Not long after that he left Albany for good. Pritchett bragged that his city was "as segregated as ever" and that King's missteps in Albany had set back the cause of desegregation "at least ten years."

King and the leaders of the SCLC learned important lessons from the experience in Albany, which they put to great use the following year in the organization's major campaign in Birmingham. King himself said as much: "The mistake I made [in Albany] was to protest against segregation generally rather than against a single and distinct facet of it," he said. "Our protest was so vague that we got nothing, and the people were left very depressed and in despair. . . . When we planned our strategy for Birmingham months later, we spent many hours assessing Albany and trying to learn from its errors. Our appraisals not only helped to make our subsequent tactics more effective, but revealed that Albany was far from an unqualified failure."

SNCC and Baker learned important lessons in Albany, too. SNCC redoubled its efforts at voter registration and community organizing in Albany and the surrounding area through its Southwest Georgia Project. Sherrod emphasized that he was in Albany for the long haul, and he proved good to his word, working on a variety of SNCC-inspired community development projects over the coming years. His voter registration campaigns transformed the region's political economy, resulting in the election of hundreds of

African American officials (including Sherrod himself, who served on the Albany city council) in the 1970s and 1980s.

The influential leftist historian Howard Zinn both participated in and observed the 1961 to 1962 protests in Albany, and he followed the progress of the Albany Movement after the SCLC left. "It has often been said, by journalists, by scholars," Zinn wrote in his memoirs, "that Albany, Georgia, was a defeat for the movement, because there was no immediate victory over segregation in the city. That has always struck me as a superficial assessment." Zinn, who admired Baker so much that he dedicated his 1964 history of the organization, SNCC: The New Abolitionists (the first of its kind) to her, wrote, "Social movements may have many 'defeats'—failing to achieve victories in the short run—but in the course of the struggle the strength of the old order begins to erode, the minds of the people begin to change; the protesters are momentarily defeated but not crushed, and have been lifted, heartened, by their ability to fight back." From this perspective—the long-term perspective that Baker insisted movements needed to assume—the Albany Movement looks like anything but a failure.

Less than two years after they began the sit-ins with little planning, the students had established their own civil rights organization and gone into the Deep South to help local people develop programs, something the NAACP and SCLC had been unable to do. They had catalyzed and supported the first locally based mass movements since Montgomery a decade earlier, and they had launched a regionwide assault on white supremacy whose goals truly were "bigger than a hamburger." Few of these initiatives met with immediate success, but Baker counseled that process and leadership development were important in their own right—more important than short-term outcomes. They may not have achieved all of their goals, but thousands of African Americans in Mississippi, southwest Georgia, and elsewhere had discovered previously unknown powers within themselves and had begun to see ways by which they *could* defeat Jim Crow for good. SNCC's early campaigns laid the groundwork for the long-term community organizing and voter registration work that would fundamentally transform the South.

By the summer of 1962 SNCC had begun to focus the majority of its energies on Mississippi. Working under the umbrella group Council of Federated Organizations (COFO) and expanding on the methodology Moses's group had developed in McComb and refined with the help of Baker, the SCLC, and Highlander Center, SNCC field secretaries moved into black communities throughout the state to register voters and help those communities build their own institutions. Bob Moses directed the statewide VEP, backed by a grant the Kennedys arranged through the Southern Regional Council. The committed cadre of Mississippi natives, southern blacks who interrupted their college studies to work full time for the movement, and a sprinkling of white southerners and black and white northerners set out to remake Mississippi through voter registration.

They established beachheads in the Delta towns of Greenwood and Ruleville, in the central Mississippi town of Canton, in McComb and Hattiesburg in the southern part of the state, and elsewhere. A half century after the fact, it is difficult to comprehend the unconscionable amounts of violence and other forms of resistance they had to endure just to register voters. Black families who dared to make the trip to the registrar's office at the county courthouse or who hosted the civil rights workers in their homes had their houses shot up or firebombed. The Mississippi State Sovereignty Commission, an otherwise bumbling state version of the FBI that would have been comical if it hadn't abetted so much of the hatred and violence, shared license plate numbers and descriptions of the cars driven by SNCC and CORE organizers with local law enforcement. It did not take long for white gangs and sheriffs' deputies—in many cases it was difficult to distinguish between the two groups—to find the cars on rural roads, whereupon they harassed, assaulted, even murdered civil rights workers.

SNCC remained committed to the ideal Diane Nash had established in the Freedom Rides, but Baker did periodically have to remind the civil rights workers of the stakes involved. After SNCC's field secretaries retreated from McComb to Atlanta following an especially brutal round of retaliation from whites, Baker bucked them up and insisted they return. "It's going to be rough now," she told them. But they simply could not allow racist violence to deter them permanently. "We just have to stick it out. We can't leave. We've got to go back to McComb."

The students did go back to McComb. They persevered in Mississippi. In 1963 SNCC helped organize the Freedom Vote, a shadow campaign meant to prove beyond any doubt that African Americans wanted to vote in the state but were systematically prevented from doing so. On Election Day, civil rights workers and student volunteers recruited from West Coast and Ivy League universities helped local people organize elections with all the trappings of official elections, only with unsanctioned candidates and unregistered voters. The Freedom Vote ticket was integrated: Aaron Henry, a black pharmacist from Clarksdale who had worked closely with Baker in the SCLC and had gone on to become the chairman of the NAACP State Conference of Branches, was the Freedom Vote candidate for governor; Edwin ("Ed") King, the white liberal chaplain of Tougaloo College, ran for lieutenant governor. Baker had wrapped up her work for the SPHR and was now employed as a staff member of SCEF with a wide-open portfolio that allowed her to participate in get-out-the-Freedom-Vote rallies throughout southern Mississippi.

She witnessed the intimidation operation firsthand on Halloween night. George Greene, a SNCC field secretary, and Bruce Payne, a graduate student volunteer from Yale, picked up Baker at a home in Natchez, where she had just addressed a mass meeting, with plans to drive her to the nearby town of Port Gibson for another mass meeting. They told her that two other cars had followed theirs to the house; indeed, when Baker looked outside she saw two cars circling the neighborhood. Baker, Greene, and Payne agreed to make the trip to Port Gibson anyway, and the cars followed. When Payne stopped at a gas station and got out to ask for directions, the hoodlums who had been following him beat his face to a pulp, punching and kicking him and beating his head against a gas pump. He did not require hospitalization, however, so the trio traveled on to Port Gibson.

Incredibly, when Payne and Greene returned to Natchez the following day, the same men followed them. This time, Payne led the racists on a 105-mile-an-hour pursuit. He and Greene made it to safety in Jackson, but only after their attackers shot four holes in their car. "Do you think those fellows really intended to kill us?" Payne asked Ed King. "Those bullets really hit the car sorta low." King answered, "In Mississippi it is an error to confuse good intentions with poor aim."

Despite many such instances of intimidation, an estimated eighty-three thousand black Mississippians cast their ballots in the Freedom Vote in November 1963. That number fell far short of the campaign's goal of two hundred thousand votes (out of roughly five hundred thousand voting-age African Americans in the state), but it was statistically significant. If the civil rights workers could register that many black voters they could conceivably tip an official statewide election, or at the very least encourage elected officials to tone down the racist rhetoric and harassment. That gave SNCC and other civil rights groups a blueprint for the future—but it also gave the racists in power an incentive to dig in their heels and resist, as if they needed one.

A faction within SNCC associated with Bob Moses began pressing for an even more ambitious program to continue the momentum of the Freedom Vote. They argued that SNCC and its allies in Mississippi should invite an interracial group of volunteers into the state the following summer to further their shared goals of registering voters and bringing national attention to the horrors average black citizens had to face every day behind the Cotton Curtain. Only that national attention, they argued, could force Mississippi to change. But there were also powerful counterarguments. The white student volunteers on the Freedom Vote project were used to being in charge, and all too often they had barged in and taken over organically created initiatives. "I came into SNCC and saw Negroes running the movement and I felt good," said field secretary Ivanhoe Donaldson, "and then the whites take over leadership. We're losing the one thing where the Negro can stand first." How could untrained white college students help SNCC reach its primary goal in the state, which was to help native black Mississippians develop into leaders and to organize black communities? Staff secretary Willie Peacock (now Wazir Peacock) argued, "I know that if you bring white people to Mississippi and say, 'Negro, go and vote,' [black Mississippians would invariably answer,] 'Yassah, we'll go and try to register and vote.'" What would that really accomplish?

SNCC engulfed itself in the question of whether or not to invite scores of white students into the Magnolia State, and then how best to make use of them, debating the issues at meeting after meeting from the fall of 1963 through the following spring. Most members of SNCC remembered Baker as having sat through these marathon meetings and listened respectfully while the students spoke, but in truth the role she played was much more complicated. She may not have offered much beyond her gnomic suggestions and questions to the students in the larger meetings, but Baker spoke up forcefully in the SNCC Executive Committee meetings where policy was made and the most critical issues were decided. The more important those decisions were, the more she took charge.

The minutes of these meetings reveal that she actively shaped debates and weighed in on the decisions she wanted the students to make. The minutes of a four-day executive committee meeting at the end of 1963 record another adult adviser, Howard Zinn, offering long lectures on how other organizations had dealt with similar problems in the past. Baker could have delivered those kinds of lectures based entirely on her own experience, but instead she emphasized what SNCC could do to make itself different from all of the organizations that had come before it. "We place too much value on action and not enough on planning," she said, and advised SNCC to develop economic education programs for the field staff. SNCC should develop a research arm—essentially, a think tank—to compile empirical evidence, she said. SNCC could use that data to bolster its arguments in the court of public opinion, thereby making it a stronger force for change. Indeed, SNCC did just that. The SNCC Research Office produced county-by-county demographic reports and analytical papers that aimed to answer questions such as "Why Are Farm Laborers Poor?" Armed with empirical evidence about their communities provided by the Research Office, SNCC field secretaries could work that much more effectively.

In an April 1964 meeting the executive committee faced the most important questions the organization had had to consider since the direct-action/voter registration debate nearly divided SNCC for good in 1961. The committee had to firm up final plans for what was now being called the Mississippi Summer Project (or Freedom Summer), debate the merits of creating an alternative political party along the lines of the Freedom Vote ticket, and decide on the curriculum and operational plan for the alternative schools SNCC would found in Mississippi. All of these discussions involved the invariably thorny issue of the role whites would play in the movement. Roughly two dozen members of the committee participated in the daylong meeting. According to the meeting minutes, no one spoke more often or more authoritatively than Baker. Despite her reputation for leading from behind, it appears that the higher the stakes rose, the more involved Baker became in deliberations.

Nor was that behavior confined to executive committee meetings. SNCC member Judy Richardson was struck by "how involved Miss Baker could become in even the minutiae of the [Atlanta] office—but only if she was concerned about something." For those such as Richardson who worked in the headquarters office, Baker emphasized professionalism. If the students approached the problems they wanted to overcome seriously, she counseled with her deeds as much as her words; if they acted serious in public, they would have to be taken seriously.

Plans for Freedom Summer coalesced during the winter and spring. COFO would recruit dozens of black and white volunteers from around the country, but mainly from the Northeast and West Coast. Baker's goals for the project were at once simple and profoundly complex: "If we can simply let the con-cept that the rest of the nation bears responsibility for what happens in Mis-sissippi sink in, then we will have accomplished something," she said. She knew from experience that the rest of the nation would only pay attention to what happened to whites in Mississippi.

Once in the Magnolia State the volunteers would work with staffers from SNCC, CORE, the NAACP, and SCLC on three main initiatives: voter registration, "Freedom Schools," and an alternative political party. Voter registration continued the work Moses and others had been doing in the state since 1961. The Freedom Schools were a commonsense approach to the state's abysmal apartheid system of public schools, which spent nearly four times more on the education of each white student than it spent on each black student. Charles Cobb, a SNCC field secretary who had worked in the Delta since 1962, conceived the alternative schools program. Cobb wrote that the Freedom Schools would:

1. Supplement what [high school students] aren't learning in high schools around the state.
2. give them a broad intellectual and academic experience during the summer to bring back to fellow students in classrooms[,] and
3. form the basis of statewide student action such as school boycotts, based on their increased awareness.

In short, Cobb wanted to create a school system that presented an alternative set of values to those that students received in Mississippi schools, to teach black students how to be critical thinkers and citizens, and to help them build platforms from which they could launch and lead their own protest movements. The summer volunteers would get the Freedom Schools up and running, and hopefully by the end of the summer the program would be firmly enough established that SNCC field secretaries and local people could continue to run it after the volunteers returned home. His plans grew organically out of his experience living and working with blacks in the Mississippi Delta who had been systematically undereducated, tracked into low-paying agricultural work, and forcibly denied their constitutional rights as citizens. They were completely powerless as a result, even more vulnerable to the violence their white neighbors used to enforce a rigid social hierarchy than they would have been otherwise.

Even before proposing the Freedom Schools, Cobb had diagnosed the ills his neighbors faced and prescribed a solution. "What we have discovered over the past few years of our activities in the South," he wrote, "is that oppression and restriction is not limited to the bullets of local racist['s] shotgun blasts, or assaults at county courthouses, or the expulsion of sharecroppers from plantations[.]" The problem was as much cultural as it was political: "What is relevant to our lives is constantly defined for us," he said, by institutions such as mass media and the school system. The only way to break that cycle was to create institutions that local African Americans could control and use those institutions to propagate their own values, not the values of the society that defined them as not worth educating.

This was to be the purpose of the Freedom Schools. Cobb emphasized that COFO should target tenth- and eleventh-graders and plan curriculum accordingly, because the schools were meant not just to educate students but to train community organizers. He hoped that the students would "form the basis of statewide student action such as school boycotts, based on their increased awareness" the following school year. The schools succeeded beyond anyone's expectations, and they did indeed generate a new crop of politically engaged young people—more than two thousand of them, twice as many as COFO had hoped for—but the high school students were not the only ones to respond to the opportunity. Hundreds of adults, some of them in their seventies and eighties, jumped at the chance to attend Freedom Schools. They hoped to learn enough there to be able to pass voter registration tests, or to expand their horizons for other reasons. As Carolyn Reese, the program's coordinator in Hattiesburg, explained, "The Freedom Schools mean an exposure to a totally new field of learning, new attitudes about people, new attitudes about self, and about the right to be dissatisfied with the status quo."

Pam Parker (Chude Pam Parker Allen), a college student volunteer, described the environment in her Holly Springs Freedom School that summer:

> The atmosphere in the class is unbelievable. It is what every teacher dreams about—real, honest enthusiasm and desire to learn anything and everything. The girls come to class of their own free will. They respond to everything that is said. They are excited about learning. They drain me of everything that I have to offer so that I go home at night completely exhausted but very happy in spirit. . . . The girls respond, respond, respond. And they disagree among themselves. I have no doubt that soon they will be disagreeing with me. At least this is one thing I keep working towards. They are a sharp group. But they are under-educated and starved for knowledge. They know that they have been cheated and they want anything and everything we can give them.

Cobb's plans for the Freedom Schools owed an obvious intellectual debt to Baker. But nowhere was the line from Baker's ideas to SNCC's actions clearer or more direct than it was in the decision to create the Mississippi Freedom Democratic Party (MFDP), a radical alternative to the so-called regular, lily-white state party. The MFDP was to be a "political vehicle for people we worked with across the state," Bob Moses said. "It wouldn't be another SNCC or CORE, but an instrument in which communities could shape and articulate ideas and one that could move into political action." The MFDP would be a community-organizing machine much more so than a political machine, certainly much more so than nearly any other political party in U.S. history. Local people and party organizers (SNCC and COFO staffers) would create the party from scratch over the course of Freedom Summer, document their exclusion from the regular state party's proceedings, and then appeal for official recognition from the national party.

If the MFDP succeeded in winning that recognition, it would castrate the "regular" party, which included nearly every elected official in the state. That seemed impossible, but the MFDP could prove that the regulars had acted both antidemocratically (by excluding African Americans from party proceedings) and anti-Democratically (by bucking the national party at nearly every turn). Only the most optimistic believed that the Mississippi Freedom

Democratic Party had even an outside shot at winning the national party's seal of approval, much less winning elections in Mississippi, but the party served several useful purposes nonetheless. According to Barbara Ransby, Baker expected the MFDP either to "win a tactical victory, providing Mississippi activists with another tool with which to push for full freedom, or . . . [to] expose the limitations of mainstream party politics and strengthen the resolve of those same activists to find creative and truly democratic methods to realize radical social change." Even if the MFDP failed to win Mississippi's seats at the national convention, it would force the nation to acknowledge and reckon with the monumentally racist system MFDP delegates had to contend with every day of their lives and build momentum for change. At the very least, it would keep the national spotlight on the need for federal voting rights legislation.

Baker was determined that the MFDP would enter the party battle at the end of the summer with all the ammunition it could muster. From April to August she commuted from her home in Harlem to coordinate strategy from the MFDP's Washington, D.C., office. (Fortunately, SCEF was willing to pay Baker to perform these duties for the MFDP; had her employer not shared SNCC's goals, or been so generous, the Freedom Democrats' challenge could not have gotten off the ground.) While COFO volunteers and SNCC staffers drummed up support for the MFDP at the grass roots and helped local people build the party at the county level, Baker ran national publicity efforts, helped attorneys finalize the MFDP's legal tactics, lobbied party leaders and raised funds from labor organizations in Washington, forged relationships with Democratic party activists outside of the South, and arranged logistics for MFDP delegates at the national Democratic convention in Atlantic City.

On August 4 investigators found the corpses of Michael Schwerner, James Chaney, and Andrew Goodman, the three civil rights workers who had gone missing in Neshoba County at the beginning of the summer, in an earthen dam near Philadelphia, Mississippi. On August 6 the Freedom Democrats held their state convention at the Masonic Temple in Jackson, where an even larger crowd had attended the funeral of murdered state NAACP leader Medgar Evers the previous summer. The members of SNCC and the MFDP had argued in their own particular way—loudly, doggedly, yet respectfully and fraternally, not unlike the members of a family—over who should address the gathering as keynote speaker. One faction argued in favor of the political scientist and diplomat Ralph Bunche, winner of the Nobel Peace Prize in 1950, who certainly would have brought prestige and press attention to the budding party. Others wanted to invite Secretary of Agriculture Orville L. Freeman in order to forge a bond with a national party insider.

Working as a staff member for the MFDP, Casey Hayden even asked Baker to extend the invitation to Bunche first and Freeman second if Bunche was unavailable. While Baker mulled that over, however, Bob Moses prevailed on her to address the convention herself.

Baker demurred; surely the party needed the attention only a political celebrity could bring to Jackson. But Moses pressed her: Hadn't Baker always said that the people needed to respect themselves enough to make their own decisions, not fawn over celebrity leaders? Hadn't she staked her entire career on the idea that only the empowerment of ordinary people, not the flowery words of elites, could lead to real social change? Baker had proved to ordinary Mississippians that she was one of them, and they responded to her message. They needed to hear from her again, Moses said. Baker agreed to make the speech and traveled from New York the morning the convention was to begin.

Aaron Henry, the president of the NAACP State Conference of Branches and chairman of the MFDP, gaveled the convention to order that afternoon in triple-digit heat. An observer at the Masonic Temple would have seen the requisite red, white, and blue bunting and streamers—the staffers worked hard to make this look like a *real* political convention—in the hot and stuffy auditorium, but her eye would have been drawn to the county names on the placards designating seating areas for the various local delegations. The mellifluous sound of the names contrasted sharply with the violent recent history of the places: Tallahatchie, Amite, Sunflower, Neshoba.

Washington attorney and Democratic Party insider Joseph L. Rauh Jr. spoke first. He detailed the strategy the MFDP would need to pursue to win the national party's recognition and gain Mississippi's seats at the national convention to take place in Atlantic City, New Jersey, later that month. Then Moses introduced Baker, who stood in an outfit an observer described as a "neat cotton suit and fashionable straw hat," and she began to speak. Another observer recalled of Baker's appearance that day, "She was a lady in charge of herself." "We must consider this a demonstration of the people of Mississippi that they are determined to be a part of the body politic of Mississippi," Baker boomed. "We are here to demonstrate the right of the governed to elect those who govern, *here*, in *this* state." She referred here to several of Mississippi's elected officials, who claimed that blacks didn't vote in the state because they did not care about politics, not because they were systematically disfranchised.

Baker had a tough row to hoe. She was addressing a group of people who were, to put it bluntly, political illiterates, through no fault of their own. Most had never voted, because they had never been allowed to register.

Before that summer not a single one of them had ever so much as attended a countywide political convention—the leaders of the Mississippi Democratic and Republican parties had made sure of that—but with help from the SNCC staffers and COFO volunteers they had formed their own political party. Most of them had grade-school educations, but they were determined to show the world that they had both the will and the capacity to act as full and equal citizens in a representative democracy. Baker had to educate and inspire the delegates. The MFDP also needed to communicate to people outside of Mississippi that it was a legitimate state party, and it could do that by putting on a show that looked like the other state parties' shows. But Baker had no use for stagecraft, and she was entirely unwilling to speak down to her audience.

She was typically militant and uncompromising. Alluding to the week's grim discovery of the civil rights workers' corpses, she thundered, "Until the killing of black mothers' sons is as important as the discovery of white mothers' sons, we who believe in freedom cannot rest." She allowed, "Now this is not the kind of keynote speech, perhaps, you'd like. But I'm not trying to make you feel good." Baker made no mention of the seats in Atlantic City in the speech. Instead she embraced the role of educator. "We have to know what we're dealing with and we can't deal with things just because we feel we ought to have our rights," she told the crowd. "We deal with them on the basis of knowledge that we gain through using people that have the knowledge . . . through sending our children through certain kinds of courses, through sitting down [and] reading at night instead of spending our time at the television and radio just listening to what's on."

She delivered a brief African American history lesson to put the MFDP's efforts in context. "It has never been true that the Negro people were satisfied," she said. "It was never true even in the darkest days of slavery. . . . True, there has been some accommodation to slavery. But the sit-ins ended the leadership of the accommodating type of leader." The audience interrupted with chants of "Freedom! Freedom!" Baker challenged the delegates to discover for themselves what truly gave meaning to their lives. "Big cars do not give meaning. Place in the power structure does not give meaning." Then she analyzed the power structure in terms they could all understand.

Why do you suppose, she asked, that white landowners in Mississippi always made the male heads of their sharecropping families deal with the landowners' wives at "settlement time," the postharvest period when the landowner settled accounts? The delegates nodded in understanding. That way, if the landowner cheated the sharecropper by shorting the amount of cotton his family had raised or added phantom expenses to the family's ledger (two common occurrences), the sharecropper could not complain, lest the white woman charge the black man with ungentlemanly behavior—a death sentence in Mississippi. It was this system, as much as the political system that had disfranchised them, that the MFDP was fighting. "You are waging a war against the closed society of Mississippi," she said. "You have not let physical fear immobilize you. And there is that other fear—the fear of communism. The red-smear which is part of the effort of the power structure to maintain itself and maintain its stranglehold" on power. "But we have sense enough to know who is using us and who is abusing us."

The delegates chanted "Freedom!" again. The stage managers led them in Freedom Songs and marched them around the auditorium behind their county placards: Issaquena, Tishomingo, Oktibbeha. "This was probably the most soul-felt march ever to occur in a political convention," one journalist wrote. The television cameras recorded all the sounds and visuals of a proper political convention, and the members elected sixty-eight delegates to represent the party at the national convention. The MFDP accomplished what it had set out to do at the state convention, but its hardest work lay ahead. Still, by Baker's yardstick the Freedom Democrats had already succeeded: The MFDP had gotten poor, rural African Americans to think of themselves as political actors. It had provided them with opportunities to lead, and they had responded beautifully.

When the MFDP delegates to the national convention arrived at the best hotel they could afford in Atlantic City, the Gem (where everyone agreed that the accommodations made a mockery of the hotel's name), they had a strong moral claim to Mississippi's seats in the convention hall, and they allowed themselves to believe that they would be seated. Baker had procured public support for the MFDP challenge from ten state delegations, several party insiders, powerful unions such as the United Auto Workers and interest groups such as Americans for Democratic Action, and civil rights establishment figures such as King, A. Philip Randolph, and Roy Wilkins of the NAACP. She had even compiled a database with the local contact information for every member of the national party's credentials committee, the expected dates of their arrival in Atlantic City, and a best guess at how likely they were to vote in favor of seating the MFDP. She had done the MFDP's homework.

Despite the MFDP's strong moral position, however, a steely-eyed, experienced observer such as Baker gave the Freedom Democrats no more than a slight chance of winning the national party's recognition. As she well knew, the all-white Mississippi regulars had no intention of relinquishing the seats. True, they refused to pledge allegiance to President Johnson, and yes, many of them had even driven cars with "AuH$_2$0" bumper stickers (barely disguised endorsements of Johnson's opponent, Republican presidential nominee Sen. Barry Goldwater) to their own state convention in Jackson. But for those steeped in national party management, the risk of offending whites far outweighed the reward of honoring the nearly all-black MFDP, no matter how loyal the latter's members were to Democratic ideals. Lyndon Johnson had bravely gambled his political capital on the legislation that became the 1964 Civil Rights Act earlier that summer, but it seemed unwise, to put it mildly, to risk further alienating white southern voters by siding with the Freedom Democrats. Such a move, he worried, would shift the "Solid South" from the Democratic to the Republican column for a generation or more.

Thanks to Baker's background work, the Freedom Democrats arrived with piles of affidavits in hand proving that the regulars had discriminated against them and had systematically denied them their rights as American citizens. They could fairly easily make the case that they had the stronger moral claim to Mississippi's seats. But the legal evidence and the appeals to party leaders' morality would have to overcome an ironclad political reality: The Democrats needed to hold on to the South to continue winning national elections. Holding on to the South meant, at a minimum, not alienating white southern voters. (Unfortunately, Texas governor John Connally spoke for many southern white Democrats when he objected to seating what he called the "baboons" of the MFDP.) Forcing the "regulars" out of the convention would be akin to committing electoral suicide, or so the party leaders feared. Then again, the MFDP only had to convince a majority of the members of the party's credentials committee, which was responsible for adjudicating exactly this sort of argument.

Baker was used to such odds, and in any case she considered the MFDP's fight a means to an end more than an end unto itself. She arranged for Rauh, Aaron Henry, Martin Luther King Jr., and Fannie Lou Hamer, a sharecropper from Sunflower County, Mississippi, who had come to embody SNCC's "Let the People Decide" mantra, to testify before the party's credentials committee. This was high-stakes drama, and the national television networks arranged to televise the testimony live on the afternoon of August 22, a Saturday.

Hamer absolutely stole the show. In plain yet electrifying language, she explained what her attempts to exercise her rights as a citizen had gotten her. Because she had tried to register to vote, she and her husband had been evicted from the plantation where they had worked for years, and nightriders had shot up the house she moved into. Because she was part of a group that had gone into a whites-only restaurant and asked to be served with dignity, she had been jailed and beaten viciously in Winona, Mississippi, the previous summer. She still walked with a limp. "All of this is on account of we want to register, to become first-class citizens," she boomed. "And if the Freedom Democratic Party is not seated now, I question America. Is this America, the land of the free and the home of the brave, where we have to sleep with our telephones off the hooks because our lives be threatened daily, because we want to live as decent human beings, in America?"

Lyndon Johnson made a choice. Rather than side with the party of political neophytes who did, after all, support his party and him personally, Johnson threw his weight behind the institution in Mississippi that may have represented the interests of white supremacy and oligarchy more effectively than any other, the state Democratic Party—the regulars. He felt threatened enough by the attention paid to the Freedom Democrats, and the possibility that the credentials committee might seat them and cause the regulars to walk out of the convention, that he called an impromptu press conference at the White House while Hamer testified. The television networks dutifully cut away from Hamer to cover the president, but his plan backfired that night when they played a tape of Hamer in full during prime time. He would have to do more than call a press conference to neutralize the threat, but backroom politicking was his specialty.

Johnson's aides began calling in favors and issuing threats to members of the credentials committee to ensure that the committee would side with the regulars and avoid a white walkout. He pulled out all the stops. FBI Director J. Edgar Hoover bugged Martin Luther King Jr.'s hotel room in Atlantic City and relayed the overheard discussions on MFDP strategy to the White House in almost real time. In the words of historian John Dittmer, the Johnson machine's performance at Atlantic City was "a Watergate that worked."

The president also presented a cynical quid pro quo arrangement to Sen. Hubert Humphrey of Minnesota. Knowing full well how badly Humphrey wanted to make it onto the national ticket as vice president, Johnson told him the spot was his if he could make the MFDP problem go away. With his ally Walter Mondale, Humphrey cobbled together a "compromise" plan that left the regulars in Mississippi's seats, awarded two at-large seats to the MFDP, and pledged that the party would not seat all-white, undemocratically selected delegations at future conventions. This could conceivably have been an acceptable half-a-loaf arrangement that satisfied Baker and the MFDP and deserved the name *compromise*, but it had been constructed without any input from Freedom Democrats. The deal was a fait accompli by the time Humphrey and Mondale even presented it to the MFDP. Baker, who believed that the processes a group used to arrive at a decision were as important as the decision itself, could hardly support it.

Party chairman Aaron Henry was inclined to accept (under the terms of the arrangement he would get one of the two seats; Ed King, the white chaplain from Tougaloo College, would get the other), but the rank and file, led by Hamer, overruled him. "We didn't come all this way for no two seats," she declared. The discussion itself marked a turning point: Baker had instructed the SNCC staff to sit back and observe rather than offer advice, but it appeared in retrospect that the party members were self-confident enough that they would not have needed the staff's guidance anyway. "The local people knew that they had done it right and they didn't buckle," Casey Hayden said. "The SNCC staff didn't have to influence the delegation. They didn't yield to pressure to accept the compromise because they knew they had legitimately elected their delegation and were correct."

The Freedom Democrats may have been unprepared for the hurly-burly of party politics, but they were determined to play the game and, if possible, learn from it. They debated the merits of the compromise and heard from a long line of labor and civil rights leaders who for the most part encouraged them to accept its terms, often in dismissive language. Bayard Rustin encouraged the Freedom Democrats to accept the deal, believing that it was time to evolve from a protest group putting on a morality play into a political party engaged in the nitty-gritty of real politics. When it appeared that MFDP delegates would vote to reject the deal, Walter Reuther, leader of the United Auto Workers, chastised them for their "completely irrational" stance. Roy Wilkins called the Freedom Democrats who wanted to reject the deal "ignorant." King acknowledged that as "a Negro leader" he believed the MFDP should accept the compromise and work from within the party, but if he were "a Mississippi Negro" in their shoes he would probably vote against the deal because it had been arrived at undemocratically and did little if anything to advance their interests. Perhaps Baker's philosophy had rubbed off on him after all.

While these discussions were ongoing, national party leaders sucker punched the MFDP. Rauh and others announced to the press that the MFDP had accepted the compromise. (Rauh insisted that he had been misquoted.) Johnson pounced, praising the decision—when in fact the MFDP had not yet come close to arriving at a decision. Baker got the news at a meeting of the Nebraska delegation, where she was lobbying members to vote to unseat the Mississippi regulars. Now the MFDP had to choose between putting on a happy public face, accepting the compromise, and supporting the national party, or appearing to renege on what had already been reported as a done deal. Rauh and other white liberals with strong ties to party leaders urged the former course—after all, Lyndon Johnson and Hubert Humphrey needed their help to lead a united party into the November election—but Baker believed that taking it would betray every one of their shared values.

At a public meeting on August 25 she said so. Following remarks from Rauh she spat, "I don't care about traitors like Humphrey" and launched into a denunciation of the man she had recruited to be the MFDP's attorney. In no uncertain terms she told Rauh that she resented powerful people like him telling desperately powerless sharecroppers from Mississippi that Humphrey's and Johnson's needs superseded their own. "She just cut me to ribbons," Rauh remembered much later in an oral history. Still somewhat in awe of the performance decades after the fact, he mused, "If you're going to get it, might as well get it from an expert . . . and I got it from an expert. She just cut me up."

Following a SNCC-style, all-night meeting in which everyone had a say, the MFDP delegates voted to reject the compromise. A handful of Freedom Democrats did obtain credentials from sympathetic delegates from outside of Mississippi that allowed them inside the convention. Once there they attempted to occupy Mississippi's seats. (Most of the regulars had refused to swear loyalty to the national party and had left the convention, but Johnson did at least avoid the televised walkout he had feared.) The attempted sit-in caused another media commotion, but it was short-lived. On August 27 Lyndon Johnson and Hubert Humphrey accepted their party's nomination as president and vice president, respectively, and in November they trounced the Republican ticket of Barry Goldwater and William E. Miller. Goldwater won 87 percent of the vote in Mississippi, where African Americans were still systematically prevented from voting.

"Atlantic City was a watershed in the movement because up until then the idea had been that you were working more or less within the Democratic party," Bob Moses said. "We were working with them on voting, other things like that. With Atlantic City, a lot of people became disillusioned. . . . You turned around and your support [within the national party] was puddle-deep." Baker concurred wholeheartedly. The experience had "settled any debate" over "the possibility of functioning through the mainstream of the Democratic Party," she said. But it had also provided the Freedom Democrats and the young people of SNCC the best political education they could have dreamed of obtaining. They returned to Mississippi with a much clearer understanding of how power operated in the American political system, to say the very least.

The Atlantic City challenge was Baker's, and the civil rights movement's, grandest failure. But what a failure! Anyone who wanted to participate in the

MFDP could and did according to the talents one could offer; one's income, education, and gender made little difference in how one participated in party activities. One of the most small-*d* democratic political parties of its size or ambition in American history to that time, it was also the least classist and least sexist. The 1964 experience forced the national party to recognize state parties that looked and acted more like the MFDP than the Mississippi regulars beginning in 1968. Never again would the Democratic National Committee seat an all-white state delegation.

The MFDP opened doors to women of all races, and women participated in much greater numbers in the MFDP relative to other parties. In fact, party chairman Lawrence Guyot, a native of Pass Christian, Mississippi, and recent graduate of Tougaloo College, noticed the lack of men in the MFDP and halfway jokingly told a group of women at a party meeting, "Y'all step back a little bit and let the men move in now." Baker took him to a corner of the meeting hall out of earshot of the other attendees and set him straight: "Ella Baker told me, 'You have proven that there are *some* men who can do a very good job but you have to learn [to] never, never make the mistake of substituting men in quantity for women of quality.' I haven't done that shit anymore," Guyot said. "In fact, I've gone the other way around."

Baker provided assistance to Hamer and two other members of the MFDP, Annie Devine and Victoria Gray, as they extended the party's challenge into 1965, but the real story here was the dog that didn't bark—the help she didn't have to provide. The three women were candidates for U.S. House seats, and they challenged the seating of their victorious white male opponents on the grounds that African Americans had been "systematically and deliberately excluded from the electoral process" in Mississippi. The House of Representatives ultimately seated Mississippi's entire all-white delegation, but the Freedom Democrats' gambit again forced Congress to acknowledge the reality of voting discrimination and added momentum to the push for what would become the Voting Rights Act. Most significantly, from Baker's point of view, the MFDP managed the seating challenge more or less autonomously, albeit with some help from SNCC and other friends. MFDP members constructed the strategy, arranged the publicity campaigns, did the lobbying—in other words, all the work that Baker had done for the party in 1964. By 1965 she could step back and allow the people to lead themselves. She had worked herself out of a job.

Baker's involvement with SNCC waned from then on. She remained on SCEF's payroll until 1967, mainly providing subject-matter expertise to community-organizing projects throughout the South and advising Anne Braden on organizational strategy. Baker consulted for and served on SCEF's board for several years thereafter, and she remained involved in an impressive array of antiracist, antiwar, and feminist campaigns and organizations throughout the 1970s even as her health declined, but she retired from full-time activism. Weaning herself from SNCC gracefully had to have been the toughest challenge. "SNCC had been her political family; the group made her feel at home more than any other organization with which she had been affiliated," Barbara Ransby writes. "In the end, there was not a sharp break but a gradual drift and erosion of the relationship."

SNCC staffers who in 1964 would never have considered making a move without first discussing it with "Miss Baker" made their own decisions and did not even bother to invite her to meetings by 1966. She took it in stride. Joanne Grant, Baker's friend from SNCC days and later her biographer, described the dynamic Baker had tried to infuse in the organization: "She instilled in them the idea that they were not organized to exist in perpetuity as an organization, that others would come along to continue the struggle, and that the struggle is continuous. 'The tribe increases,' she always said." A SNCC community organizer's job may have been to make herself superfluous, and an organizational leader's role in SNCC may have been to train others to take over that role, but that did not make it any easier on a personal level to step aside and watch the organization continue on the new leaders' terms.

By 1966 SNCC had accomplished so much so fast that the students could not agree on the organization's next steps. Congress had recently passed and President Johnson signed into law the most powerful civil rights statutes since Reconstruction. The 1964 Civil Rights Act, a direct response to the sit-ins, Freedom Rides, and SCLC's direct action campaign in Birmingham, finally outlawed Jim Crow in public accommodations. The Voting Rights Act of 1965, which finally put teeth into the Fifteenth Amendment a century after its ratification, resulted from SNCC's and SCLC's voter registration and mass mobilization campaigns in Mississippi and Alabama. Much work remained to be done to guarantee the laws' robust enforcement and to maintain pressure on the national government to end other vestiges of Jim Crow, but at this moment SNCC grew weary of community organizing and turned its attention inward.

Baker supported SNCC publicly and defended the students' right to make their own decisions while most of the rest of the civil rights coalition viciously attacked SNCC's move toward "Black Power" ideology. Baker never quite agreed with separatism or cultural nationalism, though she had organized black consumers exclusively in Harlem and had organized primarily with, among, and for African Americans in the NAACP, SCLC, and

SNCC. She emphasized that her goal had always been to organize blacks along a parallel track with efforts to organize whites, in the hope that those tracks would eventually converge. Throughout her career, Baker had emphasized the need for class-conscious rainbow coalitions. "The logical groups for blacks to coalesce with would be the impoverished white, the misrepresented and impoverished Indians . . . or the alienated Mexican American. These are the natural allies in my book," she said in 1967. She had always gladly built coalitions with whites and others, and she had a huge stable of personal friends representing all sorts of ethnic groups.

Stokely Carmichael adopted "Black Power" as a rallying cry during a 1966 protest march. The idea of Black Power was born of Carmichael's experience as an organizer in Mississippi and Alabama, but it quickly became an amorphous ideological basis for the new SNCC. Younger people within and outside of SNCC took it up as a slogan. Coming from their mouths, Baker thought, "the rhetoric was far in advance of the organization for achieving that which you say you're out to achieve." In other words, it was the opposite of a program, little more than hot air.

Carmichael defeated John Lewis in the election for SNCC's chairman in May 1966, and in December of that year the organization encouraged whites to leave and form their own group to organize in the white community, a move that many interpreted as antiwhite and certainly separatist. In this context, "Black Power" sounded like a homonym of "Black Supremacy" to white liberals, but in some ways it was merely a warmed-over version of SNCC's time-tested demand for self-determination for black communities. Baker defended Carmichael and SNCC on these grounds, but she did not identify with the Black Power mind-set, and she regretted SNCC's eventual decision to part ways with whites. Mostly, she worried that Black Power adherents quickly became too enamored of their own press coverage. "I think they got caught up in their own rhetoric," she said. "These youngsters with their own need for recognition began to respond to the press."

Tellingly, when Baker got word that the expulsion plan was in the works, she arranged to travel with Joanne Grant and Bob Zellner, arguably SNCC's most stalwart white member and organizer, to the December 1966 staff meeting at the entertainer Peg Leg Bates's hotel in upstate New York where the organization would debate and accept the plan. "She told me that she had been talking to people and that there was a strong move to make the organization [an all-] black organization so that it could be more effective in the north," Zellner said. "I kept thinking that Joanne and Ella were treating me almost like I was sick and only they could bring me comfort." They prepared him for the news and allowed him to prepare a response. The meeting was the last SNCC meeting at which whites were welcome. It also marked the end of Baker's participation in the group.

Baker had devoted her career as a civil rights activist to the core belief that interracial groups working with southern blacks over the long term could effect real social change, and she had helped the students form SNCC in that image. After 1966 SNCC embraced internationalism, pursuing coalitions with freedom-fighting groups in Africa, Asia, and the Caribbean. Baker cheered that development, but SNCC also rejected interracialism and turned its attention from the South and from developing leadership-development programs. In the words of movement historian Clayborne Carson, SNCC gradually became ineffective in these years as it "became embroiled in bitter factional battles and failed to sustain local black movements in the South." In Baker's mind, if SNCC was no longer interested in assisting local leaders in the Black South or organizing local groups who would solve their own problems, then the students had moved past a point at which she could be useful to them. It was the move away from community organizing, not the move away from interracialism, that forced Baker to drift away from SNCC.

There was little left to connect her to the organization at that point, but Baker's personal relationships with the students never wavered. She served on the board of directors, and later as president, of the New York–based Fund for Educational and Legal Defense, Inc. (FELD), a foundation created explicitly to channel funds to burned-out civil rights workers, from 1965 to 1976. FELD mainly supported students who had dropped out of college to work for SNCC and needed help with tuition payments in order to resume their studies, but among other things it also furnished legal aid for political prisoners; supported Bob and Dorothy Zellner's Grass Roots Organizing Work (GROW) Project, which organized antiracist programs in white communities, and Charles Sherrod's New Communities, Inc., a cooperative farming venture in southwest Georgia; and backed Julian Bond's legal challenges against the Georgia state legislature.

It would be more accurate to say that SNCC left Baker than that Baker left SNCC, but she betrayed no bitterness toward the students. And how could she have, after insisting that they deserved the freedom to make their own decisions—even those with which she might disagree? Besides, as she said at a mass meeting in Hattiesburg, Mississippi, at the height of SNCC's influence, "I was never working for an organization; I have always tried to work for a cause." She thought that SNCC ceased to be an effective force for social change—but from Baker's viewpoint, that was simply what large organizations working under incredible stress did. They had short shelf lives; they became ineffective, devolved into vehicles for hero worship, or imploded.

Baker kept working for a cause, and she continued to cultivate her relationships with the young people of SNCC.

Those bonds remained incredibly strong and remarkably warm. The organization's philosophy may have changed, but dozens of SNCC organizers remained committed to Baker's vision for social change, and to Baker personally. They cherished her ability to educate and empower. Bernice Johnson Reagon recalled, "If Miss Baker questioned you and then said it looks like you've thought it through[,] you really felt like somebody just slipped a foundation under you." Joanne Grant wrote, "Miss Baker, who nurtured all of us in SNCC, most certainly helped me to grow, to understand, to be tolerant, and above it all to take it slow, relax, not take anything too seriously. . . . Miss Baker kept me calm." She also emphasized that Baker's vision lived on in the work of the young people she had inspired long after she retired from full-time activism: "We are the inheritors of Ella Baker's teaching that ordinary people can do what is needed to help themselves."

SNCC women had special reasons for wanting to emulate Baker. Jean Wiley recalled, "SNCC was the first and only time in my life that my gender was not a barrier to my aspirations. I'd love it for that, if nothing else." Baker personified SNCC's ethos and organizational culture in this as in so many other ways. Because the students looked to Baker for examples of how to organize effectively, how to work professionally, and how to live a life committed to the cause of social justice, their organization was perhaps the least sexist institution of its kind in its time. This may seem faint praise in retrospect, but it meant the world to the young women of SNCC, who, like Baker, refused to accept gendered limitations in their professional or personal lives. Mary King came to believe that not only was "Ella Baker . . . catalytic to the start of SNCC and . . . became its single most important philosophical and strategic influence" but also that "she is one of this century's key voices in American political struggle. Her vision of the leadership potential in each person, the ability of each of us to take responsibility for him- or herself rather than submit to authority, and the necessity for the oppressed to define their own freedom will be as pertinent tomorrow as these insights were to us then."

Native Mississippians who got to know Baker through SNCC and the MFDP described her influence in remarkably similar ways: They marveled at her ability to say things they had always felt but until then hadn't quite known how to articulate. Victoria Gray Adams, a professional woman from Hattiesburg who gravitated to SNCC and became a leader herself in the MFDP, described the bond that formed among the members of those groups. She recalled, "When I first met [Baker] and that community of youthful civil rights activists, I realized that this was exactly what I'd been looking for all of my conscious existence. Before, I had not found a community of people who understood where I was coming from. It was like coming home." According to Adams, when she met Baker it was as though "we had already known each other. She was never a stranger, someone I had to get to know. . . . Our understanding of things was just so similar."

In 2000, when Joyce Ladner, a SNCC veteran and accomplished professor of sociology who had recently stepped down as the president of Howard University, gave a keynote speech at SNCC's fortieth anniversary conference, she described what her community of Palmer's Crossing, Mississippi, had been like before the civil rights movement changed it forever. She described all the ways that white-controlled society oppressed black Mississippians, cataloging acts of white men's sexual harassment of African American women and girls, Klan terror, and local (white-owned, of course) media sources' blackout of news about black activism elsewhere. She also described local blacks' building resistance to the "closed society." "This is what Mississippi was like before Miss Ella Baker came," she said. *Before Miss Baker came*—not before Martin Luther King or the NAACP or the Freedom Riders came. "By the time the SNCC people came in, even though direct action couldn't be carried out in Mississippi," Ladner said, "we'd also matured to a point where we realized that eating at a lunch counter was not as important as having the right to vote." In so many words, the people of Palmer's Crossing agreed with Baker's distillation of her philosophy at the original Raleigh meeting: The nature of their struggle really was bigger than a hamburger. Baker nurtured and empowered them, helped them define the problems they faced, and supported them as they crafted their own solutions. That philosophy resonated far beyond Mississippi's borders and extended beyond Baker's lifetime.

CHAPTER SEVEN

~

The Tribe Increases

In the late 1960s Baker wound down her consulting work for SCEF. SCEF was never as effective as SNCC had been in its heyday, but it became arguably the most significant interracial group organizing antiracist, labor, and social justice campaigns in the South after SNCC moved away from community organizing. (SCEF imploded, too, in the early 1970s.) Working from her home base in Harlem, Baker freelanced for church-based social justice campaigns and either lent her name to, volunteered for, or corresponded with an absolutely staggering array of groups working for international peace, racial justice, and feminist causes. Baker's personal papers reveal her interest in everything from the Free Angela Davis Committee and the Boycott South Africa movement to the Women's International League for Peace and Freedom and the Puerto Rican Solidarity Committee.

"Hers was a wonderfully eclectic style," Charles Payne concludes. "Whatever the form of injustice, she was willing to oppose it." If a group organized around a progressive or humanitarian cause in Harlem or the South, or on the national level at any time between the 1930s and the 1980s, odds are that Baker helped it organize, raised money for it, or gave a speech on its behalf. According to Julian Bond, Baker's tireless work on behalf of these sorts of "uncelebrated groups . . . provided financial and political support or the intellectual underpinning for the larger, more familiar movements or organizations."

As she neared full retirement Baker spoke of her role in the civil rights movement and in other movements for social justice as though it had been a humble one—sometimes comically so. In 1969 Vincent Harding, Bernice Johnson Reagon, and Joyce Ladner arranged for Baker to deliver a speech at Spelman College on the subject of "The Black Woman in the Civil Rights Struggle." She conjectured that she had been invited "because I have existed much longer than you [college students] and have, to some extent, maintained some degree of commitment to a goal of full freedom," as though she had some minor wisdom to impart simply because she was old. Very few if any Americans have ever maintained a higher "degree of commitment to a goal of full freedom" over a lifetime!

Baker's tongue loosened a bit as she got older. She began saying things in public that she had previously said only in private, emphasizing themes that she had previously relegated to the background of her organizing work. The tendency revealed itself most notably when Baker came out a bit more publicly as a Socialist and lent her efforts to the Mass Party Organizing Committee, a Marxist independent political party that was active in the 1970s. She came to identify herself proudly as a radical, and she was happy to explain why. In her 1969 Spelman College address, she said,

> In order for us as poor and oppressed people to become a part of a society that is meaningful, the system under which we now exist has to be radically changed. This means that we are going to have to learn to think in *radical* terms. I use the term radical in its original meaning—*getting down to and understanding the root cause*. It means facing a system that does not lend itself to your needs and devising means by which you change that system. That is easier said than done. But one of the things that has to be faced is in the process of wanting to change that system, how much have we got to do to find out who we are, where we have come from, and where we are going.

She may have phrased that philosophy more militantly in her old age, but it was absolutely true to the core philosophy she had held consistently since she entered adulthood.

By the mid-1970s various physical ailments forced Baker to cut back drastically on her public appearances and her consulting work. She may no longer have been *in* the movement on a day-to-day basis, but she remained *of* the movement until the very end. Baker's activism ended only with her death, on her eighty-third birthday, in 1986. Having done more than most other Americans of her time to end Jim Crow, to empower African Americans, and to give them a voice in the decisions that affected their lives, she bequeathed methods of community organizing that people the world over have since used to transform societies.

Baker built a wall between her public persona and her private life, but her brand of community organizing would never have succeeded had she not been able to connect with others on a deep and intimate level, to build trust, and to forge radically egalitarian bonds. A woman whose marriage was so secretive that it might as well never have happened, who met the legalistic definition of "mother" for only a few years, Baker nurtured an entire generation of warriors for social justice. In these respects she was also a living, breathing self-contradiction—which is to say, a three-dimensional human being, although a remarkable one. She was the hub in the wheel, the central figure who kept everyone else connected, even as she deflected all attention away from herself.

Joanne Grant and Bob Moses captured this dynamic perfectly at Baker's funeral at the venerable Abyssinian Baptist Church in Harlem. In her eulogy, Grant said, "We were all, no matter our color, her children." Moses agreed that he was Baker's child and asked others who thought of themselves as "Miss Baker's children" to stand and step forward. Hundreds did—people in their forties, but also people in their eighties. Some were her Harlem neighbors and comrades from the New York organizing days. Some were integrationist southern black Baptist preachers, and others were Black Power militants from northern ghettoes. NAACP, SCLC, SNCC, and SCEF colleagues stepped forward. A few were related by blood, but all considered themselves family. They held hands and prayed, remembered and sang. Bernice Johnson Reagon led them in Baker's favorite hymn: "Guide my feet while I run this race. . . . For I don't want to run this race in vain." Then Baker's pallbearers—nine men, including Bob Zellner and Kwame Ture (the former Stokely Carmichael) and five other members of SNCC—carried her body from the church for burial at Ferncliff Cemetery in Hartsdale, New York.

"I have grave reservations about what can be accomplished . . . by established political parties," Baker said in one of her last interviews, but some of those she worked with in SNCC continued to organize on behalf of the Democratic Party. Lawrence Guyot, the chairman of the MFDP, worked indefatigably to elect a fellow community organizer, Barack Obama, in the 2008 election. It was what Ella Baker would have wanted him to do, he said. Suffering from heart problems and the effects of diabetes in the fall of 2012, Guyot made sure to vote early and even made calls on behalf of Obama's reelection campaign from his hospital bed.

"We're faced with a challenge, the likes of which none of us have ever really experienced, because this challenge goes to the fundamental roots of what is humanity, what is the role of government," Guyot wrote in his last political newsletter, "From the Desk of Lawrence Guyot." He continued, "It is time for us to simply do what we know well and get into motion to do some specific things: 1) reelect President Obama president of the United States; 2) assist the Democratic Party in taking control of the House and the Senate; and 3) establish a nationwide hookup to serve several ends." By "hookup" he meant a national network of grassroots activists; he wanted to re-create SNCC for the twenty-first century. Guyot died on November 23, 2012.

Like scores of others who came of age in the SNCC of the early 1960s, Guyot considered the rest of his life's work a continuation of the path on which Baker had set him. Not everyone did so within the realm of electoral politics as Guyot did; others devoted their energies to labor organizing, feminist consciousness raising, or overseas anticolonial activism, among many various pursuits. They may not have agreed on everything, but when they approached their community work they all kept in mind Baker's maxim: "One of the guiding principles has to be that we cannot lead a struggle that involves masses of people without identifying with the people and without getting the people to understand what their potentials are, what their strengths are." No one should underestimate how difficult this work is, how much patience it requires. But neither should anyone underestimate its ultimate effectiveness.

"In order to see where we are going, we not only must remember where we've been but *we must understand where we have been*," Baker said. "This calls for a great deal of analytical thinking and evaluation of methods that have been used. We have to begin to think in terms of where do we really want to go and how can we get there." Easier said than done, but Baker was always more interested in processes than outcomes. These are wise words that anyone interested in building social movements—or just in living a fulfilling life—would do well to remember and heed. We should all ask ourselves, as Baker did repeatedly, "Why are we here? What do we hope to accomplish?" from time to time.

Anyone who wants to be part of a movement to make a part of the world more democratic, more egalitarian, more responsive to the needs of ordinary people can draw strength from Baker's ideas and her example. One can also take solace in Baker's belief that no individual could change the world by herself. Instead, like Baker, one could learn lessons from the past and connect to the rich heritage of social justice organizing. "I believe that the struggle is eternal," she said. "Somebody else carries on."

~

Acknowledgments

My colleague, Jennifer Jensen Wallach, and series editor, John David Smith, first encouraged me to write about Ella Baker for the Library of African American Biography, and Jon Sisk and others at Rowman & Littlefield saw the project through to completion. A Faculty Development Grant from the University of North Texas afforded me the time to research and begin writing the book. Thanks to all of them.

"Civil rights historian" is the best job title in the world. I am grateful for the many friendships and collaborations my occupation affords me, and I take this opportunity to thank the fellow travelers, named and unnamed, below whose work continues to excite and motivate me. Jennifer Jensen Wallach did me the favor and honor of reading chapters of the manuscript and suggesting improvements. Emilye Crosby and Monica Horowitz read the manuscript in its entirety and asked terrific questions that helped me to sharpen arguments and clarify prose. Thanks to them, too.

As always, my ultimate gratitude goes to my family—to my parents, Dot Moye and Joe Moye; to my parents-in-law, Barbara and Gene Feit; to Will and Sarah Moye; and most especially to my wife, Rachel, who organizes the community I share with our sons, Luke and Henry. Thanks to all y'all.

This book is dedicated to one of my greatest sources of inspiration, my beloved auntie Murphy Davis. A mighty good scholar-activist in her own right, she is also a loving warrior for social justice in the mold of Ella Baker. You can learn more about the work that she, Uncle Edaurd, and their partners at the Open Door Community in Atlanta are doing to bring about a world free of racism, homelessness, and the death penalty at opendoorcommunity.org.

~

A Note on Sources

Serious study of Ella Baker's life and legacy began with the work of a small group of remarkable scholars. Joanne Grant, a movement colleague and close personal friend of Baker's, produced the seminal 1981 documentary film *Fundi: The Story of Ella Baker*; authored the first Baker biography, *Ella Baker: Freedom Bound* (New York: Wiley, 1998); and collected Baker's personal papers for deposit at the Schomburg Center for Research in Black Culture, a unit of the New York Public Library system. Susan Bernice Youngblood's 1989 University of Virginia MA thesis, "Testing the Current: The Formative Years of Ella J. Baker's Development as an Organizational Leader in the Modern Civil Rights Movement", and Carol Mueller's essay, "Ella Baker and the Origins of 'Participatory Democracy,'" from the collection *Women in the Civil Rights Movement: Trailblazers and Torchbearers, 1941–1965* (Brooklyn: Carlson Publishing Inc., 1990), were among the first to take Baker seriously as a social theorist. Barbara Ransby's exhaustive and sharply argued *Ella Baker and the Black Freedom Movement: A Radical Democratic Vision* (Chapel Hill: University of North Carolina Press, 2002) brought a new level of scholarly rigor to her subject. Charles Payne's scholarship over many years, culminating with his *I've Got the Light of Freedom: The Organizing Tradition and the Mississippi Freedom Struggle* (Berkeley: University of California Press, 1995), focused attention on the modern civil rights movement's reliance on black church organizing traditions, roles played by women in the movement, and Baker's contributions to the movement. I am deeply indebted to all of these scholars.

In researching and writing this biography I have consulted the Ella Baker Papers at the Schomburg Center; the NAACP Papers at the Library of Congress in Washington, D.C.; the microfilmed papers of the SCLC, SNCC, and MFDP collections housed at the Martin Luther King Jr. Center for Nonviolent Social Change in Atlanta, Georgia; and the online materials of the King Papers Project sponsored by Stanford University. I also rely heavily on oral history interviews with Baker and movement comrades in the collections of the Southern Oral History Program at the University of North Carolina-Chapel Hill, the Ralph J. Bunche Oral History Collection at Howard University's Moorland Spingarn Research Center, the University of Southern Mississippi's Center for Oral History and Cultural Heritage, the Duke University Oral History Program Collection, and interviews with Baker published in Gerda Lerner, ed., *Black Women in White America: A Documentary History* (New York: Pantheon Books, 1972) and in Ellen Cantarow et al., *Moving the Mountain: Women Working for Social Change* (Old Westbury, NY: The Feminist Press/McGraw-Hill, 1980).

Organizational histories of the groups with which Baker worked most closely helped to contextualize the development of Baker's organizing strategies. They include Patricia Sullivan, *Lift Every Voice: The NAACP and the Making of the Civil Rights Movement* (New York: New Press, 2009); Gilbert Jonas, *Freedom's Sword: The NAACP and the Struggle against Racism in America, 1909–1969* (New York: Routledge, 2005); Adam Fairclough, *To Redeem the Soul of America: The Southern Christian Leadership Conference and Martin Luther King, Jr.* (Athens: University of Georgia Press, 1987); Clayborne Carson, *In Struggle: SNCC and the Black Awakening of the 1960s* (Cambridge, MA: Harvard University Press, 1981); Wesley Hogan, *Many Minds, One Heart: SNCC's Dream for a New America* (Chapel Hill: University of North Carolina Press, 2007); Howard Zinn, *SNCC: The New Abolitionists* (Boston: South End Press, 1964); and John M. Glen, *Highlander: No Ordinary School* (Knoxville: University of Tennessee Press, 1996).

Autobiographies and biographies of Baker's movement colleagues from the first three decades of her public activism have been especially helpful. These include George S. Schuyler, *Black and Conservative: The Autobiography of George S. Schuyler* (New Rochelle: Arlington House, 1966); Kenneth R. Janken, *White: The Biography of Walter White, Mr. NAACP* (New York: The New Press, 2003); Thomas Dyja, *Walter White: The Dilemma of Black Identity in America* (Chicago: Ivan Dee, 2008); Ralph David Abernathy, *And the Walls Came Tumbling Down* (New York: Harper & Row, 1989); Septima Poinsette Clark, with LeGette Blythe, *Echo in My Soul* (New York: Dutton,

1962); Katherine Mellen Charron, *Freedom's Teacher: The Life of Septima Clark* (Chapel Hill: University of North Carolina Press, 2009); Andrew Michael Manis, *A Fire You Can't Put Out: The Civil Rights Life of Birmingham's Reverend Fred Shuttlesworth* (Tuscaloosa: University of Alabama Press, 2001); and Myles Horton, with Judith Kohl and Herbert Kohl, *The Long Haul: An Autobiography* (New York: Doubleday Press, 1990).

Taylor Branch's three-volume, King-centric history of the civil rights years, *Parting the Waters: America in the King Years, 1954–1963* (New York: Simon and Schuster, 1988); *Pillar of Fire: America in the King Years, 1963–1965* (New York: Simon & Schuster, 1998); and *At Canaan's Edge: America in the King Years, 1965–1968* (New York: Simon & Schuster, 2006); David J. Garrow, *Bearing the Cross: Martin Luther King, Jr., and the Southern Christian Leadership Conference, 1955–1968* (New York: W. Morrow, 1986); Thomas F. Jackson, *From Civil Rights to Human Rights: Martin Luther King, Jr., and the Struggle for Economic Justice* (Philadelphia: University of Pennsylvania Press, 2006); and Clayborne Carson, ed., *The Autobiography of Martin Luther King, Jr.* (New York: Grand Central Publishing, 2001), helped me develop my understanding of King's intellectual development during the time he and Baker worked together, and of their complicated working relationship.

For the SNCC years to the end of Baker's career as an activist I drew from the following autobiographies and biographies of Baker's movement colleagues: James Forman, *The Making of Black Revolutionaries* (New York: Macmillan, 1972); Robert Moses and Charles Cobb, *Radical Equations: Math Literacy and Civil Rights* (Boston: Beacon Press, 2001); John Lewis with Michael D'Orso, *Walking with the Wind: A Memoir of the Movement* (New York: Simon & Schuster, 1998); Cynthia Griggs Fleming, *Soon We Will Not Cry: The Liberation of Ruby Doris Smith Robinson* (Lanham, MD: Rowman & Littlefield, 1998); Constance Curry, ed., *Deep in Our Hearts: Nine White Women in the Freedom Movement* (Athens: University of Georgia Press, 2000); Faith Holsaert et al., eds., *Hands on the Freedom Plow: Personal Accounts by Women in SNCC* (Urbana: University of Illinois Press, 2010); Aaron Henry with Constance Curry, *Aaron Henry: The Fire Ever Burning* (Jackson: University Press of Mississippi, 2000); Catherine Fosl, *Subversive Southerner: Anne Braden and the Struggle for Racial Justice in the Cold War South* (New York: Palgrave Macmillan, 2002); Mary King, *Freedom Song: A Personal Story of the 1960s Civil Rights Movement* (New York: William Morrow & Co., 1987); Howard Zinn, *You Can't Be Neutral on a Moving Train: A Personal History of Our Times* (Boston: Beacon Press, 1994); and Bob Zellner with Constance

Curry, *The Wrong Side of Murder Creek: A White Southerner in the Freedom Movement* (Montgomery: NewSouth Books, 2008).

I have also relied on Glenda Elizabeth Gilmore, *Gender and Jim Crow: Women and the Politics of White Supremacy in North Carolina, 1896–1920* (Chapel Hill: University of North Carolina Press, 1996); William H. Chafe et al., eds., *Remembering Jim Crow: African Americans Tell about Life in the Segregated South* (New York: New Press, 2001); Kevin K. Gaines, *Uplifting the Race: Black Leadership, Politics, and Culture in the Twentieth Century* (Chapel Hill: University of North Carolina Press, 1996); David Levering Lewis, *When Harlem Was in Vogue* (New York: Knopf, 1981); Gilbert Osofsky, *Harlem: The Making of a Ghetto, 1890–1930* (New York: Harper & Row, 1971); Jeffrey O. G. Ogbar, ed., *The Harlem Renaissance Revisited: Politics, Arts, and Letters* (Baltimore: Johns Hopkins University Press, 2010); John Egerton, *Speak Now Against the Day: The Generation before the Civil Rights Movement in the South* (New York: Knopf, 1994); Aldon Morris, *The Origins of the Civil Rights Movement: Black Communities Organizing for Change* (New York: Simon & Schuster, 1986); Richard Kluger, *Simple Justice: The History of Brown v. Board of Education and Black America's Struggle for Equality* (New York: Knopf, 1975); Raymond Arsenault, *Freedom Riders: 1961 and the Struggle for Racial Justice* (New York: Oxford University Press, 2006); Paul Good, *The Trouble I've Seen: White Journalist/Black Movement* (Washington, DC: Howard University Press, 1975); Lynne Olson, *Freedom's Daughters: The Unsung Heroines of the Civil Rights Movement from 1830 to 1970* (New York: Scribner, 2001); Sara Evans, *Personal Politics: The Roots of Women's Liberation in the Civil Rights Movement and the New Left* (New York: Vintage, 1980); and Elizabeth Sutherland, ed., *Letters from Mississippi: Personal Reports from Volunteers in the Summer Freedom Project, 1964, to Their Parents and Friends* (New York: McGraw-Hill, 1965); in reconstructing aspects of Baker's career.

Finally, in examining Baker's interactions with local people across the South and in her adopted home of New York City, the following studies of state- and local-level movement organizing have proven especially useful: John Dittmer, *Local People: The Struggle for Civil Rights in Mississippi* (Urbana: University of Illinois Press, 1994); William H. Chafe, *Civilities and Civil Rights: Greensboro, North Carolina, and the Black Struggle for Freedom* (New York: Oxford University Press, 1980); Glenn T. Eskew, *But for Birmingham: The Local and National Movements in the Civil Rights Struggle* (Chapel Hill: University of North Carolina Press, 1985); Adam Fairclough, *Race & Democracy: The Civil Rights Struggle in Louisiana, 1915–1972* (Athens: University of Georgia Press, 1995); Hasan Kwame Jeffries, *Bloody Lowndes: Civil Rights* and *Black Power in Alabama's Black Belt* (New York: New York University Press, 2009); Martha Biondi, *To Stand and Fight: The Struggle for Civil Rights in Postwar New York City* (Cambridge, MA: Harvard University Press, 2003); and Clarence Taylor, ed., *Civil Rights in New York City: From World War II to the Giuliani Era* (New York: Fordham University Press, 2011).

~

Index

Abernathy, Rev. Ralph David, 86–88, 105, 112–13
Abyssinian Baptist Church, 167
ACMHR. *See* Alabama Christian Movement for Human Rights
Adams, Victoria Gray. *See* Gray, Victoria
Agar, Herbert, 50
Alabama Christian Movement for Human Rights (ACMHR), 102
Albany, Ga. *See* Albany Movement
Albany Movement, 138–44
Allen, Chude Pam Parker. *See* Parker, Pam
American Baptist Home Mission Society, 23
American Communist Party, 79
American Jewish Congress, 80
American League for Peace and Democracy, 44
American Socialist Party, 122
American West Indian News, 33
Anderson, Jervis, 80
Arsenault, Raymond, 130, 141
Ashmore, Susan Bernice Youngblood, 41

Atlanta Committee on Appeal for Human Rights, 111
Atlantic City, N.J., 153–59
Auburn University, 136

Baker, Anna G. Ross (mother), 13–17, 20–23, 27, 43, 66, 93
Baker, Blake (father), 14–17, 43
Baker, Blake Curtis (brother), 16, 21, 22–23, 66
Baker, Ella J.: as parent, 66–67; experiences with sexism, 3, 25–26, 67–68; general philosophy, 5; ideas about community organizing in the civil rights movement, 1–7, 45, 47–48, 50–51, 53–55, 59–63, 65, 86–87, 89–90, 93–94, 104, 160–62, 166–68; ideas about democracy and the political process, 1–7, 50, 64–65, 69–71, 92, 167–68 (*see also* Mississippi Freedom Democratic Party); ideas about education and teaching, 22–25, 27–28, 31–32, 35, 37, 40–43, 168; ideas about organized labor, 39, 40–41, 60–61; ideas about racial

177

integration/separation, 23, 31, 43, 69–71, 160–63; ideas about religion and religious leaders, 19–22, 24–25, 27, 51–52, 90, 92–3, 40–41, 73–75, 79, 166; reticence about sharing details of private life, 5–6, 41, 167; travel on behalf of the NAACP, 51–53. See also group-centered leadership

Baker, Margaret (grandmother), 10

Baker, Margaret Odessa ("Maggie") (sister), 16, 22–23, 66

Baker, Prince (brother), 16

Baldwin, James, 4

Bates, Daisy, 71

Bates, Peg Leg, 161

Battle, Clinton, 78

Birmingham, Ala., 51, 102–3, 127–29, 143, 160

Black Power, 160–61

Blackwell, Randolph, 109

Blake, James F., 83–84

Blair, Ezell, Jr., 109

Bond, Julian, 4, 110–11, 120, 162, 165; Boycott South Africa movement, 165

Branch, Taylor, 100, 102

Braden, Anne, 116–18, 138, 159

Braden, Carl, 104, 116

Brawley, Benjamin G., 25, 28

Brockington, Jacqueline ("Jackie"), 66, 99

Brotherhood of Sleeping Car Porters, 43

Brown, Earl, 69

Brown-Nagin, Tomiko, 108

Brown v. Board of Education, 69–70, 72, 77–78, 82, 84, 88

"The Bronx Slave Market," 37–39

Bryant, C.C., 130

Bunche, Ralph, 151

Carmichael, Stokely, 2, 161, 167

Carson, Clayborne, 115, 139, 162

Carter, Robert, 64–65

Cason, Sandra ("Casey"). See Hayden, Sandra ("Casey") Cason

CED. See Consumer Education Division

CEP. See Citizenship Education Program

Chaney, James, 151

Citizens' Committee for the Integration of Negroes in the Brewery Industry, 68

Citizens' Councils, 77–79, 80, 103

Citizenship Education Program, 102, 105

Civil Rights Act of 1964, 72, 160

Clark, Kenneth, 70, 72

Clark, Mamie Phipps, 70

Clark, Septima, 81–82, 98, 102

Cobb, Charles, 148–50

COFO. See Council of Federated Organizations

Colvin, Claudette, 83

Commission on Integration, New York City Board of Education, 71–72

Congress of Racial Equality (CORE), 2, 67–68, 100, 112, 126–28, 132, 145, 148, 150

Connally, John, 155

Consumer Advisory Council, President's Council of Economic Advisors, 68

Consumer Education Division (CED), 42–43

Cooke, Marvel Jackson, 37–39

CORE. See Congress of Racial Equality

Council of Federated Organizations (COFO), 144, 148–51

Courts, Gus, 78

Cox, Courtland, 123

Crawford, Samuel, 72

The Crisis, 37, 38, 44

Crusade for Citizenship, 94–96, 97, 100–2

Current, Gloster, 65
Curry, Constance ("Connie"), 118, 122

Dabney, Virginius, 58
Davis, Ben, Jr., 74
Davis, Benjamin O., Sr., 57
Day, F.B., 84
Debs, Eugene, 38
DeLaine, J.A., 78
Delany, Hubert, 70
Democratic national Committee,
    152–59
Devine, Annie, 159
Dexter Avenue Baptist Church, 86, 93,
    98–99
Dittmer, John, 156
Donaldson, Ivanhoe, 147
DuBois, W.E.B., 9, 31, 34, 38, 49,
    53–54, 60, 79
Durr, Virginia Foster, 81

Ebenezer Baptist Church, Atlanta, Ga.,
    95, 100, 120
Eisenhower, Dwight D., 71
Elams, William D., 12
Evers, Medgar, 151

Fairclough, Adam, 91, 141, 142
Farmer, James, 128
Fayette County, Tenn., movement,
    124–26, 131
FELD. See Fund for Educational and
    Legal Defense
Fellowship of Reconciliation, 67, 112
Field Foundation, 132
Forman, James, 126
Fort Huachuca, Ariz., 57
Fosl, Catherine, 117–18
Free Angela Davis Committee, 165
Freedom Rides, 67–68, 126–33, 140,
    145, 160, 164
Freedom Schools, 148–50
freedom songs, 141

Freedom Summer, 148
Freedom Tent City. See Fayette County,
    Tenn., movement
Freedom Vote, 145–47
Freeman, Orville, 151
French, Rev. Edgar N., 87
Friendship Baptist Church, 107
Fund for Educational and Legal Defense
    (FELD), 162

Gandhi, Mohandas, 80, 88, 89, 100,
    102, 111, 134
Garvey, Marcus, 30–31
"Give Light and the People Will Find a
    Way" workshops, 62–63
Goldwater, Barry, 155, 158
Goodgame, Rev. J.W., Jr., 51
Goodman, Andrew, 151
Granger, Lester, 39
Grant, Joanne, 36–37, 49, 59, 68, 81,
    160–61, 163, 167
Grass Roots Organizing Work, 162
Gray, Fred, 83, 84, 87
Gray, Victoria, 159, 163
Great Depression, 33–44
Greene, George, 146
Greensboro sit-ins, 104, 109, 111
Grinage, Martha, 16, 22, 29–30, 66, 67
group-centered leadership, 2, 115–16
Guyot, Lawrence, 159, 167–68

Hamer, Fannie Lou, 155–56
Harding, Vincent, 135, 141, 166
Hardy, John, 130
Harlem, N.Y., 29–36, 41, 56, 66,
    165–66
Harlem's Own Cooperative, Inc., 35
Harlem Public Library. See New York
    Public Library, Schomburg Center
    for Research in Black Culture
Harlem Renaissance, 30–31, 38
Harlem Riot, 72
Harris, Rutha, 140

Hastie, William, 59
Hayden, Sandra ("Casey") Cason, 5–6,
   122, 136–37, 152, 157
Hayes, Curtis, 131
Henry, Aaron, 145, 152, 155, 157
Higginbotham, Evelyn Brooks, 93
Highlander Folk School, 81–82, 98,
   102, 122, 131, 144
Hoover, J. Edgar, 156
Horton, Myles, 81–82
Howard, T.R.M., 78
Hubbard, Rev. H.H., 86
Hugo, Victor, 109, 111
Humphrey, Hubert H., 156–58

In Friendship, 79–81, 89, 128
Indianola, Miss., 77–78
Intergroup Committee on Public
   Schools, 70
Internal Security Committee, 73–74,
   79–80

Jackson, Bernice. See Reagon, Bernice
   Johnson
Jackson, Geneva, 72
Jackson, Miss., 129, 133
Jackson, Jacob, 72–73
Jansen, William, 70
Jim Crow laws, 1, 5, 16, 52–53, 56, 58,
   63, 67–68, 70, 75, 77, 79, 82, 90,
   101, 110, 131, 144, 160, 166
Johnson, James Weldon, 30
Johnson, Lyndon B., 154–58, 160
Jones, Charles, 138
Jones, Madison S., 44, 74
Journey of Reconciliation, 67–68, 80,
   126
Judkins News Service, 33
Judson House, 32

Kelly, Asa, 143
Kennedy, John F., 128, 130

Kennedy, Robert F., 128, 132
King, Ed, 125–26
King, Edwin ("Ed"), 145–46, 157
King, Lonnie, 111
King, Rev. Martin Luther, Jr., 2, 60,
   86, 88–108, 109, 112–17, 120, 122,
   141–44, 154–55, 157, 164
King, Mary, 4, 124, 137–38, 163
Kluger, Richard, 78
Ku Klux Klan, 78, 90, 127

Ladner, Joyce, 6, 164, 166
Lampkin, Daisy, 74
Lawson, Rev. James, 102, 112–15, 118,
   122, 124
Leadership Training Conferences,
   NAACP, 62–63
LeFlore, J.L., 65
Levison, Stanley, 79–80, 89–90, 92, 94,
   99, 108, 119
Lewis, Alfred Baker, 59
Lewis, David Levering, 36
Lewis, John, 117, 126–27, 132, 161
Liberal Party, 69
Littleton, N.C., 9, 15, 17–22, 66
Locke, Alain, 30
Long, William Worth, 55
Long, Worth, 55

Malcolm X, 103
Marshall, George C., 57
Marshall, Thurgood, 48–49, 51, 53, 59
Mass Party Organizing Committee, 166
McCain, Franklin, 109
McCarran-Walter Act, 79
McComb, Miss., movement, 130–34,
   138, 144–45
McDew, Charles ("Chuck"), 118, 123,
   131
McGuire, Danielle, 62, 87
McNeil, Joseph, 109
The Messenger, 34

MFDP. *See* Mississippi Freedom Democratic Party
MIA. *See* Montgomery Improvement Association
Miller, William E., 158
Mississippi Freedom Democratic Party, 150–61, 167
Mississippi Summer Project. *See* Freedom Summer
Mixon, D.W., 84
Monahan, 73
Mondale, Walter, 156
Montgomery, Ala., 62–63, 81–91, 127, 136
Montgomery bus boycott, 111, 114. *See also* Montgomery Improvement Association
Montgomery Improvement Association (MIA), 87–92, 96, 100, 105–8
Moore, Amzie, 78, 121, 130
Morgan v. Commonwealth of Virginia, 67
Mormon, Natalie, 67–68
Morrow, E. Frederic, 51, 58, 74
Moses, Robert P. ("Bob"), 5, 119–21, 130–33, 144, 146, 150, 152, 158, 167
Mount Zion Baptist Church, 140–41
Murray, Pauli, 36, 67–68

NAACP. *See* National Association for the Advancement of Colored People
Nash, Diane, 128–32, 145
Nashville student movement, 114, 117, 128
National Association for the Advancement of Colored People (NAACP), 2, 6, 44–45, 47–64, 67, 71, 73–74, 77, 80–81, 83, 87–89, 91, 95, 99–100, 103, 108–10, 112, 113–15, 121, 124, 128, 130, 132–33, 138, 140, 148, 152, 160, 164, 167. *See also* "Give Light and the People

Will Find a Way" workshops, New York City branch
National Association of Colored Women, 19
National Council of Churches, 102
National Student Association, 112, 118, 122
National Student Christian Foundation, 112
National Urban League, 39, 66, 70, 132
Negro National News, 33, 34
New Communities, Inc., 162
New Deal, 39–40, 43
"New Negro," 30
New York Amsterdam Star News, 58
New York City branch, NAACP, 68–75. *See also* Internal Security Committee
New York Cancer Committee, 66–67
New York City Council, 68, 69
New York City Welfare Council, 68
New York Housing Authority, 44
New York, N.Y. *See* Harlem, N.Y.
New York Public Library, 32, 36–37, 39, 41, 42, 44. *See also* Schomburg Center for Research in Black Culture
Nixon, E.D., 62–63, 82–86, 87–88, 106
Noonan, Martha Prescod Norman, 138
Norfolk Journal and Guide, 33
Norfolk, Va., 9, 14–17
North Carolina A&T College/University, 104, 109

Obama, Barack, 7, 167–68
Office of Price Administration, 68
Ogbar, Jeffrey O.G., 31

Palmer Institute, 134
Parchman State Penitentiary, Miss., 129–30

Parents in Action Against Educational Discrimination, 71, 72
Parker, Pam, 150
Parks, Raymond, 63, 84
Parks, Rosa, 62–63, 81–87, 88, 106
Payne, Bruce, 146
Payne, Charles, 3, 71, 79, 165
Peacock, Wazir. *See* Peacock, Willie
Peacock, Willie, 147
Pickens, William ("Bill"), 49, 56–59
Pittsburgh Courier, 33, 34, 49
Plessy v. Ferguson, 14
Pritchett, Laurie, 140, 142–45
Puerto Rican Solidarity Committee, 165

Randolph, A. Philip, 34, 44, 50, 60, 80, 154
Ransby, Barbara, 5, 18, 20, 23, 53, 59, 69, 103, 105, 113, 151, 160
Rauh, Joseph L., Jr., 152, 155, 157–58
Reagon, Bernice Johnson, 6, 140–41, 163, 166–67
Reagon, Cordell, 138–41
Reconstruction, 18
Reese, Carolyn, 150
Reuther, Walter, 157
Richardson, Judy, 148
Richmond, David, 109
Richmond Times-Dispatch, 58
Roanoke Baptist Church, 12, 17–18
Roberts, T.J. ("Bob"), 5, 26, 36, 41, 66, 99
Robeson, Paul, 79
Robinson, Jo Ann Gibson, 82–85, 86, 87, 90, 106
Robinson, Reginald, 130
Robinson, Ruby Doris Smith. *See* Smith, Ruby Doris
Robinson, T.J. *See* Roberts, T.J.
Roosevelt, Franklin D., 39–40, 43, 57
Rose, Ernestine, 36, 37
Ross, Anna Georgiana. *See* Anna G. Ross Baker

Ross, Josephine Elizabeth ("Bet") (grandmother), 11–13, 17–20
Ross, Mitchell R. (grandfather), 11–13, 17–20
Rustin, Bayard, 68, 79–80, 89–90, 92, 94, 97, 108, 119, 122, 157

Salvation Army, 66
SCEF. *See* Southern Conference Educational Fund
Schomburg Center for Research in Black Culture, 6, 24, 36. *See also* New York Public Library
Schuyler, George, 33–34, 44
Schuyler, Josephine, 34
Schwerner, Michael, 151
SCLC. *See* Southern Christian Leadership Conference
Scott, John B., 87
SDS. *See* Students for a Democratic Society
Seaboard Airline Railroad, 53
segregation. *See* Jim Crow laws
Shaw Academy, 23–24
Shaw University, 23–27, 112–13
Sherrod, Charles, 131, 138–40, 143–44, 162
Shiloh Baptist Church, 141–42
Shuttlesworth, Rev. Fred, 102, 104, 105, 111
Shuttlesworth, Ruby, 102, 105
sit-ins, 111
slavery, 9–12
Smith, Howard K., 127
Smith, Mary Louise, 83
Smith, Ruby Doris, 129
SNCC. *See* Student Nonviolent Coordinating Committee
Social Security Act, 39
Southern Christian Leadership Conference (SCLC), 2, 6, 92–108, 110, 112–14, 117–22, 128, 132–33, 135, 141–46, 148, 160, 167

Southern Conference Educational Fund (SCEF), 104, 116, 120, 122, 146, 151, 159–60, 165, 167
The Southern Patriot, 116, 125
Southern Regional Council, 132, 145
Southwide Youth Leadership Conference, 112
Special Project in Human Relations (SPHR), 135–37
SPHR. See Special Project in Human Relations
Stembridge, Jane, 118–22, 138
Stern Family Fund, 132
Stimson, Henry L., 57
Student Nonviolent Coordinating Committee (SNCC), 2, 4, 5, 118–35, 136–51, 158–65, 167–68. See also Mississippi Freedom Democratic Party
The Student Voice, 119, 124–25
Students for a Democratic Society (SDS), 112, 122, 138
Sullivan, Patricia, 45

Taconic Foundation, 132
Thrasher, Sue, 5–6
Tilley, John, 99–101
Tinsley, J.R., 51
Totten, Ashley L., 43
Travis, Brenda, 133–34
Tri-State Bank, 80
Truman, Harry S, 79
Ture, Kwame. See Stokely Carmichael
Turner, Nat, 10
Turner, Walter S., 25
Tuskegee Army Flying School, 57
Tuskegee Civic Association, 136
Tuskegee Institute, 135–36

UCM. See United Christian Movement
United Auto Workers, 154, 157
United Christian Movement (UCM), 96–97

Urban League. See National Urban League
U.S. Civil Rights Commission, 97, 104

VEP. See Voter Education Project
Voter Education Project (VEP), 132, 144–45
Voting Rights Act, 159–60

Wagner Act (National Labor Relations Act), 39
Wagner, Robert F., Jr., 70, 71
Walker, Rev. Wyatt Tee, 104, 105, 113, 119, 121
Warren County, N.C., 10, 14, 19. See also Littleton, N.C.
Washington, Booker T., 23
Watkins, Curtis, 131
WEP. See Workers Education Project
White, Alvin C., 60–61
White Citizens' Councils. See Citizens' Councils
White, Walter, 44, 47–51, 55–56, 58–59, 63–65, 94
Wiley, Jean, 163
Wilkins, Roy, 47, 51, 54, 154, 157
Williams, Robert F., 77
Womanpower Unlimited, 133
Women's Auxiliary Progressive Baptist Convention (N.C.), 20, 23
Women's International League for Peace and Freedom, 165
Women's Political Council, 82, 84–85
Woodard, Sgt. Isaac, Jr., 52
Workers Education Project (WEP), 39–43
World War I, 30, 34, 49, 57, 60, 72
World War II, 35, 49–50, 56–58
Works Progress Administration (WPA), 39–43, 44
WPA. See Works Progress Administration

Yancy, Roberta ("Bobbi"), 137
Yazoo City, Miss., 78–79
Yergan, Effie, 26
YNCL. *See* Young Negroes Cooperative League
Young, Rev. Andrew, 102
Young Communist League, 79, 80
Young Negroes Cooperative League (YNCL), 33–36, 37
Young People's Socialist League, 122

Young Women's Christian Association (YWCA), 26, 36, 135–37
YWCA. *See* Young Women's Christian Association

Zellner, Dorothy, 162
Zellner, Robert ("Bob"), 4, 138, 161–62, 167
Zinn, Howard, 144, 147

About the Author

J. Todd Moye is an associate professor of history and the director of the Oral History Program at the University of North Texas.